# Some Far and Distant Place

Some Far and

JONATHAN S. ADDLETON

University of Georgia Press • Athens and London

© 1997 by the University of Georgia Press
Athens, Georgia 30602
All rights reserved
Designed by Erin Kirk New
Set in 11 on 14 Fournier
by Books International
Printed and bound by Maple-Vail Book Manufacturing Group
The paper in this book meets the guidelines for
permanence and durability of the Committee on
Production Guidelines for Book Longevity of
the Council on Library Resources.
Printed in the United States of America
01  00  99  98  97  c  5  4  3  2  1
Library of Congress Cataloging in Publication Data
Addleton, J. S. (Jonathan S.)
Some far and distant place / Jonathan S. Addleton.
p. cm.
ISBN 0-8203-1858-2 (alk. paper)
1. Pakistan—Description and travel. 2. Pakistan—
Social life and customs. 3. Addleton, J. S. (Jonathan S.)—
Childhood and youth. I. Title.
DS371.2.A313 1997
954.91—dc20
96-768
British Library Cataloging in Publication Data available

What should I say, if anyone asks of me:

"What did *you* do while you lived on this earth?"

—Mir Taqi Mir (1722–1808)

کہیں کیا جو پوچھے کوئی ہم سے میر
جہاں میں تم آئے تھے کیا کر چلے

# Contents

# Acknowledgments

This manuscript was started in the fall of 1990, when I worked in Yemen and was waiting for the Gulf War to begin. Fiona was in Scotland, about to give birth to our long-awaited first child. The loneliness of separation, the anxiety of pending war, the prospect of becoming a father—all somehow contributed toward a growing introspection about what increasingly seemed like my own remote and improbable childhood in Pakistan.

The story is to a certain extent also rooted in rural Georgia. Unaware of the ways and requirements of the publishing world, I sent a partial manuscript, unsolicited, to Karen Orchard, director at the University of Georgia Press. It was she who picked the first three chapters off the proverbial "slush pile." Her first letter, suggesting that she would like to see more, ensured completion of the remaining seven. An anonymous first reader, selected by the University of Georgia Press, further convinced me that publication might be possible, and made a number of suggestions that led to a much improved final manuscript. I am also grateful to those who participated during the publication process, including Jane McGarry and Kristine Blakeslee.

My parents, Hubert Franklin Addleton and Bettie Rose Addleton, freely made available their personal papers, including letters, diaries, photographs, and a short personal memoir of their own. My brother

David and my sister Nancy shared in the experiences described and offered important encouragement along the way.

A number of other readers have since offered support, kind words, and occasional suggestions, including Janet Bogue, Daniel Brown, Jan Campbell, Joel DeHart, Doug Francomano, Brooke Isham, Myron and Janice Jesperson, Scott Kennedy, Farooq Mangera, John and Kate Mitchell, Karen Rushworth, Paul Seaman, Steve Spielman, Ben Steinberg, John Stonham, Rocky Staples, Bob and Rowena Tebbe, and Helena Yee. Many classmates from Murree Christian School commented on the incomplete manuscript, particularly those attending a twenty-year reunion of our class held in Wisconsin in July 1995: Tom Brown, Sharon Erb, Virginia Feldman, Rebecca Ketcham, Nancy Kennedy, Robert Lotze, Stephen McCurry, Mark Pegors, Susan Pietsch, Frank Pressley, Martha Rasmussen, Elaine Roub, Margaret Tebbe, Alison Thompson, and Linda Walsh.

Finally, I owe a large debt of love and gratitude to my immediate family who patiently endured while the manuscript went through its various stages. Fiona was at all times supportive and must share in any dedication. The rest of it is for Iain at four, Cameron at two, and Catriona just recently born: may their own childhoods be filled with as much wonder and astonishment as the one recounted here.

Some Far and Distant Place

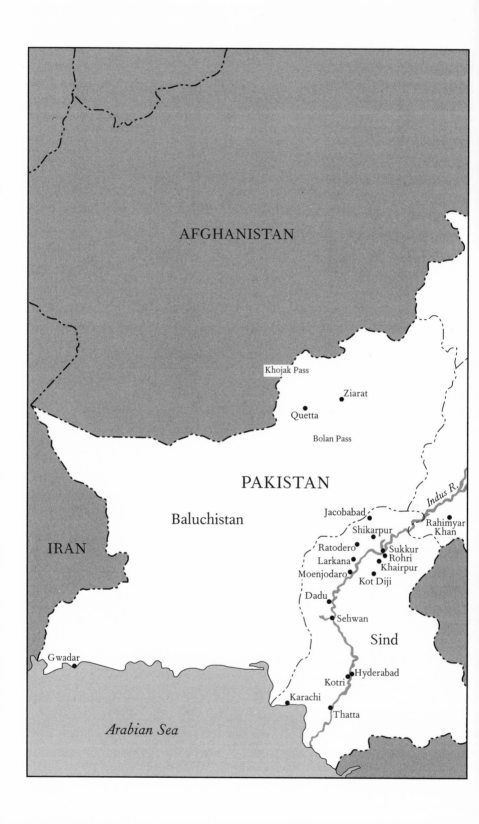

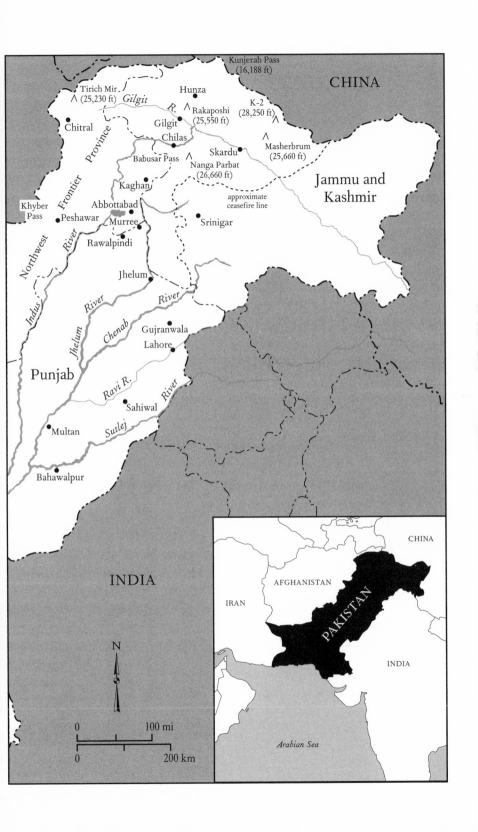

Kunjerab Pass
(16,188 ft)

CHINA

Tirich Mir
∧ (25,230 ft)   *Gilgit*   Hunza

Chitral        Gilgit        Rakaposhi        K-2
                            (25,550 ft)   (28,250 ft) ∧
               *R.*
               Chilas                    Masherbrum
                                          (25,660 ft)
               Babusar Pass   Skardu

Northwest                    Nanga Parbat
                             (26,660 ft)

Frontier Province            Jammu and
                             Kashmir

               Kaghan

Khyber         Abbottabad
Pass
Peshawar       Murree        approximate
                             ceasefire line
               Rawalpindi    Srinigar

*Indus*

               Jhelum

*River*        *Jhelum River*   *River*

Punjab                        *Chenab River*

               Gujranwala
               Lahore

               *Ravi R.*

               Sahiwal        *River*

Multan         *Sutlej*

Bahawalpur

INDIA

N

0          100 mi

0          200 km

CHINA

AFGHANISTAN

IRAN           PAKISTAN

               INDIA

*Arabian Sea*

# I Am Born

I was born in the mountains of northern

Pakistan, in a small town looking out over

Kashmir.

The name of the town is Murree. According

to local legend, Jesus Christ himself had passed

through after his crucifixion, on his way from

Palestine to India. His mother died en route,

within sight of the distant mountains above

Srinagar where her son the Messiah, the healer,

would at last find peace. Hence the name—

Murree, as in Mary, the mother of Jesus.

A small shrine built of loose stone marked the place where she was buried. Local village women made their way up the mountain to burn incense and pray. Some lit candles and cried desperately for male children. Others pleaded for healing, for wealth, for spiritual guidance. Colored strips of cloth decorated the nearby bushes, signs of prayer and supplication, the dark reds and blues fading into white with the next monsoon.

Murree's more recent history was better documented. For a time, the villagers paid tribute to Ghulab Singh, ruler of Kashmir. Later, the mountains marked the northeastern border of Ranjit Singh's Punjab empire, reverting to the armies of the East India Company only in 1849 when the Sikhs were finally defeated by the British. Cool in summer, the high altitude offered relief from the burning heat and disease of the plains below. It was a perfect hill station. Soldiers and bureaucrats arrived first. The club, the church, the hotel, and the graveyard followed.

"Oh Mama, if you could only see these lovely hills," wrote a British army officer's wife to her mother in England in May 1858, not long after the first British child had been buried in the small field below the tonga stand where visitors first arrived, after travelling overnight by horse and buggy from the garrison town of Rawalpindi forty miles below. "Our house is on the top of the highest hill here, seven thousand feet up from these horrid plains. Oh, the deliciousness of having no hot weather, no punkahs to endure. From our verandah we have a view of the whole of Murree, and of the snowy range, and at the back Rawalpindi, and down to the plains where the poor wretches are now stewing in all the miseries of another hot season." These lines could just as easily have been written by my mother to her family in America exactly a century later.

Local villagers had stories of their own, told and retold around dung and pinecone fires on the short winter days when the snow was deep and the winds blew cold from Tibet. According to one account, the British had not conquered Murree from the Sikhs; they had leased it from a local Muslim tribe for a nominal fee of sixty rupees a year. The tribal chief who negotiated the contract turned his face in shame upon seeing the naked ankles of an approaching Englishwoman. As he got up to leave, he returned ten rupees to the English official and admonished him to "keep this with you and buy some trousers for your madam." (It was a legend that grew larger in the telling, passed down from family to family unto the fourth generation.) One hundred and twenty-five years later, the descendants of that haughty tribal chieftain stood in line outside the courts of law across from the General Post Office and just off the Murree Mall, challenging the government for grazing rights on the denuded hillsides they claimed had been promised to them by the British so many years before.

After independence, Murree became Pakistan's foremost hill resort, a fashionable place where young honeymooners from Lyallpur and Lahore could walk about in freedom, hand in hand, scandalous skin touching scandalous skin. Some had only just met on their wedding day, a few days before. The pleasures of Murree were the same that the British had once enjoyed. An army pipe band still played on Sunday evenings, the tartans of the MacDonalds and Campbells now decorating the shoulders of a later generation of Mohammeds and Khans. There were donkey rides for children and horses for adults, hired out by the day for longer trips on the unpaved mountain paths. Rickshaws were also available for hire, the heavy wooden carriages manhandled up and down the steep slopes by four stooped Kashmiri coolies wearing rope thongs, two trotting along at each end. Other attractions included tea at Lintott's, shopping at Mohammad Ismail & Sons, badminton on the lawns outside Brightlands. Fur hats, painted Kashmiri boxes, and carved wooden canes remained in special demand.

On weekends, gangs of students from Lawrence College at Lower Topa paraded up and down the Mall in their dark blue blazers and ties. On occasion, police constables rounded up some of the more boisterous boys on charges of "Eve teasing," that peculiar phrase used by English-language newspapers to describe the young teddy boys, virgins well into adolescence, desperate to grow moustaches, passionate in their silliness, lusting for the time when they too might take a languid honeymoon in the wet greenness of the Murree hills. Sometimes the boys wore dark glasses and carried metal-tipped canes, for added effect.

Their targets were often the schoolgirls from the Convent of Jesus and Mary toward Pindi Point, dressed in red uniforms, or those from St. Denny's at Kashmir Point, further up the Murree ridge, dressed in blue. One school was run by Irish nuns, the other by an elderly headmistress from the Church of England. The schools at least survived independence, offering an exclusive education to the sons and daughters of the new elite in the Islamic Republic of Pakistan. A long line of prominent Pakistanis, including Benazir Bhutto, attended such schools. Pakistan may have been founded as the homeland for the Muslims of the Indian Subcontinent, but Christian missionary zeal was still welcome, as long as it remained strictly in the service of education. Morning mass and Sunday evensong continued without interruption. There were few if any conversions.

Lawrence College later changed its name to Pine Hills College, then to Ghora Gali College—and finally back to Lawrence College once again. The alumni society, the "old Galians," formed almost entirely of Pakistani military officers, civil servants, and businessmen, was simply too strong. The original name had to stay, even if a new populist government in Islamabad did not approve, even if Sir Henry Lawrence himself had blood on his hands because of his role in the Indian Mutiny of 1857 in which Murree had played a small and undistinguished part.

Fifteen nameless local villagers were hung from a hastily constructed gallows on a nearby Murree hillside, on orders from local British administrators, after one disorganized rebel skirmish in September 1857, heroes to a post-independence Pakistan searching desperately for heroes. Newly published history texts called the Sepoy Revolt the First War of Independence. Nonetheless, the name Lawrence College remained intact, decades after the enormous statue of Queen Victoria, once seated prominently in a pseudo-Moghul cupola at one end of the Mall in Punjab's capital of Lahore, had been placed in a museum warehouse to gather dust. Her place of honor sat empty for years until, in a surge of religious enthusiasm, a later government set a large, carved, glass-encased copy of an open Koran in the very spot once reserved for Queen Victoria, Empress of India, Defender of the Faith, and Ruler of the Large Mass of Pink Spots on the battered world maps that hung from every grammar school wall in England, Ireland, Scotland, and Wales.

Holy Trinity, St. Margaret's, and the Roman Catholic Chapel, just up the road from the General Military Headquarters in Murree, also survived, decaying memorials to a people who would have no permanent memorial, who had perished as though they had never been born, and their children after them. The Church of England, the Church of Scotland, and the Roman Catholic Church, diminished stones of empire kept alive by small native congregations, the sons and daughters of *chowkidars,* cooks, bearers, and sweepers, the low castes and undesirables of one era becoming the outcasts and despised of another.

In the year I was born, St. Margaret's was literally sliding down the hillside above the Murree bus station, near what had formerly been the Murree Club. Not long afterward, a visiting civil engineer from England pronounced the massive Gothic church, built in the 1850s, structurally unsound. Services were immediately cancelled until another engineer was called out to render a second opinion. He conducted his own inspection and announced that the old building was not a danger after all and might yet survive a few more decades. The first Sunday School class I ever attended was held at St. Margaret's, on hard wooden pews built originally for battalions of Scottish soldiers. The lectern was in the shape of a golden eagle made of brass, wings outstretched. The whitewashed walls at times seemed almost haunted with the names of casualties from another generation, soldiers dying young of cholera and dropsy so far away from home. The brass plaques at Holy Trinity, recalling children of another age, were still more moving. I memorized the first verse of a poem written in memory of Hyacinth Swinhoe, buried in 1913, two weeks before her third birthday, almost before I had memorized John 3:16:

I wonder, oh, I wonder, where
The little faces go
That come and smile and stay awhile
Then pass like flakes of snow?

The Christian cemeteries of Murree also survived, for another generation at least, until the headstones crumbled into ballast and became building material for local road works. A marker that spoke of the eternal and everlasting memory of a long lost, fondly remembered King's Own Scottish Borderer who rested in peace became the lintel in a nearby mountain farmer's mud-brick home. In one cemetery on a ridge near Gharial, crosses were systematically chopped off and used for bricks. George Edward, Darling Son of the Pearsons, accidently killed at Murree on the 8th of May 1928, aged three years. "Ray of Sunshine, Show us the Way." Archibald McKinnon, Beloved Son of Private Archibald McKinnon, Her Majesty's 93rd Sutherland Highlanders who died at Murree 12 April 1863, aged six months. "Of such is the Kingdom of Heaven." Jane, Beloved Daughter of Private Alexander and Jane his wife, 79th Cameronian Highlanders, and also of John, their son, who followed soon after. "Mourn not for us my parents dear, we are not dead but sleeping here. We was not yours but Christ's alone. He loved us best and took us home." Years later, even the grammatical mistakes were somehow affecting.

Along with the bones of their children, the British left their red-roofed summer cottages behind. Many were taken over by newly formed "real state" companies that arranged expensive leases for the hundreds of middle-class Pakistani vacationers venturing up into the mountains in growing numbers each summer. Rumors that a new capital called Islamabad, "abode of Islam," would be built on the plains outside Rawalpindi, thirty miles to the south, increased real estate prices still further. Norwood, Bexley, O'Spring, Mount Pleasant, Sunshine Villa, Alpine Lodge, Helen Cottage—all held memories of a colonial past, a little England on which the sun would never set, a place where the soldiers would parade and pipe bands would play God Save the Queen on every public holiday, forever and always, amen.

By the late 1950s, only a few survivors of the British Raj were still left on the Murree hillside, the handful of retired civil servants and military officers who had "stayed on" in a drunken or senile stupor, awaiting death. Most of this dwindling number lived in collapsing villas or hotels with names like Mrs. Davies' Boarding House or Lockwood's or the Golf Hotel at Bhurban, their pensions worth little enough in Pakistan and even less in England. One pink-faced, white-haired gentleman roamed up and down the Mall each afternoon, campaign medals dangling loosely on a black overcoat. When accosted by local schoolchildren, he waved his wooden cane shakily, shouting obscenities in a garbled Hindustani that sounded as stilted and unnatural as the day, no doubt, when he first walked down the gangplank in Bombay five decades before.

•    •    •

This was the mountain town into which I was born in late June 1957, on the heavy wooden dining room table of a gray house with a corrugated tin roof situated just below the Murree Water Works, near Kashmir Point, looking toward Srinagar. Srinagar, which should have belonged to Pakistan. Srinagar, in the beautiful Vale of Kashmir, where one heretical sect claimed that Jesus Christ himself was buried and another sect had placed a hair of the Prophet Mohammed, Peace Be Upon Him, on permanent display. Or rather almost permanent display, because there came a time not long after independence when the hair was stolen and riots broke out throughout Kashmir, killing dozens and almost causing a war between India and Pakistan, two countries that were destined to fight one another again and again.

Murree was not far from the Kashmir cease-fire line and tensions ran high, dying down only when the prodigal hair was finally returned. Or, at least, a hair that a Select Committee of Imminent Religious Scholars certified was the original hair was returned, soothing communal passions until the next time a butchered cow was thrown across the wall of a Hindu temple or a pig's head was placed in a mosque in Kashmir or Punjab or Uttar Pradesh. Then hotheads would once again be fomenting destruction, reviving the horrors of partition in 1947 in which independent Pakistan and India were born and as many as a million Hindus and Muslims died. Stories were told of trains in which every passenger had been killed, of whole villages in which every man, woman, and child had been butchered by neighbors with whom they had lived peacefully for centuries.

According to Islamic belief, I was in fact born a Muslim—all babies are born Muslim, as the Ahmediyya apologist once told my father in a heated debate over religious truth that took place in a Christian bookstore on the Murree hillside several years later, amid a collection of religious tracts in a dozen languages. "All babies are born Muslim," he said. "It is only their parents who make them Hindus, Christians, or Jews."

My parents were Christian missionaries, as the birth certificate on file at the Murree Registry Office so plainly stated under the section marked "occupation, caste, and religion of the father." They too were recent arrivals, strangers in this land, in this sparsely furnished summer house in Murree overlooking a steep cliff, below which terraced fields gleamed invitingly in the sun, in the far and distant valley where, if you hung your head over, you could see the smoke of distant chimneys, hear the howls of jackals, feel the gentle wind blowing from Kashmir. Like most other houses on the Murree hillside, the house had been given a descriptive name, Rock Edge. For some unknown reason, a Star of David had been carefully incorporated into the design motif, on the lintel above the door.

On a clear day it was possible to see Nanga Parbat in the far distance, technically the most difficult of all Himalayan climbs. Nanga Parbat, "Naked Peak," the mountain on which the finest in a generation of German mountaineers, nearly a dozen world-class climbers, had been wiped out in a single awful avalanche, shortly past midnight on a cold evening in June 1937, exactly twenty years before my birth. One member of the team, resting at base camp, followed the tracks the next day, only to come across a white expanse of unbroken snow, unmarked by footsteps, unspoiled by human tracks. The flower of German mountaineering, heroes all, dead in seconds, buried forever beneath the eternal weight of the unforgiving Himalayan snow.

Years later, I came to think that the task my parents, still in their early twenties, had set for themselves while embarking on a lifetime of Christian missionary service in the Islamic Republic of Pakistan was no less difficult. For, struggling through the difficulties of Sindhi and Urdu language study in their summer months in Murree, far from the desert hundreds of miles to the south where they would spend most of the rest of their lives, they had higher goals on their minds, etched on their hearts, embedded in their souls. They would introduce an entire Muslim people to the saving grace of Jesus Christ who was not, after all, buried in an obscure tomb in Srinagar but alive for all the world to see, if only someone told them about it and showed them the way. Never mind the two centuries of British bones littering the subcontinent. God had called, as He called even the sparrows by name. The cross before, the world behind. If no one comes, still I will follow. Bearing witness even unto the ends of the earth, until the day when He returns. It was the great commission that, according to Christian belief, Jesus Christ had given to his disciples shortly before he ascended to heaven to sit at the right hand of God the Father Almighty, Maker of Heaven and Earth.

We were part of a great cosmic drama that went back to the beginnings of time, a drama that had reached a climax nearly two thousand years earlier, in Palestine, at Golgotha, place of the skull, where time and eternity intersected, where in one afternoon a mighty event occurred that forever altered the fate of the universe. To be sure, we had only small, walk-on parts and would not be long remembered. But we were nonetheless honored to be assigned a tiny role in the working out of God's plan for the human race. Our lives mattered and were known, even as the sparrows were counted and known by name.

•   •   •

It was a difficult birth, as I later learned, many years later, when I came across an old letter that my mother had carefully typed to a close friend only a week after I was born. The letter was sent to an Allen Way address in Macon, Georgia. Ten thousand miles from Pakistan, ten thousand miles from the coolness of a blessed Murree monsoon when mountain streams in minutes became flooding torrents, tearing down the Himalayas, inch by inch, carrying red clay from the mountains into the fertile Indus plains below.

The Islamic green aerogram with a green four-anna stamp featuring a half-empty hourglass was signed Bettie Rose, for the four of us. My brother David had been born two and a half years earlier, at Macon Hospital. The three of them had left the United States on April 7, 1956, setting sail from New York on a 7,700-ton ocean freighter belonging to the Isthmian Steamship Line and flying under an American flag. The freighter, a Liberty ship built in 1944 at the Pascagoula shipyards in Mississippi, had been christened during World War II as the

*Westermorland* and was now known as the *Steel King*. There were only four other passengers, all of them missionaries. The ship's captain, a Mr. Williams, was from Mississippi. The ship's radioman, predictably enough known as "Sparky," enjoyed Scrabble and played with my parents often during the long voyage. He found their journey incomprehensible and told frightening stories of the diseases that awaited missionaries in Asia, to no avail. My mother and father had already set their eyes firmly toward the other side of the world, toward the mission fields of Pakistan, white unto harvest, where the laborers were few but the harvest plentiful. Reading material during the trip included *A Sailor's Life, Doctor at Sea* ("a vulgar book," my father commented in his diary), and the missionary classic, *When Iron Gates Yield.*

Each evening during their several weeks aboard the *Steel King* my parents met in their small cabin with Sam and Grace Pittman, Baptist missionary colleagues from Minnesota, for prayer, for thanksgiving, for readings from the Book of Acts. Their missionary enterprise was no less real than Saint Paul's, the great Saint Paul who had at first persecuted the church and then become its greatest apostle. "May the Lord give us something of Paul's fire and passion," my father wrote. It was Saint Paul who at one point in his own ministry had made the fateful decision to leave Asia and go west to Europe and ultimately to Rome where he would meet his heroic destiny as a martyr for the early church.

"If Paul had turned east and travelled deeper into Asia, we would have Indian and Persian missionaries in Europe and America today," my father used to say with conviction in his sermons back in the United States, to our partners in America who faithfully paid their tithe each month that we might live out our lives in Pakistan. The Apostle Paul was not merely a distant historical figure, shrouded in mystery. He was the greatest of all missionaries and his Epistles were for us living documents, useful road maps in the missionary enterprise to which my mother and father had dedicated their lives. Paul's Epistles became prototypes for the letters my parents wrote to our friends and supporters back home. They demonstrated the power that we too might have if we placed our lives wholly and completely in the hands of God. The closing lines of my father's letters to our supporters reflected this faith. "Yours because of His unspeakable gift." "Yours in His wonderful service." "Yours in Calvary's bonds." "Yours in His amazing grace." "Yours in Christ's Love." "Yours for the saving of souls in Pakistan."

The crystal stillness of the Mediterranean Sea reminded my parents of Saint John, the last of the Apostles, surviving his lonely exile on the Greek island of Patmos, writing his warning to the churches, recording his Revelation about the catastrophic events that would mark the end of time. The state of Israel was not yet a decade old, and in some missionary circles it was widely believed that the reestablishment of Zion would hasten the events John had foretold. We ourselves could well be living in the end times, among the final, faithless generation who would suffer under the Antichrist, receive the Mark of the Beast, and be destroyed at Armageddon. The end of the millennium was hardly half a century away. Christ would not return until Christians were represented among every tribe and nation on earth. Viewed from this perspective, a missionary calling took on added urgency and significance.

After sailing through the eastern Mediterranean the *Steel King* docked for a few days in Beirut. My parents were met there by Bible school classmates and fellow missionaries who had been called to serve in Arab lands, who could already read the New Testament Scriptures in another tongue. The city was not yet divided by barbed wire, and cedars of Lebanon still graced the nearby hills. During their short stay in Lebanon, my father left the ship and visited the ancient Roman and Phoenician ruins at Byblos and Balbeck, thinking perhaps of nearby Nineveh and of Jonah's fate when he turned his back on his own missionary calling and rebelled against God.

Alexandria brought other images, of ancient Egypt, of the years in captivity, of the call of Moses and his own claim that he was a stutterer, incapable of addressing a crowd and unworthy to ever lead his people out of bondage. It was a startling image that my father would come to appreciate even more in later years, when a fear of public speaking temporarily threatened his own public ministry. Farther on, the Suez Canal brought Scripture even more to life. When my father described the trip in later sermons, he recalled especially the gathering of the clouds over Sinai, deep red at sunset, taking on the appearance of the pillar of fire described in Exodus that God had used to direct his chosen people toward the Promised Land, exactly as the Old Testament had depicted it so many centuries ago.

The eastern Mediterranean evoked more than biblical images in my parents' minds. It was also their first introduction to the world of Islam. "We observed a longshoreman in Beirut cease to work long enough to take off his shoes and prostrate himself toward Mecca in prayer," my father wrote in one of his first letters to financial supporters back in America, moved by his first glimpse of the unexpected piety and faithfulness of the people he had come to serve. "During the long, hot days in Alexandria when the Egyptians were observing the month of fasting we saw that the people neither ate nor drank. During these days at Jeddah, we have seen several ships from Africa and the Far East unload hundreds of devout Muslims on pilgrimage to Mecca. We have been deeply stirred by these multitudes so earnestly seeking peace with God."

On arrival in Karachi at the end of the holy month of Ramadan, my parents and my brother David were met by Ralph Brown, a Baptist missionary colleague who drove them to the train station for the thousand-mile journey to Rawalpindi. It was the height of summer. Two huge blocks of melting ice were placed in a tin tub in the middle of the six-berth compartment, directly below a small ceiling fan, providing cool relief as the train rattled north across the deserts of Sind and into the fertile plains of Punjab. A Pakistani Christian family was waiting at Multan, a railway station halfway up the line. A colleague had telegraphed ahead, asking them to meet my parents with a fresh supply of boiled drinking water contained in several large, disposable clay pots—an arrangement that, nonetheless, did little to delay the onset of the first of many bouts of dysentery. Warren Webster, a fellow missionary who later became director of the Conservative Baptist Foreign Mission Society for which my parents worked, was waiting on their arrival at Rawalpindi station, where they boarded a Willy's jeep for the two-hour drive up the twisting road to Murree, the mountain town where missionaries habitually congregated each summer for language study, for vacation, for spiritual refreshment—and to have babies and educate their children.

•        •        •

"You have probably read in the papers about the influenza epidemic sweeping across this part of the world," my mother wrote from Murree to Hilda Young in Macon, seven days after she had brought me whimpering despairingly into the world. "It started on the hillside and I was one of the first to get it. On Sunday my temperature went up to 105 and Maybel, our doctor, was a little alarmed."

It was Dr. Maybel Bruce's first delivery in Pakistan. She herself had only just arrived, travelling by ship and train exactly as my parents had twelve months before. She was from Massachusetts. Her fiancee, Bill Harro, had been killed in the closing months of World War II. His commitment in life was to become a missionary doctor, a vision that Maybel Bruce now chose to fulfill on his behalf. I still remember the time that she spoke in a chapel service in Murree on the three loves that had dominated her life. Her first love, the young soldier who wanted to be a missionary doctor, was killed in action in the Ardennes, a few days before Christmas 1944. Her second love was the profession she adopted, medicine. Her third love was the God who called her, like my parents, to a lifetime of missionary service in Pakistan.

"I had these horrible spells of coughing and vomiting," my mother wrote. "Maybel kept me in bed all day and she even gave me a bath in bed. Hu planned to buy some ice and make some sherbert for me, a real luxury here in Murree because ice is so expensive. At about ten I started coughing again and began feeling quite nauseated. I didn't have the heart to tell him that I didn't want the sherbert so he made lemon sherbert and I ate just a few spoonfuls.

"Maybel and Hu kept towels rung out of cold water on my body, from head to toe. Still the fever kept getting higher and finally it reached 106. My pulse rate was measured at 140. Now Maybel sent for ice and another doctor. The ice came and they soaked the towels in ice water and kept them on me for what seemed like hours. I have never been so hot in all my life. I didn't get delirious but sometimes I think I was close to it. We were so concerned about the baby and I kept asking her over and over again if the fever would hurt the baby, but she didn't say."

I have since wondered if, even then, they contemplated the possibility of yet another little tombstone set into a decaying Christian cemetery on the green Murree hillside, a white marble cross with only the dates and names of the deceased, brief facts: infant Jonathan, beloved brother of little David, fondly remembered son of Hubert Franklin and Bettie Rose Addleton, Missionaries of the Gospel to Pakistan, died at Murree, 27 June 1957, Aged One Day. And then the epitaph drear, so many to choose from among the neighboring stones. "Before our bud had time to blossom, it was taken away." "Until the day break and the shadows flee away." "Of such is the Kingdom of Heaven." "He Giveth his Beloved Sleep." "We do all Fade as a Leaf." "Lead Kindly Light." "I am where the weary are at rest." "Sometime, someday, we'll understand."

But my parents were spared such an ordeal. Healing somehow came to my mother, like the soft footfalls of a desert breeze, like the gentle touch of the Messiah's metaphorical hand, which the village women prayed for at Mary's tomb, on the other side of the Murree ridge, not two miles distant from Rock Edge. No more white crosses on the green hillside in the summer of 1957, at least not just yet. That would have to wait for another summer, for the Australian child who died of diphtheria, for the British son who died of a strange and undiagnosed paralysis, for the young daughter of a Finnish missionary couple who broke into the medicine cabinet and swallowed too many malaria pills. "We all went down to the European Christian cemetery on the side of the mountain," my father wrote at the time, in April 1959. "I don't think I could have borne up under it." Burial services for Europeans continued to be held on the subcontinent, even years after the last of the British soldiers, bagpipes skirling, stepped off the pier at Bombay Harbor for home. Missionaries, at least, stayed on.

"When Dr. Hamm came the fever had gone down to 102. He suspected malaria and decided the best and quickest thing to do was to give quinine in the vein. Quinine will usually start labor in a pregnant woman and since it was time for the baby to come anyhow they didn't hesitate. By nine that night the contractions started. All day Wednesday I was in labor. Maybel went to prayer meeting and it was during this time that real labor started in. After prayer meeting she examined me and told the nurse to stay because the baby would soon come. Hu dozed on the sofa, Connie on a cot and Maybel got in bed with me. At about two in the morning she and Hu got up and made coffee and they got Connie up and then things started happening so they put me on the delivery table.

"The baby was coming in a posterior position which would prolong labor and make it much harder. Maybel sent for Dr. Hamm again to consult about using forceps and she prayed. Before Dr. Hamm arrived, the baby turned himself and was born. Before his shoulders came out he cried and you can't know what rejoicing we had to hear him cry out. I think all of them said Amen, Praise the Lord!

"The baby came at 5:22 A.M. and David woke up at 5:30. They took him next door and an hour later he saw his brother. He loves him very much and hasn't showed any signs of jealousy. The baby is real sweet and healthy and normal as could be. I'm nursing him and he eats and sleeps all the time. He is different from David, lighter hair and different features. We are so thankful for him and really praise God for his nearness at this difficult time."

My mother slept for twenty-four hours after I was born. I slept too, drugged with a dose of quinine that has made me immune to malaria ever since. When my mother finally woke, the house was quiet and she stood up on her bed and screamed, waving the top sheet and looking like a ghost. Dr. Bruce came running, as did my father. There, nestled near the edge of the bed, was a litter of six tiny mice, pink in their nakedness. They had evidently fallen from the ceiling, entering the world in the same harsh manner in which I was born, seeking warmth in the small of my mother's back. My father picked up the half-dozen mice, slid them onto an old newspaper, and then dumped them out the back window, off the cliff that faced Srinagar in distant Kashmir, down into the valley where the wind whistled softly and into the green terraced fields glistening brightly in the warm sun below.

# TWO

# Living in Sind

For my parents, Murree was never more than a temporary home, a place to come to for a brief rest during the summer months when the heat in the rest of Pakistan became intolerable, when the thermometer in some areas reached more than 120 degrees in the shade. Our permanent address was always in Sind, Pakistan's southernmost province seven hundred miles to the south, squeezed between Baluchistan, Punjab, Rajasthan, and the Arabian Sea. We lived in Upper Sind with a handful of other Baptist missionary families from September to May each year, in the village of Ratodero first and then in nearby Shikarpur, a larger market town once dominated by Hindu merchants.

For us, the Sindhi landscape always took on biblical proportions. The small towns, the mud-brick houses, the fields, the deserts, the camels, the date palms outlined against the distant horizon—it looked like something out of the posters hanging in Sunday School classrooms back in rural Georgia, where my parents had been born and raised. The bearded patriarch leading a group of migrating gypsies (*khanabadoosh,* they were called; "those who carry their houses on their shoulders") through the streets of Shikarpur during the winter months could just as easily have been Abraham. The shepherd boy tending his flocks outside Ratodero might as well have been a young King David.

My father later became something of a Sindhi scholar, but early attempts to learn the language did not come easily. There were no textbooks or tapes or even trained language teachers. Young college students were usually hired, for a few rupees an hour, to go through grammatical constructions and introduce new vocabulary. The Sindhi college students were curious about Americans, and the American missionaries in turn looked upon their language teachers as potential future converts. Lessons invariably included readings from Scripture, followed by discussions on what the verses might mean. Most of the Sindhi college students quickly became bored with the rote monotony of language teaching, but a few began to look upon their unexpected encounters with Americans as a possible passport to a new and different life.

To the dismay of almost the entire Baptist mission, one young language teacher, already a Christian, struck up a romance with a newly arrived single missionary. They eventually married. She had to resign from the mission immediately afterward, returning with her Pakistani husband to the flatlands of distant Louisiana, one of the first in what later became a steady stream of Pakistanis moving west to America, in the opposite direction from whence my parents came. "At times I wanted to see the couple breaking up simply because of their two different races and my background was against the marriage for this reason," my father wrote, trying to come to terms with a difficult situation. "Our own desires and prejudices can get in the way and we must get the victory over them."

When the wedding was scheduled, my father was asked to give the bride away. Another missionary declared that he would interrupt the service at the point when the minister publicly announced that, if anyone in the congregation knew of any reason why the two should not be joined in holy matrimony, they should speak up now or forever keep their silence. He was adamant that he would not remain silent, then or ever; he fully intended to voice his deep disapproval in front of the assembled guests, starting with the biblical injunction that believers should not be unequally yoked. It would be impossible to bridge the cultural divide. The marriage was doomed from the outset. There was a long and pregnant pause during the order of service when the minister finally asked the fateful question. He was met only by a gratifying quiet—the missionary who had been most vocal in opposition had dysentery on the wedding day and was unable to attend. Several in the congregation later commented that his sudden sickness was no coincidence; it was the hand of God that had struck him low, ensuring that he could not attend the wedding and thereby embarrass the entire community.

There were embarrassments of a different kind in the early attempts to use a new language in religious settings. At one memorable communion service, this time in Urdu, a missionary asked God's blessing on the wine, the *sharab;* instead, he inadvertently substituted another word, *peshab*. After the service, he realized to his horror that he had stumbled upon the word for urine rather than wine. On another occasion, a missionary opened a prayer with a reference to *Khuda ke bundee,* the servants of God. What came out instead was a plea of mercy for *Khuda ke bunder,* God's monkeys.

Some aspects of the Sindhi language seemed to defy all description, especially the unique Sindhi diphthong, a guttural sound emanating from deep within the throat, like the last gasp of a man strangulated. It was something a dictionary could not explain and even a linguist had difficulty describing. My father eventually mastered the sound but my mother was never quite able to pull it off, or indeed much of the Sindhi grammar. When she finally left Pakistan nearly four decades later, she continued to speak a stilted Sindhi wrapped within a distinctive southern drawl. She was nonetheless one of the very small number of Americans who had ever even tried. It did not seem to matter; communication in Sind involved far more than grammar rules and vocabulary. Accents varied across districts and between tribes. Every group had its own dialect, separate mode of expression, and unique turn of phrase. We represented just one more community, a recent arrival, with our own way of speaking, a not unusual situation in a land that had been accommodating new arrivals for centuries.

Local scholars, proud of the language, its literature, and its history, usually linked Sindhi to nearby Moenjodaro, "city of the dead." The ancient ruins there had been excavated earlier in the century by Sir Mortimer Wheeler, late of the Indian Archeological Service, whose extensive publications had been reprinted in Pakistan after independence and informed our own views about the place. The discovery revolutionized historical views on the Indian Subcontinent, demonstrating that an Indus Valley civilization developed independently and became the equal of anything found in Egypt, China, or Mesopotamia. There was even an Indus Valley script, still undeciphered. Some claimed that the Sindhi language had originated in Moenjodaro, that continuing links between modern Sindhi and the language of ancient Moenjodaro would be firmly established once the secrets of the script had finally been deciphered and the mysteries of ancient Moenjodaro were finally revealed.

Moenjodaro was less than sixty miles from Ratodero and we visited there often for picnics, collecting flint stones and pottery shards from underneath the rubble. We occasionally stumbled across children's toys, like the kind displayed in Moenjodaro's small museum: a wheel on one occasion, a set of clay oxen on another, exactly like the ones that still trampled the road outside our house in Upper Sind. One winter, after we moved to Shikarpur, my brother David and I combined collections and established our own private museum on a shelf in a half-empty storeroom, attaching labels to artifacts we had unearthed at Moenjodaro.

We often imagined what life must have been like for people living in the Indus Valley in ancient times, for those who had once held these same objects in the palms of their hands. Perhaps the broken bowl, the shards of which we so carefully collected and displayed, had been knocked off the table by an ancient Moenjodaroan three thousand years ago. Had his mother berated him in anger at his clumsiness? Had it been broken during a late-night brawl in some ancient tavern? Who knows, the pieces from a broken china plate and the handful of modern-day Pakistani copper coins that we ourselves buried in our own front garden that very morning might one day be discovered, thousands of years from now, by people exploring the ruins of our own habitation. Would they too wonder about our childhood games, the sports we played, the food we ate, the shoes we wore? Would someone in a distant age ever stop to reflect upon the brief lives of those who, once upon a time, long ago, as in a far and distant dream, walked across the Sindhi landscape, shaped animals out of Sindhi clay, breathed deeply the Sindhi air?

.　　.　　.

Closer to home, there was a strangeness and wonder in the mix of Hinduism and Islam that we saw around us every day, in the customs of a society that even the seemingly all-encompassing British Raj had only superficially penetrated. Sindhis never had the romantic appeal of the "heroic" Afghans and Pathans, the warlike tribes who faced the British army in repeated mountain battles and skirmishes and who had been romanticized by Rudyard Kipling. Neither had they been stereotyped in the fashion of the "hard-working" Punjabis, the aggressive and independent small farmers who readily adopted new agricultural techniques and turned their province into one of the breadbaskets of the British Raj. Sindhis were usually perceived as too passive, too rooted in the land, overly steeped in old feudal traditions, utterly resistant to change.

For the most part, Sindhis had simply been ignored. The British fought a single major battle in Sind in 1843, in the thick forests of Miani outside Hyderabad city, near the Indus River, at a place now used by the Pakistan Forestry Department for experimental tree plantations. The battle was brief and ended with the ill-prepared armies of the Talpurs, a Sindhi-Baluch dynasty, the last to rule in Sind, fleeing in terror from the cannon and rifle shot. The subsequent annexation of Sind by the British East India Company was controversial. European public opinion, even in the nineteenth century, thought of the country as a peaceable kingdom, a buffer between India and Persia that ought not to be disturbed. Sir Charles Napier, the British general who conquered Sind, was well aware of these feelings when he used a single Latin phrase to notify England of yet another acquisition for the empire. *"Peccavi,"* he reportedly cabled back to his empress in Britain after the Battle of Miani. "I have sinned."

It was a play on words that my father appreciated and he sometimes used the apocryphal story in his own sermons back in America, to startle drowsy church congregations out of their lethargy. "You may find this difficult to believe," he would say, "but for the last several years I, as your missionary, have been living in Sind."

Ratodero, our first home, was a large village trying to become a town, a run-down place of seven thousand souls with an ancient Hindu past and an increasingly Islamic future. The more wealthy Hindus—the landlords, merchants, and moneylenders—had all left for India at independence. Low-caste Hindus—the untouchables, Gandhi's harijans—mostly stayed behind, sweeping streets, cleaning drains, and washing toilets. Although despised because of their occupations, the remaining Hindus nonetheless seemed to be keepers of a deep and mysterious spiritual tradition, with an access to the ancient soul of Sind that had somehow been lost in the intervening centuries. They had a link to Moenjodaro, a city built long before Christ and Mohammed, before Buddha even, a link that later generations of Christians and Muslims could never fully understand.

Years later, my parents told me that it was an old Hindu woman from Ratodero who first announced my coming birth. A snake charmer and a cobra were also involved. It happened in November 1956, when my parents had hardly been in Pakistan for six months and were only just beginning to understand the local language. "A snake charmer came by today and we took pictures of the cobra," my father wrote in the notebook he used to record his first impressions of Pakistan. "An old toothless woman standing nearby became very excited when she saw Bettie looking at the snake. She kept pointing to Bettie's stomach. Finally I got someone to tell me that the old woman was saying that Bettie was pregnant, that if she looked at the snake then she would lose the baby. It is considered bad luck for a woman to look at a snake. This was very strange for us and gave us an eerie feeling since we are not aware that Bettie is pregnant."

A short while later, my parents travelled by Land Rover to the mission hospital in Sukkur where tests confirmed that a baby was indeed coming; a baby conceived in the deserts of Sind, born in the mountains overlooking Kashmir, raised in the shadow of a cobra. Who knows when ears are formed, when the gift of hearing is bestowed, when the first neuron of memory is permanently emplaced in the brain? It just may be that the first sound I ever heard, deep within my mother's womb, was the shrill piping of a snake charmer in a small brick courtyard in Ratodero, near a colony of Hindu sweepers, under the watchful eye of a toothless Hindu woman who foretold the future.

•   •   •

There was always something strange about the fleeting Hindu presence in our lives, something otherworldly and faintly evil from the perspective of both the missionary community and our Muslim neighbors. We occasionally attended Hindu weddings, where an elderly priest dressed entirely in white would officiate. His gums were red from chewing betel nut and he spoke in strange Sanskritic syllables, mouthing words that even the bride and groom could never understand. Occasional visits to Hindu temples were equally disturbing to monotheistic minds, with their wall-to-wall displays of countless gods and goddesses, endless rows of strange and unfamiliar figures, molded in clay, painted in many colors, each with the brightness of a glaring sun—Shiva the sustainer, Kali the destroyer, along with hundreds of other, lesser deities, stacked cheek by jowl like some enormous congregation of unemployed extras from an abortive spiritual Disneyland.

My favorite Hindu temple was on an island in the middle of the Indus River at Sukkur, near Bukkur, close to the ancient town of Rohri. The island was called Sadhbello. The *barakat*, the grace that abounded there, was said to be strong, so strong that, as a sign of respect, even the fish swimming past pointed their tail fins upstream rather than toward the island. We sometimes crossed over on a small wooden boat, carrying a picnic lunch to eat in the coolness of the gardens, beneath the spacious embrace of a wide and ancient banyan tree, guarded only by the noise of a thousand screeching parakeets. For a few rupees the solitary Hindu holy man who inhabited the island would greet us and show us around, occasionally commenting on the significance of one figure or another. Ganesh, the elephant god, was always my favorite, a laughing deity who, I was told, signified prosperity. He seemed to introduce a humorous element into religion, a kind of playfulness that was absent in our own worship and in the all-encompassing monotheism of Islam that we saw around us every day.

The shadows of a Hindu past also survived in Shikarpur, twenty miles from Ratodero, the larger town to which we moved when I was four years old. It was decaying now, but boasted of a more glorious history, of a time when it controlled the major trading routes to central Asia and was fleetingly known by local civic boosters as the "Paris of Sind." The disintegrating mud walls of an old caravanserai outside town remained from the times when caravans of a hundred camels and more passed through Shikarpur, on their way to Kabul, Bokhara, Samarkand, and the other trading towns of central Asia. Kandahar, the first city on the other side of the Afghan frontier, even had a Shikarpur gate facing east toward the Kojack Pass and then to India. The gate survived into the 1980s, when it was finally destroyed by Soviet tanks.

Old Shikarpur was also falling apart, because of neglect rather than war. Its mile-long covered bazaar, where dozens of Hindu merchants and moneylenders once sat cross-legged in their tiny stalls, was still a vibrant marketplace. But the Victorian-style mansions with their distinctive wrought iron grillwork, erected by an earlier generation of Hindu merchants, were already beginning to crumble into the desert dust, helped along by a rising water table and the canker of saltpeter that infested and then destroyed everything it touched. A decade after the Hindu merchants left, Shikarpur was already a town that seemed to have a past but not a future. Even its population had declined, from perhaps sixty-five thousand at independence in 1947 to only forty-five thousand less than a decade later when my parents first arrived in Pakistan.

When my brother and I pedalled through the streets of old Shikarpur on our all-metal Eagle cycles in the middle 1960s, we occasionally looked up at the decay wrought by time, across the rusting iron banisters, into the broken lattice windows, toward the marble memorial plaques placed by builders who imagined that their works would last at least a hundred years. The Sethi Asood Amal Menghra Jasrani Building, grandly constructed in A.D. 1915, was already falling down. The botanical garden outside Shikarpur, reputed to have once been one of the wonders of western India, was turning into a wilderness of weeds and thorn bushes. The Mereweather Pavilion, named after a former commissioner of Sind, was rarely used. The crocodile pool was empty and the heavy steps of domesticated elephants no longer echoed in the quiet of a late afternoon. The impressive Shikarpur Civil Hospital, built by Rao Bahadur Udhawdas Tarachand and opened by His Excellency Sir Lancelot Graham, governor of Sind, as recently as 1937, was a memorial that should have lasted at least a generation. Its doors were still open, but the English and Hindi scripts that explained its origins were incomprehensible to most passersby, as incomprehensible as the undeciphered script at Moenjodaro, less than ninety miles away.

In both Ratodero and in Shikarpur, we lived in houses that had been vacated by departing Hindus. The house in Ratodero had five rooms and a large verandah. The windows were barred but contained no glass. The shutters were made of unvarnished *sheesham* wood and banged noisily in the late afternoon, when an occasional gust of hot wind broke the stillness of a late spring day, before we migrated by train to the coolness of the Murree hills. The house had electric lights and ceiling fans, but the municipal power station only operated a few hours each day. During much of the year we slept upstairs in search of an evening breeze, on the flat roof made of mixed mud and straw that characterized all the houses of Upper Sind, on a rope-strung bed, beneath a sagging army surplus mosquito net held up by four thin bamboo poles, stretched out in the shape of a St. Andrew's cross.

At night, the sky seemed to come alive with the brilliance of the planets and the hazy splendor of the Milky Way. A National Geographic map of the stars, given to us by friends in America, was carefully taped onto the whitewashed wall in my brother's room. We located the constellations on the map and then gazed up at them at night, at Orion, at Taurus, at the Pleiades, imagining ourselves as Greek shepherds or Phoenician sailors, imagining the stars as so many pinpricks in the dome encompassing our own small universe. Who could doubt that the heavens declared the glory of God, who could question that the firmament sheweth his handiwork?

By day, it seemed like we would live forever, in our small world where only the chuk-chuk-chuk of a distant diesel-fired irrigation pump or the quiet laughter of a group of girls in a cradle swing next door would break the silence of morning. We were aliens, to be sure, but over time we also became a part of the landscape in a land that had enveloped and then absorbed generations of invaders, going back before the time of Alexander the Great. His hardest battles had been fought in Sind and he had almost been killed laying siege to one of the Indus towns. The Greeks came, the Persians, the Arabs, the Turks, the Mongols, the British, even the Baptist missionaries from America, as curiosities at first, then as strange warriors who unaccountably abandoned their families and endangered their lives, all for the clash of battle in a distant and unknown land. Finally, and with the passage of time, it was almost as if we too were absorbed into the very depths of Sind, into the fabric of a country that outlived all who tried to change it.

The train of oxcarts going past our door before dawn each morning signified something about a seemingly eternal Sindhi past. A single kerosene lantern was affixed above each turning axle, to light the way. One pair of oxen followed another, all the way to the farmer's markets in Larkana, Shahdadkot, and Jacobabad. The farmers themselves remained fast asleep atop their produce, confident that their oxen would know the way. Remarkably, the carts in Sind had remained unchanged for centuries. Unlike in neighboring Punjab, there were no spokes, no mechanism by which the wheels operated separately from the axle. The result was a high-pitched squeaking, the sound of wood against wood, a noise that first fascinated and then delighted, like nostalgic music from a distant and dimly remembered past. In matters of design, the oxcarts in Sind were exactly like those on display in the Moenjo-daro museum, exactly like those that slowly trod the roads of Upper Sind nearly three thousand years before. Even when the farmers in neighboring Punjab turned discarded truck tires into the latest in ox-cart technology, the farmers in Upper Sind continued to build and op-erate their much smaller, spokeless oxcarts with all-wood wheels that squeaked incessantly, like an out-of-tune orchestra in the darkness of the ancient Sindhi night.

Our house in Shikarpur had been a Hindu assembly hall, a place hired out to local officials and businessmen for large weddings and other social events. There was a single large room with a high ceiling in the middle of the house, surrounded on three sides by a long ver-andah. We planted a small garden outside, with a neem tree on one corner and a mulberry tree on the other. High walls surrounded the house on three sides and, on the fourth side, there were three separate out-rooms. One became a storage place, a second a servant's quarters, the third a small *otak*, a book room where my father met with male guests, mostly students from the local college, inquiring as to the way of salvation.

Although the brick floors in our Shikarpur house were buckling in the middle and the poison of saltpeter was already making its way up the sides of our walls, there was a feel of luxury that we had not enjoyed in Ratodero, an echo of a time when the music of sitars and tablas and perhaps even the soft steps and clanking bangles of a nautch girl entertained party guests numbering in the hundreds. The doors were made of Burmese teak rather than *sheesham* wood. The windows were fitted with Italian stained glass, greens mostly with some red or blue or lilac panes mixed in. A band of pale blue tile work stretched along an upper wall. The Conservative Baptist Mission in Pakistan, renamed as the Indus Christian Fellowship to indicate its new roots, spent twenty-five thousand rupees to buy the house in the early 1960s and another five thousand rupees for necessary repairs, six thou-sand dollars in all. It seemed like a small fortune at the time. Even now, when I recall my growing-up years, I think most often of the converted wedding hall that we turned into our Shikarpur home.

●      ●      ●

We lived as part of an extended family, much as other middle-class Sindhis in the town. My father, who inhabited a man's world, never brought male guests into the inner sanctum of our home but entertained them from the *otak* outside. My mother, who ruled the family nest with a firm hand, supervised the water carrier and the part-time sweeper, managed the kitchen, and kept the daily *hissab*, recording expenses in a lined notebook kept specifically for that purpose in an upper kitchen drawer. My brother David, two years older, and I were close enough in age that we could entertain each other, playing tag on the courtyard walls, riding our cycles through the dusty streets of Shikarpur town. My sister Nancy, two years younger, vulnerable and with dark eyes, as a female never had a bicycle of her own and could never walk the streets alone.

Baroo, the water carrier, watchman, gardener, and general handyman, had been with us since Ratodero days. My father later said that when he started working for us he did not have much more than a dhoti in which to wrap himself. He stayed with us for two decades and then worked for another missionary family in Hyderabad for another twenty years. He was a Muslim but sometimes attended church services held on Sunday afternoon on our verandah, fascinated by stories about the same prophets who inhabited the pages of the Koran. He bowed his head during the prayers and joined in when we sang choruses from the Punjabi Psalter. I saw Baroo years later, when his hair had turned gray and a paunch the size of a small tractor tire had grown up about his middle. "Sahib, I have grown old," he said. It was an emotional moment and there was a kind of glistening when our eyes finally met, as if we both were holding back feelings that should have been expressed long ago.

The notion of "servants" was always an uncomfortable one, though children for a time could at least maintain the fiction that it did not really matter, that we were instead members of the same family, each with our own assigned roles, feelings, and peculiarities. But the basic inequalities in the relationship were inescapable. One cook, briefly in our employ, lost his job for stealing sugar, which was heavily rationed at the time. I had not yet started school and was still struggling with the meaning of words. When I heard that he was going to be "fired," I briefly feared that it meant he was about to be turned over to the police and shot.

Gopal, our part-time sweeper, lived in one of the Hindu ghettos in Shikarpur town. He was employed by the Shikarpur Municipal Committee to sweep the streets, but he also worked for us two afternoons a week. He was short, used henna to dye his hair red, and always looked years younger than his actual age. He fathered eleven children by a single wife. His seven sons survived into adulthood. His four daughters died as infants, before they were old enough to hold a broom. Years later, my mother told me that Gopal once came to the house, carrying his youngest son. "He is yours," he said. "Take him to America, make him a Christian, raise him and care for him as if he were your own." Instead, my parents urged Gopal to educate all his children, to send them to school so that they could learn to read and write. "This I cannot do," he replied. "Even if they go to school, they will never be anything more than sweepers. Why give them an education, only to make them miserable and unhappy in the only job they will ever have?"

Once, when I was in high school, Gopal took me aside and said with some urgency that he wanted to show me something in private. He carefully unwrapped a scrapbook out of its cloth covering, and together we spent the next hour going through it: page after page of cuttings, clipped out of the magazines that we had discarded during the last many years, photographs from *Time*, from *Life*, from *National Geographic*, from *Good Housekeeping*, advertisements depicting strange appliances, automobiles, airplanes, scenes of distant countries—the endless wheat fields of America, the snowcapped mountains of Switzerland, strange animals from Africa, beautiful women in swimming suits dancing across the distant beaches of the South Pacific.

It was a fascinating glimpse into the imagination of someone who never learned to read or write, who never expected to travel outside

Sind Province, whose children were destined to spend out their own lives as sweepers in the employ of the Shikarpur Municipal Committee. I knew something about the spirit that inspired his scrapbook, because Nancy and I had developed a game of our own that we called "I got." We would look through the pages of a Sears catalog sent from America and take turns laying claim to an item on a particular page, a stereo on one page, a camera on the next, a set of living room furniture on a third. Like a cargo cult, almost. Blessed are they who lack for everything, for some day they will inherit the earth.

Gunga, the deaf-mute who operated the Shikarpur Municipal Committee watering hole across the street, was also almost like family. He pumped by hand, keeping the concrete water troughs filled for passing horse-drawn tongas and donkey carts. My father often slipped rupee coins into his hands for small favors—washing our Land Rover, watching the outside door, occasionally carrying water. Gunga means deaf, and he could easily have been the prototype for Rudyard Kipling's "Gunga Din." His family had either turned him out or all passed away. He had long hair, a silver earring, and sometimes wore a colored bandana that made him look vaguely like a pirate. He was mostly pleasant but on rare occasions became angry when he felt he was being taunted or misunderstood. Then he would grunt and gesticulate wildly, as if to express emotions that words alone could not properly convey. He once watched with curious interest as I tried to mime the Gospel story, the birth of Christ, His death and resurrection, and His final return to glory. As I concluded my earnest meditation, he smiled, hoisted his leather water bag, and then was gone.

The family beyond included the small number of Baptist missionaries posted in the other small towns in Upper Sind, isolated sentinels standing fast at their lonely posts at the farthest reaches of Christendom. We practiced the old colonial custom, inherited from earlier generations of missionaries and adopted in another context even by middle-class Pakistani families, of addressing adults associated with our family as aunt and uncle. There was Uncle Ralph and Aunt Polly in Ratodero, Uncle Ray and Aunt Jean in Larkana, Uncle Sam and Aunt Grace in Dadu, Uncle Will and Aunt Mildred in Jacobabad. In Shikarpur, the center of our missionary activity, there was

Uncle Larry and Aunt Connie, Uncle Ben and Aunt Betty, and the several single missionary women, including Auntie Maybel who had delivered me and Auntie Phyllis and Auntie Hannah, the nursing sisters. My parents later told me that the first time I ever went to the United States, I took one look at a crowded New York street and, in that distant time, associating pale skin with kinship, shouted with delight—"look at all the aunts and uncles in America!"

Occasional gatherings for prayer and fellowship gave us an opportunity to mix with the rest of our extended family, cousins as it were, the couple of dozen Baptist missionary children of Upper Sind: Mark, Thomas, Philip, John, Paul, Stephen, Timothy. The list of names went on and on, reading almost like a roll call of the early Apostles, a gathering of the disciples who would one day transform the world. Remarkably, almost all of them were boys, a sign of singular honor and good fortune in the largely Muslim society that surrounded us. The entertainments for missionary children rarely varied: bicycling the dusty Shikarpur streets; tag on the walls and rooftops of our houses; kite flying, sometimes using glass-covered string to detach and "capture" kites flown by other neighborhood children; picnics in a park nearby, under the shade of a large mango tree; and an occasional afternoon resting along the banks of an irrigation canal outside town, where small blue kingfishers hovered above the water reeds, where cattle egrets hopped back and forth along the thick backbones of sleeping water buffalo, where tufted hoopoe birds occasionally flashed red, white, and black against the cloudless blue of the sky, the sky, the never-ending Sindhi sky.

One afternoon gathering alongside a canal outside town nearly ended in tragedy. We went for a picnic, with Auntie Polly and her three boys. Ralph, her husband, the fellow missionary who had first welcomed my parents to Pakistan, was away at the time. A jeep jolted by in a cloud of dust on the unpaved canal road and the three adults turned to look. When they looked again, beyond the muddy canal bank, a homemade wooden boat was floating gently by—one of the Brown children, not yet six years old, had fallen in. My father said a brief prayer, removed his shirt and trousers, and dived into the deep water. "With the Lord's guidance, I made my way out to the middle of the canal and worked downstream," he wrote several days later, in a mimeographed letter sent to other missionary families in Upper Sind to describe the miracle that had somehow touched our lives. "I would go to the bottom, feeling along with my feet. Suddenly I touched Eddie with my feet. I dived down and prayed that I would not lose him. The Lord placed my hands on him and I brought him to Polly, who was on the bank praying. He had been under water for at least five minutes." As it happened, Auntie Polly had read an article on mouth-to-mouth resuscitation in a copy of *Reader's Digest* only the day before and was able to breathe into him the breath of life. He recovered at the mission hospital in Sukkur. None of us doubted that a miracle of almost biblical proportions really had occurred.

Local Pakistani Christians represented kinfolk of another kind. They were few in number and, along with the Hindu sweepers, lived mostly at the bottom of the social order. They too lived in *bustis*, ghetto-like communities that smelled of sewage and lacked running water, fertile breeding grounds for disease and despair. Most of the Christians had migrated from villages in Punjab within living memory, looking for work as day laborers or as sweepers in municipal sanitation departments scattered across the country. Their parents or their grandparents had been low-caste Hindus, darker-skinned tribal folk who changed religions during the British period in a mostly unsuccessful effort to escape the chains of history.

The presence of a small colony of Christian sweepers in Shikarpur came as something of a surprise. My parents had not expected to find any Christians at all in Upper Sind and they had not foreseen that much of their own work would eventually be centered around social uplift and spiritual nourishment for one of the most despised and depressed communities in Pakistan.

I visited the *busti* from time to time with my father, tagging alongside when he made his pastoral calls. The pattern never varied: a walled courtyard, sometimes with a single cast-iron hand pump; a verandah with a small fireplace and cakes of dried cow dung stacked in a far corner; a single brick room with barred windows and wooden shutters; a naked lightbulb hanging from the ceiling, the electric wire heavy with flies; several tin trunks stacked in a corner, enough to contain all the family's possessions; two or three rope-strung beds, one for the parents, a second for a surviving grandmother, a third for all the children; one or two posters on the wall, pages from an old calendar donated by a visiting priest—a picture of Jesus as a shepherd looking for his lost sheep, a painting of Mary and a well-fed Christ child, his head encased in a shining halo; a shelf decorated by a cracked teapot and, just beyond, a mixed set of teacups, several with broken handles. In better-off households, our tea would be sugared. When visiting poorer families, the tea was always flavored with salt.

Whether we liked it or not, we could not help but be drawn into the joys and sorrows of the small Christian sweeper community in Shikarpur, a community that found it difficult to distinguish between the visiting Catholic priest from Italy or Ireland and the Protestant pastor from America who occasionally entered their lives. Into their weddings, where a European almost automatically became the guest of honor. Into their illnesses, when priests were asked to anoint the forehead of a diseased relative with oil and offer a prayer, in the manner of James the Apostle. Into their court cases, where the influence of even a missionary might sway the judgment of a senior police officer and bring about swift release. Into their unemployment, where a note from a European might at least bring a job interview. Into their deaths, when having a foreign priest or pastor say a final prayer might yet bring respect and dignity to a grieving family.

Relations with local officialdom were more distant, though even here there was sometimes politeness and even a show of friendliness along with occasional undertones of suspicion and disgust. Many people in both Shikarpur and Ratodero wrongly assumed that the American missionaries were paid by the American government, that they were civil servants with salaries drawn from Washington accounts. When Baptist missionaries first arrived in Upper Sind in the middle 1950s, some officials hoped that they might bring with them hospitals and schools. My father bought six acres of land for a women's hospital, which was eventually built in Shikarpur. One small primary school was later started in Jacobabad, mainly for the *busti* Christian sweeper community living there. But evangelism remained central to the ministry, and the Baptist missionaries were determined not to be captured by institutions in the way, they believed, previous generations of missionaries on the Indian Subcontinent had been. There was always the fear that a bad word from a local police official or magistrate would result in a visa rejection or in a refusal to extend necessary work permits.

Before leaving town for more than seven days, my parents were required to sign in and out at the local police station. Detailed records on our every movement were maintained in the local magistrate's office, amid dusty piles of old ledgers, files, and report forms dating back to British rule. The Civil Intelligence Department—the CID—also visited from time to time, to gather information for the reports they maintained on the small number of foreigners living in the district. "The CID officer called me over to his office today to meet me," my father wrote in his diary, shortly after we moved to Shikarpur in September 1961. "I had a very good talk with him. He had much contact with the CMS missionaries as a boy in Sukkur and Karachi. He seems to have a deep respect, if not love, for the Lord. He said to me that the most important thing in the life of a missionary is sincerity and love."

·     ·     ·

Sincerity and love, twin emotions that appeared in surprising ways, even in talks with the more educated Sindhis who lived in Shikarpur town, who might well have reason to fear or resent the arrival of evangelists representing another faith from half a world away. Work with the sweeper community did not exclude friendship with such leaders, some of whom were driven by missionary impulses of their own. I well remember Dr. Shaikh, an elderly Sindhi doctor with thick plastic glasses, white hair, and an aristocratic bearing that set him apart as one of the most venerable of Shikarpur's town elders. He had been something of an athlete in the 1930s, active in cricket and field hockey during the days of empire. He took a personal interest in my own undistinguished athletic career, discussing with me what type of strides made the most sense for long distance running and which kind of starts were best suited for sprints. His own children and grandchildren lived far away, in Karachi, in Canada, and in the United States. One son was in the Pakistani diplomatic service.

At times, conversation drifted toward more spiritual directions. "You are my close friends," he told my parents on one occasion, sitting on a wicker chair in our front garden in the early evening while David and I played badminton in the shadowy light of a single outside bulb. He was nearing eighty and about to leave Shikarpur for Karachi, possibly for the last time. "I am getting old and I cannot expect to live much longer. Therefore, I want to take this opportunity to share God's message with you."

With great sincerity, he catalogued a long list of traditional Muslim objections to Christianity. The Scriptures had been changed. Jesus could not have been divine. God would not have let him die on a cross. "As you know, we Muslims have great reverence for the Prophet Jesus. He is one of the prophets sent by God to show the way to Himself. But you must go one step further and accept the Prophet Mohammed as the last prophet. God gave his final message to Mohammed, and that message is contained in the Koran. The Koran summarizes the message in your Bible and goes on to complete God's revelation to man. As a friend who loves you very much, I enjoin you to take Mohammed and embrace Islam."

It was a moving recitation from someone so old, an exposition of faith and commitment that my father might well have envied. Take Mohammed and embrace Islam, take Mohammed and become a Muslim. It would have been a wonderful story, a young Baptist missionary couple from America and their three young children becoming Muslims in the depths of Sind. It might even have been written up in *Dawn* or the *Pakistan Times*, like any number of European conversions reported regularly in the local press. Visitors passing through from Britain, Germany, Australia, or the United States who embraced Islam were sometimes listed by name. The conversion of celebrities figured in headlines. Cassius Clay become Muhammad Ali and the world of Islam rejoiced. Cat Stevens became Yusuf Islam and the world of popular music would never be the same.

Long afterward, there was a rumor that Neil Armstrong, the first man to walk on the moon, had become a Muslim. He had heard the Islamic creed spoken as if from God as he stepped out of the spacecraft into the Sea of Tranquillity—"Laillahailallah, Mohammed Rasul

Allah, There is No God But God, and Mohammed is the Prophet of God." The rumor lingered on for years, until it was finally dismissed through a direct phone linkup, arranged by the United States Information Service, from America to the Indian Subcontinent. A panel of religious scholars was asked to pose the fateful question, and Neil Armstrong replied that, while he respected Islam greatly, he had not yet embraced it for himself. A decade later, there were similarly enthusiastic reports in the Urdu and Sindhi press that the entertainer Michael Jackson, formerly a Jehovah's Witness, had embraced Islam; word of the boxer Mike Tyson's conversion was met with the same rejoicing.

When I had left Sind long behind and the scenes of childhood were becoming more distant and remote, almost as if it had all happened to someone else, I met Dr. Shaikh's grandson Asif in the United States. It was incredible when we both realized the connection. He told me that his grandfather had eventually come to America, to be with his daughter who had moved there some years before. He lived into his late eighties before dying in Chicago, ten thousand miles from the deserts of Upper Sind, ten thousand miles from the wilderness where my parents still labored in the vineyards of the Lord. We got on surprisingly well together, comparing life histories, contrasting experiences, empathizing with each other's rootlessness—Asif the son of a Pakistani diplomat who retired in Canada, I the son of American missionaries who spent a lifetime in Pakistan, both of us linked somehow and forever to the far-off land of Sind.

Asif had married an American woman and did not seem religiously inclined, at least in a traditional sense. He had one son, aged twelve. The three of them were going on vacation in a month's time, to Scotland, to the islands of the North Sea, to the desolation and loneliness of the Outer Hebrides. I remembered a program I had heard on a BBC shortwave radio broadcast some weeks before, about several families of Pakistani peddlers who set up businesses in the Outer Hebrides during the 1950s, in Stornaway, on the island of Lewis. Several dozen Pakistanis now lived there, shop owners and itinerant merchants mostly, Muslims bearing faithful witness in a distant place where the ancient Celts had once built circles of stone in honor of the summer solstice, a far country where the Gaelic tongue somehow survived. A Pakistani child, born on the island, had recently won a local competition for his rendition of a haunting Gaelic song, as strange on his lips as an Urdu *ghazal* on mine. The latest local controversy was about whether or not a building permit would be granted to construct a mosque.

We met briefly, and then departed. "Make sure to look up the Pakistani Gaels in Stornaway," I told Asif, just before we separated to go our different ways. It seemed no less odd than the idea that I should somehow have spent so much of my own childhood living in Sind.

# THREE

# Father's House

I have often wondered what brought my mother

and father from rural middle Georgia to the

hardscrabble mission fields of Sind. Even now, I

do not completely understand. The few surviving

photographs give little enough away and it is

harder still to imagine parents who were ever

young. It seems almost unimaginable that the

handsome, earnest man with piercing eyes

looking out from the missionary prayer card

published in the early 1950s should have been

my father. It is just as far-fetched that the young

woman with the dark eyes and hopeful look seated beside him should have been my mother. The publicity material issued by the Conservative Baptist Foreign Mission Society to help raise financial support mentioned that the two of them had "grown up together in a small farming community, but were separated before either of them entered high school." Years later, after they both had gone to Bible college, "God brought them together again."

My father, Hubert Franklin Addleton, was born in Bibb County, Georgia, in November 1929, on the eve of the Great Depression, in the year the stock market crashed. He was the eleventh in a family of fourteen children, all of a single mother who had married when she was sixteen years old. Six brothers and six sisters reached adulthood. A seventh brother, Robert, nearest to my father in age, was born sickly and lingered on for several months before dying. My father later told me that his older brothers were more like uncles to him because of the differences in age. By the time he entered first grade, they were already getting married and starting families of their own.

Parts of rural Georgia in those years resembled life in much of rural Pakistan. The large families, the bare feet, the tenant farming, the lack of plumbing—his father might as well have been an unknown Sindhi farmer, living precariously from year to year off the land, putting his children to work, gathering up the grain at harvest, trying to postpone for another year the final day of reckoning when debts came due, when the tax collector or the moneylender might yet again repossess the slight and rocky acreage that gave sustenance to what often seemed like an entire tribe. One of my father's earliest memories was of learning to plow in straight rows behind a mule.

The history of the Addleton clan was no less undistinguished, despite our best efforts to find heroism and family honor somewhere in our lineage. In Shikarpur, upper-class Sindhis tended to think of Americans as barbarians, especially if they had no sense of family history. It was a standing joke that most Americans did not even know the names of their grandparents. In contrast, family names in Pakistan formed the basis for entire sagas. A Moghul would be descended from one of the major Muslim dynasties to rule in India, a Durrani could claim ties to the royal house of Afghanistan, and a Bokhari could relive the days of ancient Islamic glory in Bokhara, in central Asia. A Sayyid, descended as he was from the family of the Prophet Mohammed, On Whom Be Peace, merited special respect. Our own family history seemed shabby by comparison. My father scoured telephone books across America for other Addletons and found none. In the end, he concluded that we were related to every one of the dozen or so Addletons living in the United States, almost all of whom lived in middle Georgia. Even those dozen or so seemed in danger of dying out. For some reason, almost all the surviving male Addletons in any generation tended to have only daughters.

According to one family legend, the first Addleton to come to North America arrived before the American Revolution, having been sent there as an indentured servant. In fact, the records at the Old Bailey Court near St. Paul's Cathedral in London do include a reference to a "John Eddleton" held at Newgate Prison, a possible ancestor. In 1741, he, along with a partner, Will Brown, had been found guilty and sentenced to seven years of transportation for stealing five perokes valued at four shillings ten pence. *Peroke* is the old English word for a powdered wig. Judging from the other cases appearing in the same court report, he had been lucky not to hang.

Throughout the second half of the 1700s, the Addleton family name appears several times on Massachusetts census ledgers, in court records, and on lists of births, deaths, and marriages. One Addleton lived on Nantucket Island. Others lived in Boston, the names surviving among brief references that hint of scandal. In 1751, alongside the entry in the marriage intention list for a Susanna Addleton, is the word *forbid*, suggesting impropriety or, perhaps, the fact that she was underage. Another eighteenth-century Addleton is mentioned in the Boston selectman's minutes, in records from a town meeting held on June 28, 1762. "William Baker informed the Selectman that he had taken into his family a maid servant, one Addleton from the town of Milton. Ordered that Mr. Adams be directed to warn said Addleton to depart this town in the manner the law directs."

By the early 1800s, a diminishing number of Massachusetts Addletons were being listed in the various census reports. Only one male, Cyrus, the grandfather of my own grandfather, survived to carry on

the family name. He made his way south to Georgia in the years before the Civil War. There he met and married a woman named Eliza
Kitchens and had two sons, Horace and Robert. Robert in turn had
nine children, five with his first wife, Penny, and four with his second
wife, Mary Wilson. One of these children, Benjamin Lark, was my
grandfather.

When Ben Addleton was in his eighties, I tried to record his stories of what it had been like to grow up in middle Georgia in the early
part of the twentieth century. By then it was too late. He recalled
something about a runaway horse and buggy on Vineville Avenue in
Macon. He mentioned that his wife, Bessie Gordon, then sixteen, had
brought a can of snuff with her on their wedding day. He told me that
he did not believe that the astronauts had ever walked on the moon;
the government was capable of staging anything to win elections and
keep public morale high, he said. The entire event had probably been
filmed in Hollywood.

The recollections of my father's brothers and sisters were equally
hazy. Otha, his oldest surviving brother, did recall that all his paternal
uncles had died before they reached the age of fifty. When my grandfather turned forty-nine, he became convinced that his life too was
almost over and approached the half-century mark with fear and trembling. "He went around the entire year depressed, sure that his time
had come," Otha recalled to me. "He was surprised when he turned
fifty and was still alive and well." In fact, almost half his life was still
ahead. He died in 1982 at the age of ninety-four, outliving three sons
and a daughter, his life having spanned almost half the history of the
United States.

My father grew up in a household that nowadays would be considered "disadvantaged" and "below the poverty line." Steady work was
as much as most people ever aspired to. When times were good, his
father was a "masher" for Central Georgia Railways in the Macon
marshalling yards, banging old boxcars back into shape. More often,
he alternated between a series of tenant farms and the cotton mills. In
this, he followed a pattern set by his own father, who had worked for
the Bibb Manufacturing Company for $1.50 a day and, at the age of
sixty-two, had almost lost an arm in a carding machine. The children

helped work the farm, until the agricultural economy of Georgia collapsed and stands of pine were allowed to grow up where rows of corn had once been cultivated. By then the children were growing up and they too began to move on, to wage employment in nearby Macon. Most found jobs in the nearby Willingham Cotton Mills, earning weekly salaries in the single digits.

The shift toward wage employment was accompanied by another move, a movement toward the church. There was a Willingham Baptist Church not far away, built by the same family who owned both the Willingham Cotton Mills and Willingham Village, a small mill town at the edge of Macon. A young and dynamic student preacher from Alabama, E. C. Sheehan, married a mill foreman's daughter and also preached at local revival services there. He spoke of heaven and hell in a matter-of-fact way and asked for nothing less than the emptying out of one's entire soul before God the Father Almighty, maker of heaven and earth. The growing congregation consisted mostly of dispossessed Georgians who were only then just beginning to migrate from the countryside to the city. It was almost like Pentecost. Onetime farmers, previously more at home in late-night country taverns, suddenly got saved. Sin, salvation, the figure of Christ, and the presence of the Lord suddenly took on new meaning. Contrary to received wisdom about the spirituality of those who work the land, it was not as tenant farmers that the Addleton family came into the church. It was as a salaried working class; as mill workers, railway mashers, and day laborers trying to make sense of a strange new world. One by one, family members walked down the aisle. Ben Addleton responded to the altar call last of all. He had been known as a strong man, a ladies' man, a formidable baseball player who gambled in pool halls and got drunk on weekends. After he finally walked the aisle, he never touched a drop of alcohol again.

The Second World War brought still more change. In retrospect, there is a clear family divide between those of my father's brothers and sisters who came of age before the war and those who grew up afterward. Those who started work in the 1930s had little more than a primary school education and worked in the cotton mills first, often as teenagers. All of the women later got married to local men, most in blue-collar trades such as fire fighting or building construction. One by one, the brothers also started to leave the cotton mills. One joined the Army Air Force and another became a life insurance salesman. Several became Baptist or Pentecostal preachers, lack of formal education being considered much less important than spiritual maturity when it came to ministering from a pulpit. Most also eventually sat and passed their Georgia High School equivalency exams and some, later in life, went on to college or Bible school. The wives worked as office secretaries or manned cafeteria lines in public school lunchrooms. All the brothers and sisters married and had children of their own. There were twenty-seven Addleton grandchildren, followed by more than fifty great-grandchildren. True to historical pattern, almost all the grandsons had daughters and almost all the granddaughters gave birth to sons.

My father, the eleventh of Ben Addleton's fourteen children, had more opportunity than his older brothers and sisters, at least in matters of education. He graduated from Sidney Lanier High School in Macon in the spring of 1947, just as the post-World War II prosperity was about to begin transforming the old impoverished South into the new Sunbelt. When he travelled by bus to Columbia Bible College in Columbia, South Carolina, in the fall of 1947, he was the first in his family to finish high school and go immediately on to college. He joined the school barbell club, participated in mission prayer groups, and was elected vice president of his class. He was driven by many concerns, but more than anything he was driven by a desire to yield his life completely to the Lord, even if it meant serving Him in the farthest regions of the globe, unto the ends of the earth. He told me later that he had made this commitment underneath a pine tree, near the house not far from Macon that he was helping his father build out of old railway two-by-twos. The tree was still standing when we visited the United States in 1965 and again in 1970, as if to give added validity to what was, after all, a historic commitment made to a historic person who walked the shores of Galilee and, two thousand years later, still offered hope and comfort to all who called upon His name.

•     •     •

One other event occurred not long after the end of World War II that, in retrospect, takes on added meaning, a crossing of two lives that eventually determined my own. It happened in September 1946, when my father was walking alongside Walnut Creek, which ran through Jones County and flowed into the Ocmulgee River near Macon. He was near the bridge on Old Clinton Road when he saw a funeral party passing by, a black hearse followed by a solemn and slow-moving procession of other cars. "They're burying Mr. Simmons," someone said, breaking the silence. "He died yesterday on the Gray Highway. He fell out of the back of a truck and never said another word again." It was my mother's father who was being carried away. A circle was broken, a family would never fully recover. My mother was sitting in the back seat of one of the cars.

My mother was born Bettie Rose Simmons in October 1931, on a farm in Jones County, Georgia. Her material circumstances were somewhat more elevated than those of my father, but the psychological burdens were almost certainly harder to bear. The Simmons family aspired to the comforts of middle-class life and almost reached it. In the end, the dream was destroyed, partly because of random tragedy and partly because of drink.

Her father, Melton Simmons, started his professional career as a meat-cutter at the Broadway Super Market in Macon. The family had come from counties farther south, toward Savannah, "from down Jesup way." The family tree was just as hazy as my father's, but there were stories of ancestors who fought with Francis Marion in the American Revolution, of a grandnephew scalped after crossing the Altamaha River in the early 1800s, of a great-uncle who lost an eye while serving as a sharpshooter with the Forty-ninth Georgia during the Civil War, of a family estate that had been burned to the ground during Sherman's march to the sea. One surviving last will and testament does in fact mention slaves—and a no-good son-in-law who inherited a single dollar, "because I have no desire for him to enjoy any more of my wealth." According to one story, passed on through my great-grandmother who lived to be a hundred, the winter after the war was so bad that the family was reduced to scratching for salt amid the sand scattered on the smokehouse floor.

Years later, the Simmons family had become yet one more rural family that was gradually moving toward town, part of an army of people transforming Georgia within a single generation from a mainly rural society to a largely urban one. The transformation itself was never neat or tidy. For the Simmons family, at least, there were several shifts back and forth, between countryside and town, between the security of a salaried job in the city and the uncertainties of farming life. At times, they kept one foot in both camps. When my mother was born, her mother managed the farm while her father worked as a butcher in nearby Macon, both jobs having been provided by Greatuncle Monroe who owned the farm in Jones County as well as the Broadway Super Market in Macon.

Not long afterward it became apparent that Uncle Monroe's farm was a front for a bootleg liquor operation that crossed state lines. Melton Simmons, my mother's father, was often away for days at a time, driving his truck to distant towns in Ohio and Michigan and Florida "to pick up a load of dishes," as the children were told. My mother recalled that she was often awakened by the clatter of dishes. Only later did she realize that it was the sound of ceramic and glass whiskey bottles, clanking against each other in the dead of night.

During those years, the farm became to the family an idyllic dream, almost a Garden of Eden, a vision of how things might have been. There was the usual mix of goats, cows, and mules. There were the peach, pear, and apple trees, canning in the summer, butchering hogs and making cane syrup in the fall. A stream ran nearby and there was a large rock in one of the pastures where arrowheads were often found, evidence of Indian tribes who had once inhabited the same landscape. As I was growing up, I wondered if perhaps my mother had imagined, as my brother and I imagined when we walked among the ruins at Moenjodaro, what it might be like to have been born into a past century, into another family, into a civilization that worshipped other gods. Did she too wonder about those who came before, walked the same piece of ground, and vanished almost without a trace, leaving only a few small artifacts behind, the cups and glasses and arrowheads, shreds of surviving evidence that lived on long after the hands that fashioned them had finally ceased to move? The psalmist was right, our lives were brief, brief as the morning dew, as feebly remembered as the disappearing embers of an evening fire.

The Simmons family was smaller than my father's—eight children rather than the fourteen who formed the Addleton clan. Six of the eight Simmons children were girls. Dr. Zachary was there for one home delivery and announced that yet another girl had been born. "Well, put her back in that bag and take her away," my grandmother exclaimed while my mother, then six years old, listened quietly in the next room. My mother later said that even as a child she had been embarrassed by the steady progression of children. She wished her mother would stop.

Nonetheless, by rural Georgia standards, the Simmons family at that time lived comfortably. "We may have been poor," my mother once told me. "But it wasn't like the Addleton family. There were so many of them. Everyone knew they were as poor as church mice." Children on welfare got free lunches at school; the Simmons children were able to buy their own. Poor children ate brown biscuits made of whole wheat flour; the Simmons children ate biscuits made of white flour and made no attempt to hide the fact. Meals were never a problem. On occasion, clothes were even ordered by post, out of a Sears mail order catalog. "There was no inside plumbing," my mother told us later. "However, we had a very fine outhouse. It had a cement floor and a large raised seat with a cover. It was well-built and modern for its time." This description could only have come from my mother: the recollection of small detail, the sense for the comic, the view that even outhouses could somehow be used to define class. The Simmons family may have had an outhouse, but it was one of the finest outhouses in the length and breadth of Jones County, Georgia.

Among the closest neighbors were the Barkers, who owned a dairy farm nearby. Frances Barker was remarkable, a woman who aspired after culture, who wrote poetry by the ream, and who, in later years, became a correspondent for the weekly *Jones County News,* filling her columns with a mixture of local happenings, philosophical ruminations, and quotations from the great writers of history, Shakespeare sometimes and, more often, the Bible. Her husband, physically immense and with a foul temper, made life difficult. "I am certain that he beat his wife regularly," my mother told me. "I can remember one time hearing her shriek while she was helping him down in the milk barn." By some accounts, her husband later committed suicide. Her only son became a bouncer in a nightclub, I was told, a good ole country boy who kept hound dogs and flew a ragged Confederate flag from the roof of the family homestead. His mother continued to write newspaper columns for the *Jones County News* into the 1980s, finally concluding a journalism career that lasted sixty-seven years. When she was placed in a nursing home outside Gray, her son, by some accounts, began to sell off parts of the Barker farm—in fact, the Simmons farm, because the Barkers had later bought the land and farm houses that once belonged to Uncle Monroe—as plots for new suburban housing, for commuters interested in recovering their rural roots and, at the same time, escaping higher Macon city taxes. She died in 1993, two years after I had last seen her in a crowded county nursing home, rocking slowly and with a distant look, as if she had already taken her leave.

The Simmons family did not attend church, though my mother says she sometimes went on her own to First Baptist in Gray. In the summer months, Mrs. Barker organized an informal Vacation Bible School for children in the neighboring farms. The group was known as the Sunbeams, their theme song beginning with the words, "Jesus wants me for a sunbeam, a sunbeam" and ending with the refrain, "I'll be a sunbeam for Him."

"That was the first time I thought that I would love to be a missionary in some far and distant place," my mother once told me, recalling Frances Barker's Vacation Bible School classes. In some far and distant place: in China perhaps, where Lottie Moon had labored for the Southern Baptist Foreign Mission Board; in Burma, where another Baptist hero, Adoniram Judson, had taken two successive wives to early graves; or even in India, the land of yet another Baptist saint, William Carey the humble cobbler, who grew up in poverty and almost single-handedly inspired the modern Protestant missionary movement, which survived long after the British Empire had disappeared and which inspired even my mother and father to leave their family and home in middle Georgia and go to a far country among a people who had not yet had an opportunity to hear about the saving work of Jesus Christ.

The rest of the Simmons family remained unmoved by such inspiration and dwelt on more mundane concerns. Uncle Monroe went legitimate and opened the Macon Liquor Store, a package shop on Broadway. This was followed by a chain of upmarket taverns, each one known as the Brass Rail. "Respectable saloons," a relative later recalled, "the kind of place where a man could get a drink without also getting into a fight." Melton Simmons too moved back into town, to a job cutting meat at the Mulberry Market. He also began to drink heavily. His wife cried the day they left the farm.

Bennie Simmons, formerly a Sheffield, had grown up in the country and had stopped school at the end of seventh grade, on account of her mother's poor health. She had met her husband at seventeen at a cane-grinding party and then eloped a year later, at age eighteen, to marry him. She knew her father would be upset and wrote home saying, "If you are mad and don't want me to come back, I won't—but please send me my clothes." Her father later reconciled himself to the marriage and over time grew to like his son-in-law.

Perhaps it was the move to Macon that started the downward spiral. Melton lost his meat-cutting job and became a carpenter, then a bricklayer. He was often unemployed. He kept drinking, sometimes spending the night away from home. At other times, he stumbled inside and sobered up with a cold bath. His wife talked often of the country, of how much better it was when they had a piece of land and she could grow vegetables and raise chickens, where the air was clean and the children could run and be free. Some time later they moved once again, to a four-room house on the edge of town that rented for six dollars a month. The house even had a telephone, a six-party line with the number 285 W-3. The Simmons family answered after three rings.

Then the war came and my mother's oldest brother, Raymond, was drafted into the army. He went by Greyhound bus to Atlanta for his induction and travelled to Texas before being sent to the Pacific, to Okinawa and finally to Japan. My mother wrote to him all the time he was away. When he finally came home, he presented a Japanese bayonet to his mother as a memento of the war. After the war, he became a butcher, like his father before him. James, my mother's youngest brother, lied about his age and joined the Army Air Force. He was disappointed when the war ended before he too could be sent overseas. Instead he left the service and moved to Detroit with a service buddy, in search of a job in the rapidly expanding automobile industry, one of an army of southerners, black and white alike, who moved north in search of work.

Sister Sara quit school and went to work at Cleo's Barbecue, a short distance down the road from the house on Gray Highway, the small clapboard house that rented for six dollars a month. Sara was still a teenager then, young and beautiful, with suitors at every turn. She was not allowed to walk to work alone; someone had to accompany her at least halfway. Ordinarily it was my mother's job. On one occasion, when Bettie Rose was eleven years old, after a visit to Frances Barker's, she complained that she was tired and asked her mother to let the two younger sisters, Jenelle and Shirley, take her place. And so the three of them walked up the road together, three small shadows disappearing around a corner.

Only one figure returned, a stout black woman who came running down the road toward the Simmons house, breaking the quietness of the afternoon, waving her arms like a slow-moving windmill, shouting hysterically, an image of the Angel of Death almost, a portent of things to come. Jenelle was not coming back. She had been hit by a wrecker belonging to the Dunlap Chevrolet Company. She had a fractured skull and was taken by ambulance to Macon Hospital. A neighbor suggested that the family file a legal suit against the truck company, a suggestion that was immediately dismissed out of hand. Accidents just happened; it was nobody's fault.

My mother remembered the heartbreak and tragedy the rest of her life and grew fearful even when her own children returned home late or walked the streets alone. Jenelle was ten years old, in retrospect her favorite sister, the sibling closest to her in age. She came into the world a little more than a year after my mother had been born. Perhaps, if my mother had not been so tired, she would have walked with Sara to Cleo's Barbecue and Jenelle's life might have been spared.

"She died with her hand looking as if she was clutching Shirley's," my mother later remembered. The funeral was held in the school auditorium in Gray, near the county courthouse. Hundreds attended from farms across the county. At one point, Frances Barker got up in front of everyone and said, "When Jenelle left us, it was like the sunshine had gone out of our lives."

After Jenelle died, Melton Simmons drank more and more and worked less and less. His temper was at times terrifying. One night, in a fit of anger, he returned home and went through all the family picture albums, systematically destroying every photograph in which he appeared. Only one picture survived, a framed portrait of a middle-aged man with a receding hairline, a large round face, brown eyes, and a closed mouth that gave away no secrets. When I grew up, one of my mother's sisters told me that I looked exactly like her father. I often wondered what else I had inherited from him, besides his looks, besides his tight-lipped expression, besides the genes that produced what my mother always hopefully referred to as a "Roman forehead" and what I knew with resignation to be simply the first sign of impending baldness.

In September 1946, when my mother was fourteen years old, there was another accident, near the same spot where Jenelle had been hit by a wrecker and killed four years before. This time, Melton Simmons, then aged forty-six, was sitting on the back of a truck; he tapped the window, to signal the driver to stop and let him off. The driver braked immediately and my mother's father lost his balance, hit the pavement headfirst, and never regained consciousness. The same black woman, arms waving like an out of control windmill, ran toward the house to announce the news. The county coroner, W. T. Pitts, signed a death certificate that said "chest crushed, fractured skull, accidently run over by a truck." His occupation was listed as carpenter.

My mother was in school at Jones County High at the time and overheard the school bus drivers talking quietly among themselves about an accident down the road, about a man who had fallen off a pickup truck and been killed that very morning. "I will never know why it came to me, but I was pensive all the way home and when we got home and I saw all the cars around I knew in my heart what had happened," she recalled. "I was devastated. I had had a conversation with my Dad that morning before going to school. We stood on the back porch and he told me that he thought I could get some new shoes now as he had been working again. I remembered that for a long time afterward. In spite of everything, he was a very good Dad."

The second tragedy brought still more dramatic change to what was left of the Simmons family. Another move had to be made, back to Macon, to a new house on Flamingo Drive. The insurance money and Raymond's GI loan privileges helped out. My grandmother went to work as a seamstress at the Happ Pants Factory in Macon. Sara was already married and Raymond and James got married in turn. My mother, now the oldest child still at home, looked after her three younger sisters. In 1948, at the age of sixteen, she graduated from Miller High. She did what she was supposed to do and got a job, first with a local telephone company, then as a helper with Jimmy Perkin's Florists, later as a clerk at the Banker's Life and Insurance Company. She also came to know the Lord.

It is hard in retrospect to recreate the spiritual experience of one's parents, to understand encounters with the Almighty God that affected not only my mother and my father but their children also after them. The sociologist would offer one explanation, about the Great Depression, about migration from farm to city, about the influence of race and class. The psychologist would explain events differently, perhaps with talk of childhood trauma, an alcoholic father who failed, an adolescent who needed to believe. And yet it all seems so inadequate, a comic book version of what really happened in the life of a single soul who happened to be my mother, thrown unaware into the confusion of what became the postwar generation of Americans, producing babies, raising families, making even missionary families wealthy by the standards of rural Georgia in the 1930s.

Respectability, not money, is what drove my mother most of all. Uncle Monroe, the bootlegger who employed relatives, first on his farm and later in his liquor stores, offered one view of the world that was momentarily exciting but ultimately seemed to be built on sand. "His entire life was spent in the pursuit of money and what it could buy," my mother said. It was not one that she could ever countenance or wish upon her children. In this at least she was successful, because all of her own children grew up with an inherent inability to manage anything even remotely involving risk, dollars, or salesmanship.

Still, there was something exciting about Uncle Monroe and the life he chose for himself, a life so different than what any of us would ever experience. He lived on Merritt Avenue in Macon, just off Ingleside Drive. His wife was an Italian Catholic woman who brought with her a son by a previous marriage. He maintained a second home where, it was rumored, he kept a secretary from South Georgia who doubled as his mistress. According to one surviving uncle, he was convinced that everyone had a price, that money could buy the allegiance of anybody. He was a hard taskmaster and reportedly beat his employees.

My mother once stayed in the Merritt Avenue house for several days, when Uncle Monroe was away on one of his frequent business trips. She was horrified to discover a cache of black and white studio photographs, pictures of girls with whom he had presumably become involved. On another occasion, she drove and almost wrecked his Cadillac. Nonetheless, Uncle Monroe continued to shower his niece with gifts—one hundred dollars upon her high school graduation, and a still larger check on her wedding day. The money was used to pay for my parent's honeymoon in the Smokey Mountains. They spent the first night together at the old Georgia Hotel in downtown Athens on their way north.

Looking back, I can only barely imagine what kind of man Uncle Monroe must have been. The bootlegger, the entrepreneur, the tight-fisted boss who beat his employees, the suave man of the world who married an Italian Catholic and kept his mistress in a second home. Was it true, or was it my mother who was imagining things, embellishing the story of a relative who lived in a large house in town, owned a Cadillac, and operated a chain of bars and liquor stores? I met Uncle Monroe face-to-face only once, when I saw him as an ill-tempered old man with a thin remnant of gray hair, confined to a wheelchair, hunched up against the cold, unlikely to live out another winter. When we visited, my parents only told me that he had fought in the First World War, had been shot in the leg, and was still carrying the fragments of a German bullet in his right knee. At eight years old, I never imagined the places he had been, the stories he could tell, the memories that would soon disappear forever. Only much later did I realize why my parents always talked in hushed tones whenever we drove by the liquor store on Broadway.

.    .    .

It was in February 1948, at the age of sixteen, that my mother became a Christian, taking the fateful decision that would determine the course of her life. She spoke of it to us only on rare occasions. "One Sunday morning I went down to Houston Avenue and took a bus going south. I followed the crowd who got off the bus and ended up at Mikado Baptist Church. I attended that church for a long time. A great change came over me and I found acceptance and love. I became an active part of the young people there, sang in the choir and even began to teach Sunday School." Her own mother was horrified and feared her daughter, now unwilling to go to dances, was becoming some kind of "religious nut." E. C. Sheehan, the same minister who brought most of the Addleton family to the Lord during his revivals at Willingham Baptist Church, had started preaching at Mikado and was having a similar impact on neighborhoods and families living in South Macon.

Her mother's apprehensions took on a new urgency when Bettie Rose began talking about going to college to prepare for a life of "full-time Christian service." My mother, always determined, visited Tennessee Temple College in Chattanooga and was convinced that she had to cut her family ties and begin a life of her own. Like my father, she was the first in her family to finish high school, the first and only child in her generation ever to go on to college. Brother Sheehan was encouraging at every step of the way. The ladies at Mikado Baptist Church arranged a shower, giving her everything from clothes to a travelling iron to a footlocker to put it all in. They also gave her a one-hundred-dollar check as a parting gift. My mother's mother was much less pleased. At one point, she said that if her daughter went off to Bible school she would not be welcome at home again. She went anyway, supporting herself by working in the library during the week and at Mangel's Dress Shop in downtown Chattanooga on weekends.

Soon after starting at Tennessee Temple, my mother received an unexpected letter from Hubert Addleton, by now a senior at Columbia Bible College. They had met at Mikado Baptist Church in Macon during the summer and chatted briefly before Hubert left on a summer mission project sponsored by the Southern Baptist Home Mission Board in the Ozarks in rural Arkansas. They met once more, after he had returned to Macon and had been asked to give a devotional at a church youth party at a friend's house. His devotional was entitled "Demas Hath Forsaken Me" and had been taken from Timothy's Second Epistle. "Do your best to join me soon, for Demas has deserted me because his heart was set on this world." It was a revealing commentary, a text that could only have been selected by an aspiring minister of the Gospel, an expectant missionary whose own heart and soul was even then directed toward other continents. Unbeknown to my father, my mother too had already forsaken the world and committed herself to a life of full-time missionary service abroad.

The correspondence turned into a romance the following summer, when my mother returned to Macon and my father found a temporary job at Sears, Roebuck and Company. "We dated all summer and really got to know one another well," my mother remembered. My father had by this time been accepted at New Orleans Theological Seminary, one of several operated by the Southern Baptists. He persuaded Bettie to follow him and begin nursing training at Baptist Hospital, also in New Orleans. "Hubert visited me there. Since he did not have much money, we went to a drugstore and had a soda and walked along St. Charles Avenue. We saw a synagogue that was open. It was the Jewish New Year. We went inside and sat down for most of the service. Afterwards we walked back to the dormitory and sat outside in the balmy September evening. It was then that he proposed to me."

They were married nine months later, at Mikado Baptist Church in Macon where the two of them had first met as young adults, where my mother had come to know the Lord. Brother Sheehan, the preacher who played such a significant role in both of their lives, read the marriage vows. More than forty years later, Brother Sheehan still lives in Macon and remains active in the church, a powerful and persuasive preacher whose own ministry now spans well over sixty years. There are more than a few old Maconites who hope he will still be around to conduct their funerals. Willingham Baptist Church and Mikado Baptist Church, the sites of so many revivals in the past, have been sold to mainly black congregations that, in their turn, are continuing in the tradition of powerful preaching, stirring music, and inspired prayer.

It took one more year for my own father to complete his degree at New Orleans Theological Seminary. During that time, he served as part-time pastor at O'Zion Baptist Church in Meadville, Mississippi, north of New Orleans. Payment included a bag of farm produce to help see them through the following week. Practical seminary work included evangelistic missions in the bayous, from which the image of an elderly black woman, tears streaming down her face as she sang "All My Trials," stayed with him the rest of his life. He passed the image on to me, a scene so vivid that I sometimes imagine I was there myself.

It was doubtless in seminary where my father also read Thomas Merton's *Seven Storey Mountain* for the first time, the book, he once told me, that was the most important he ever read. Merton found truth and comfort in the Catholic Church, but his story of a spiritual quest set against the backdrop of a morally bankrupt postwar American society had obvious parallels for a Baptist country boy from middle Georgia who had already dedicated his life to God. Much to my surprise, my father also told me that he wished there had been a monastic tradition within the Protestant church. In another lifetime, he could easily have imagined himself as a monk living the contemplative life. Instead, he wrote away to foreign mission societies. The Southern Baptist Foreign Mission Board at that time had not yet opened up a work in either India or Pakistan, the foreign lands where my father felt God had called him to serve. In the end, he sent an application to the Conservative Baptist Foreign Mission Society, then based in Chicago, Illinois, and only recently formed as an alternative to the more theologically liberal American Baptist missionary organizations. He and my mother were accepted almost immediately, setting them firmly on the course needed to realize their lifetime calling of serving as ministers of the Gospel to Pakistan.

Trying to be a Sindhi, c. 1960: aged three, wearing local clothes outside our house in Ratodero.

Atop a borrowed Land Rover during a family vacation in Kaghan Valley, northern Pakistan, c. 1964.

This photograph must
have been taken in
Murree during the
summer of 1964, not
long after I turned
seven. I had recently
completed my first
term at boarding
school.

CONSERVATIVE BAPTIST FOREIGN MISSION SOCIETY
P. O. Box 5                                    Wheaton, Illinois

*"Ye also helping us together by PRAYER
for us . . ."* —II Cor. 1:11
*"For we are labourers together with God."* —I Cor. 3:9

HUBERT and BETTIE ADDLETON
David          Nancy          Jonathan
*SERVING CHRIST IN WEST PAKISTAN*

"Prayer Card" circulated among supporters
back in the U.S. during our first furlough,
c. 1960.

## MISSIONARIES TO PAKISTAN

*Lord, show me what I need
And teach me how to pray,
And help me when I seek Thy grace
To mean the words I say.*

— John Burton

<u>Home Address:</u>

Conservative Baptist Foreign
  Mission Society
P.O. Box 5
Weaton, Ill.  60187
<u>In Pakistan:</u>

Box 11
Shikarpur, West Pakistan

### THE ADDLETON FAMILY

| Jonathan | | David |
| Hubert | Nancy | Bettie |

"Prayer Card" circulated among supporters back in the U.S. during our third
furlough ten years later, c. 1970.

Sandes Home, built during colonial times as a place of rest for convalescing
British soldiers and later turned into a boarding hostel for students from
Murree Christian School.

Jhika Gali, the small mountain village below Sandes Home and a mile from the main school building at Gharial.

Jhika Gali by Alistair Bavington.

David's 1973 high school graduation photograph outside Holy Trinity in
Murree. One church in the U.S. dropped their support on account of this picture:
David's hair was too long, Nancy's dress was too short, and my mother was
wearing a pants suit.

Chess tournament
at the American-
International School
in Kabul, Afghanistan,
c. 1974. I seem
to already be in deep
trouble and promptly
lost all four games.

The 1974 edition of the Murree Christian School Jesters. Standing from right to left: Colin Old, Paul Johnson, Graham Duncan, Mark Pegors, Frank Pressley, Stephen Rasmussen (captain), Stanley Brown, Stephen Rock, Larry Cutherell; sitting from right to left: Stephen McCurry, Timothy Old, Nathan Irwin, Thomas Brown, Jonathan Addleton.

Trying to be an American, c. 1975: aged seventeen, following a basketball game at the International School of Islamabad during my final year in Pakistan.

# FOUR

# The Getting of Wisdom

Murree became the defining geographic feature

of my early life, even as middle Georgia served

that purpose for my parents. It was not only

that I happened to be born there, that it was

stamped into my passport, that it caused comment

and consternation among officialdom whenever I

applied for a visa, went through a customs

clearance, or filled out any government form that

demanded information on date and place of birth;

it was also because I went to school there. I lived

in Murree for nine months out of every year, until

I reached the age of eighteen. I was first sent off to boarding at Murree Christian School in the spring of 1964, at the age of six. I graduated twelve years later in a class of fifteen, the largest graduating class the school had ever had.

Murree Christian School was founded in 1956 specifically for the children of Protestant missionaries working in Pakistan. With Pakistan's independence in 1947 followed so quickly by conflict over Kashmir, the more usual boarding schools—Woodstock in north India, Kodikanal in the south—became much less accessible. Several foreign mission societies banded together to organize a comparable missionary school for Pakistan. The search committee established to survey possible sites concentrated on smaller towns with cooler climes, located where possible at higher altitudes. Quetta, a popular choice among the Conservative Baptists because it was relatively close to Upper Sind, was briefly considered. Abbottabad, a scenic northern valley that was also home to Pakistan's military academy and several of the country's leading private schools, was another candidate. Families associated with the Evangelical Alliance Mission, popularly known as TEAM, championed this choice, partly because Abbottabad was the center of much of their own work in Pakistan. In the end, Murree was chosen, mostly because acceptable facilities were offered virtually free of charge. The Anglican Bishop in Lahore agreed to hand over an empty garrison church, built for British soldiers at Gharial, less than five miles from the Murree Post Office, as a site for the main school building. At the same time, the United Presbyterian Mission offered the use of Sandes Soldiers' Home, only a mile away from Gharial and also inherited from the British Raj, as a hostel.

In retrospect, the tiny school for missionary children that developed in the Murree Hills was at once one of the most peculiar and heroic ventures in international education ever attempted. Enrollment in all twelve grades never exceeded 180 and more usually hovered around 130, an average of just over ten students per class. Recruiting the required number of teachers and houseparents needed to begin a school term was almost always a matter for urgent prayer. At one time or another, as many as two dozen missionary agencies representing virtually all major Protestant denominations figured on the school board. Each agency was "assessed" according to the number of "their students" who were enrolled. Fees were based partly on this assessment, partly on the number of full-time staff that any particular mission board contributed. The school board set the strong moral tone and most of the rules governing day-to-day behavior. There were discussions every year about whether dancing or card-playing would be permitted, about rules for dating, about the number of nonmissionary children allowed to attend. In the end, the most conservative views usually prevailed. Teaching methods and curriculum, ostensibly based on those of an American high school, reflected a strong British influence. Students and staff came from throughout the English-speaking world: the United States, Canada, Britain, Australia, and New Zealand. From time to time, Norwegians, Swedes, Finns, Danes, Poles, Germans, and even Japanese, Iranian, and Sri Lankan students also attended.

The school architecture, together with the mountains, helped shape early attitudes about the world surrounding us. I came to love both. It was the mountains that were most spectacular and seemed to go on forever, to Kashmir first and then on into Tibet in one direction, toward the Pamirs and then the steppes of Soviet Central Asia in another. During the monsoon season, in July and August, it was as if we lived at the far edge of a finite, four-cornered universe. Clouds lay heavy with rain in the mountain valleys below and, from the cliffs above, it looked like we could simply step off and fall freely in space forever. Lightning flashed often against the sky, thunder broke loud and lasted long and the sun often stayed hidden for days at a time. Sometimes, days became so dark it seemed as if the world was about to end. "This morning it was really strange," I reported home to my parents in one letter, written when I was twelve years old. "Part of the sky was dark, the other blue. The wind would blow furiously, then it would quieten down. The thing that really amazed me was the two rainbows. It was really beautiful. There was a tint of red in the sky. To me, it was a sign that God was not forgetting us down on earth and that He was still alive."

The farthest peaks, Nanga Parbat most notably, were always covered in snow. By late September, when the last of the monsoon clouds had begun to dissipate, late summer gradually gave way to early autumn and, ridge by ridge, the deep snow moved closer. Finally, by December at the latest, the first snow flurries began to appear on the Murree ridge. For some reason the heaviest snow usually came late at night. "After lights went out, I looked out at the snow coming down," I wrote home to my parents when I was ten, describing a night that I still remember well. "It was really beautiful." And again, the following year: "It snowed on the mountain away from us. It looks so beautiful." A sixth-grade vocabulary was somehow inadequate to describe the scenes we saw around us every day, on the mile walk to and from school when through the pines the setting sun set fire to the distant mountains and then, in the dim light of early evening, charred them first to blue and then to deep purple before enveloping them completely in the darkness of another Himalayan night. It was hard to move beyond the word *beautiful* without sounding ridiculous.

The physical solidity of the school buildings also left a lasting impression. The deconsecrated garrison church at Gharial, which became Murree Christian School, was a drafty, barnlike edifice constructed, according to the inscription on the tiny bell tower, in 1909. A family of flying squirrels lived in the rafters, occasionally making a dramatic appearance during school concerts and plays. The building was shaped like a cross and built of cut stone. The casement windows were small and narrow, admitting only a minimum of light. Classrooms were constructed along the sides of the sanctuary and the central part of the nave became a basketball court. The north transept was turned into a library, the south transept into a chemistry laboratory. The entire altar area was retained as a stage. Enough old pews had been salvaged to seat the entire student body for plays, special events, and Friday morning chapel services. A single granite memorial plaque that had once adorned an earlier church also survived and was kept polished in the English literature room, in remembrance of eight British soldiers (Lieutenant Boothby and Privates Dripot, Tubb, Keating, Ponting, Clement, Goodman, and Humphries) who had died at Gharial in the cholera epidemic of 1876. It would have been hard to recreate a more suitable site for a Christian school, like a monastery almost, dedicated to instilling faith from an early age.

The architectural atmosphere at the main hostel a mile away was equally impressive. Sandes Home had been built decades earlier, in the late nineteenth century, under the auspices of a Lady Sandes from England who had devoted her life to funding a network of soldiers' homes across British India. Most were constructed in hill stations such as Murree or Simla, where soldiers were sent for rest and recuperation during the hot summer months. The goal was to combine relaxation with spiritual nourishment, an ideal that was not always successful.

When I was older, as part of my usual and often quixotic quest for historic documentation of any kind, I came across an odd reference to Sandes Home in an old diary kept by a Scottish chaplain, which somehow had survived at St. Paul's Presbyterian Church in Rawalpindi decades after the British had finally left. "Sergeants Wilson and Lambert of the Black Watch at tiffin and tea," the chaplain had written in July 1903, when he himself was vacationing in Murree. "They are returning to the plains before their furlough is over, because they find the food at the Soldier's Home too disgusting to keep them fit. It is very extraordinary that in such a Soldier's Home, men's souls may be diligently looked after, though their bodies are neglected. This is scandalous." It was the sort of sentiment with which any number of Murree students of a later generation would have wholeheartedly agreed.

Sandes Home was as windy and barnlike as the main school, though in this case it had at least been originally constructed with the needs of a hostel in mind. The ground floor consisted of two staff apartments, a kitchen, a large dining room, and a larger lounge area; upstairs was for sleeping. A long wooden verandah stretched along the front, decorated in places with white latticework. The doors and window frames were painted forest green. The front facade looked vaguely like a Victorian barracks masquerading as an alpine chalet. The interior was made mostly of wood. There were fireplaces throughout Sandes Home but, because of fears of fire, heating was allowed only in a single sitting room. A heavy iron gong hung from a tree in back of the kitchen, mainly to signal mealtimes but also for use as a makeshift fire alarm. Fire drills were arranged at frequent intervals, to test how long it would take to vacate the building in case of fire.

Over the years, several other buildings were added to the physical plant that formed Murree Christian School. Three separate cinder block boarding houses were built above Sandes Home and, in the opposite direction, four apartments were constructed to house staff members and their families. At the school a mile away, the old manse was turned into quarters for the principal, followed by construction of an outdoor basketball court, a larger hostel for girls, and a separate elementary school block. It seemed like construction was always going on, that we were always praying for relief from the latest cement shortage, that appeals were continually being made for more funds to construct a new building or refurbish an existing one. Our parents always felt like their sojourn in Pakistan would be temporary, that all missionaries might be expelled from the Islamic Republic of Pakistan at any time. And yet they built as if their work would last for generations. Four decades on, Murree Christian School continues to educate a new generation of missionary children, in the coolness of the hills looking out over the Jhelum River, in the shadow of distant Nanga Parbat, within full view of the mountains of Kashmir.

· · ·

One school rule stated that a child had to be at least six and a half years old before he or she could be sent off to boarding school. My turn came in March 1964, four months before my seventh birthday. I travelled the seven hundred miles from Shikarpur to Rawalpindi by train, then boarded a rented bus belonging to the Pindi Murree Transport Company for the two-hour trip into the mountains to school. Looking at my own two sons growing up now, I can hardly imagine how my parents could have done it. At the time, it seemed as natural as boarding a school bus for a county school half a dozen miles away.

Part of my early enthusiasm was based on a colossal misunderstanding about travel arrangements. Every term, Murree Christian School, like virtually every boarding school servicing Pakistan's middle and upper classes, hired a railway bogey, or carriage, that was in turn hitched to one of the major express trains such as the *Tez Gam* or *Khyber Mail*. We usually travelled third class, on hard wooden bunks that often dated back to British times. At the start of the journey, the Pakistan Western Railways conductor responsible for the train invariably scrawled in large chalk letters *MCS School Party* across each side of the green and yellow railway bogey. As six-year-olds boarding an ancient railway car for the first time, our first response was always to wonder when the balloons, cake, and party hats would arrive. Our parents compounded the misunderstanding by their frequent references to a forthcoming "train party" weeks ahead of time. Eagerly anticipating my first train party, I could barely wait for the festivities to begin.

Prior to that first train party, and before each of the couple of dozen other train parties that followed, my father gathered the family together and led us in prayer, a long and detailed prayer commending us to God's safekeeping in the weeks and months to follow. It was as if we would not be separated by seven hundred miles after all, that God at least would bridge the difference, binding us together in the chains of His everlasting love, holding us fast in a dimension where space no longer mattered, where distances became immaterial. Even from an early age, I regarded these as among my father's most moving and powerful prayers. The words were so heartfelt, the expressions so meaningful. I felt like crying at the end of them, not only because it meant we were about to depart; it was an emptying out of my father's feelings, in seemingly total sincerity, not only to God, but also to the three children whom he had helped bring into the world and was now sending from him, for three months at a time.

We usually boarded the train at Rohri Junction, thirty miles and an hour away from Shikarpur by Land Rover. Although a formal party never materialized, we nonetheless enjoyed every minute of the long train ride north. There was pleasure in the view from the window, particularly as the dust and date palms of Upper Sind gave way to the green of Punjab, with its enormous orange groves and endless wheat and mustard fields. The first sight of the mountains was even more wonderful, especially in March when the peaks of Kashmir were invariably covered in snow. The brief stops at railway stations along the way gave happiness of another kind—the smoke of tea stalls, the smell of freshly fried *pakoras*, the color of the sweetmeat stalls. Even at night, under the soft glow of dozens of kerosene lanterns, the stations came alive with a profusion of people and smells and sounds, the mingled cries of "baksheesh" and "gharam gharam chai" followed in turn by the high-pitched conductor's whistle, a billow of steam, and then the laborious heaving of train wheels finally beginning to move. Other classmates joined the train party along the way, at out-of-the-way stations like Rahim Yar Khan, Khanewal, and Wazirabad as well as at the better-known stops such as Multan and Lahore.

On occasion, some of the more adventuresome among us introduced ourselves to the railway engineers, riding for part of the way in the train engine cabin. By the early 1960s, most of the coal-fired steam engines inherited from the British Raj on the main railway lines were being replaced by new General Electric diesel engines, painted green and bearing a red, white, and blue emblem centered around two clasped hands—the familiar sign of American aid, gifts to the people of Pakistan from the people of America. When my turn came and I finally had an opportunity to ride in the engine cabin, I pulled the chain that activated the whistle with a special pride and satisfaction, as if I too had been partly responsible for the donation. Later, as an adult, I came across another, more cynical version of the familiar American aid sign in a popular Pakistani publication, a cartoon depicting a hand squeeze rather than a hand shake—an aggressive white hand grasping a limp brown hand tightly, hard enough to draw blood.

At other times, the railway carriage itself turned into a free-for-all, a game of darts with paper airplanes or banana peels. On at least one occasion, a thrown sleeping bag missed the intended target and instead fell out an open window. The train happened to be crossing a bridge at the time and we all gaped in astonishment as the sleeping bag began to unfurl and then fell into the muddy river below, all of us no doubt wondering what would have happened if it had been a person rather than a sleeping bag that had slipped away. One story, based at least partly on fact, had been drilled into each of us for years. Apparently, it concerned a similar train party in India, with missionary children involved in similar antics. In one version, a young boy was hanging out from an open door; in another version, several students had clambered onto the roof. Both accounts ended with a tunnel and a decapitation, a chilling conclusion that always filled me with special dread whenever we reached one of the several tunnels marking our final approach to Rawalpindi. I always made sure I did not stick my neck out too far, not only when we approached tunnels but also for fear of nearby electric wires or signal towers. I could almost feel the clash of metal on skin. It was an early lesson that served me well, a graphic example of the getting of wisdom in even the most unlikely places. Never stick your neck out too far; it might get chopped off.

My father served as an adult escort on that first train party, in March 1964 when I went away to boarding school for the first time. We arrived at Rawalpindi in the late afternoon and it was dark by the time we reached Sandes Home. The next morning, my father left early for the return journey to Sind, just as we were lining up on the verandah outside for the mile walk to school. There was snow on the ground. We said our final good-byes, hugged briefly, and then he walked away. I turned for a final wave just as a tightly packed ice ball broke across my nose. I cried briefly and my father never looked back. Years later, my father told me it was one of the hardest things he had ever done, to hear his six-year-old son cry and decide that he should not look back. I suppose a psychologist would make a meal, maybe even a banquet, out of the incident. I am not sure. I did cry, softly and for a few minutes. Perhaps I would have died of embarrassment had my father simply retraced his steps and returned to try and comfort me.

•     •     •

This is where the stereotypical themes of boarding school life would ordinarily be catalogued: the chill of unheated classrooms, the terror of corporal punishment, the torments of upper-class bullies, the rigidities of institutionalized religion. It would be easy enough to elaborate on these matters, to draw caricatures of particular teachers, to belittle the moral framework, to sneer at the rules and regulations. Most rooms did lack heating. It was cold in winter. Chapel services were mandatory. Some Sunday night sings did border on the maudlin. The fears and insecurities of particular teachers were inflicted on their students. On occasion, shoes, belts, branches, rulers, and even bare hands were used to administer discipline.

Taken selectively, the accumulation of such experiences could have scarred me for life, as was perhaps the case for certain classmates, some of whom are still trying to come to terms with it all. For some, it was the constant separation, the idea that we were always saying good-bye. For others, it was the unbelievable notion that our parents should have uprooted us and raised us in a foreign and at times hostile land, thousands of miles from what should have been our home. Another former student once told me that it was the belittling of the self that was hardest to bear, the drumming into young heads that our priorities ought always to be "God first, others second, and ourselves last of all." Viewed within the psychological framework of a later generation, it probably was a sure formula for disaster, an approach to child rearing specifically designed to undermine fragile self-esteems and scarify small children into deep emotional caverns from which it would be impossible to ever emerge unscathed.

Reading between the lines, there is at times a deep loneliness in some of my own early letters home, short epistles scrawled on lined notebook paper with all the earnestness of a grade school student. "I get homesick every night," I wrote in September 1964, not long after I had turned seven. "One night I had a dream that you were up here," I commented a few days later. "I don't know who my best friend is," I replied sometime afterward, in response to the kind of question my mother was forever asking. "I guess I'm a good boy," I wrote during another term, in answer to a question from home. "I have gotten only one spanking. Some people have missed quite a few meals for talking and laughing during devotions." Another letter, written at the end of a school term, ended on a happier note. "The next letter I send will be myself. It will be coming special delivery on the train."

Perhaps the saving grace was that, in the end, I somehow decided to never take any single event too seriously. At one level, fleeting unpleasantness never represented more than one dimension of a much more complicated private universe. Things happened, on occasion unpleasant things; but life went on, and there were many extraordinary compensations. At another level, I came to respect and even appreciate the ordering of my life, bound as it was by rules and regulations that at the very least were animated by an attempt to realize a moral vision, by the view that thoughts and aspirations mattered, that personal actions had real consequences. In any case, community life was never as rigid or as mean-spirited as it might have seemed at the worst of times. I saw many examples of devotion, selfless service and, on occasion, true love. The worst memories were laughed away; the best became part of the spiritual framework on which my own life came to be built. "If you lose your memories, you lose your soul," I once read. I made sure that I kept mine, intact and for as long as possible.

Some aspects of the culture we developed in that small place were truly hilarious. In the late 1960s, cigarette box collecting suddenly became the rage at Murree Christian School. I was in fifth grade and had never smoked. Nonetheless, there was something compelling, even manic, about owning as many different brands as possible. The commoner makes were cut into pieces and used for cigarette box chains; over time, virtually all the boys in my class had collected enough blue and white K-2, red and white Scissors, and yellow Woodbine cigarette boxes to make chains measuring several feet long. "I hope you don't mind me making cigarette box chains," I wrote home in March 1969, when the fad was at its height. "Dad knows what they're like. They are really fun." I went on to boast that my cigarette box chain now measured nine feet and asked if Baroo and Gopal could save up their own discarded cigarette boxes and post them to me from Shikarpur so that I could expand the length still further. A year later, I reported with pride that my collection had grown from thirty to forty-five different brands, including several foreign varieties.

At one point, the mania grew so strong that, during the noon lunch hour, several fifth graders watched in eager anticipation as an elderly Pakistani gentleman dressed in a suit lit up a cigarette and then casually dropped a rare red and white packet of Navy Cuts in mint condition onto the pavement. Our eyes followed his every move. I could hardly contain myself beyond the necessary decent interval. Unfortunately, Colin Old, a more daring classmate, was first, racing ahead of more timid souls such as myself to pick up the discarded packet almost before it had hit the ground. The Pakistani man, cigarette in hand, was still gaping in astonishment when he finally rounded the corner.

It was doubtless around this time that the school arranged for a visitor from Australia to give a public lecture on the evils of smoking. He stuck purely to the medical facts, with hardly a reference to the more standard religious views such as the admonition that our bodies were the temple of the Holy Spirit and ought not to be abused. In the Saturday night lecture for older students, there was some film footage of parts of a diseased lung being removed because of cancer. We younger students, spared the gruesome film scenes, were nonetheless intrigued by the dummy with the movable mouth and inane smile that the Australian man used throughout his demonstration. The dummy was dressed in jeans and a checked shirt and had normal arms and legs, but the chest cavity was clear, so clear that we could see the plastic lungs. At the end of the demonstration, the man from Australia lit up a cigarette and had the dummy "smoke" it; within seconds, the lungs became black with carcinogens. As soon as the lecture ended, I made a dash for the front. "Please, mister, could I have the empty packet?" It was an Australian make, a brand that no one else at school had yet acquired. Unfortunately a classmate of mine, Joel DeHart if I remember rightly, got there first.

The visit by the public health man from Australia was unusual, but the special programming on a Saturday night was not. Films were shown virtually every Saturday evening, some provided by a religious film distributor, most others courtesy of the United States Information Service, known simply as USIS and first based in Rawalpindi and then in Islamabad. There were Moody Science Films, produced by Moody Bible Institute in Chicago and devoted to such topics as the social order of bees and how the very complexity of their lives pointed to the existence of a creator—God. There were missionary documentaries and historical dramas based on the biographies of heroes of the faith such as John Bunyan and Martin Luther. On one occasion, someone somehow managed to acquire the rights to a full-length commercial film, *The Sound of Music*. Parental permission had to be sought before it was shown; in a few cases, such permission was denied and the students in question were excused from the showing.

More commonly, there were the USIS documentaries on everything from the Rocky Mountains to new manufacturing techniques to the latest military developments in Southeast Asia (the latter bearing such predictable titles as *Vietnam Profile* and *Spotlight on Vietnam*, titles that only a bureaucrat back in Washington could have dreamed up). Like the huge new General Electric train engines with their United States aid insignias stamped in red, white, and blue, the American films seemed to offer reassurance that, though a minority in Pakistan, we still belonged to a larger and more powerful civilization that commanded attention and displayed its largesse in even the farthest reaches of the globe.

During the 1960s, these links with America were reinforced by the friendship shown by several well-wishers at the United States Air Base outside Peshawar, near the Khyber Pass and only a few minutes' flying time from the Soviet Union. A few students from Murree Christian School had even visited the air base, taken a dip in the swimming pool, and seen the impressive bowling alleys firsthand. Dollars were the only acceptable form of currency; rupees were useless there, as if to emphasize the continuing reach of the United States in as remote a place as Pakistan.

The base had taken on a kind of infamy in the early 1960s when Gary Powers, flying out of Peshawar in a U-2 spy plane, was shot down over Soviet Central Asia and captured alive, causing Nikita Khrushchev to draw a red circle around the city and announce that, in the event of nuclear war, the Peshawar air base would be one of the first targets. The Pakistan public was outraged and, several years later, the last of the American military personnel finally left. When they departed, a portion of the base commissary seems to have been gifted to Murree Christian School. One Saturday night, during an intermission in the inevitable showing of the weekly USIS films, we stood in line to receive a Three Musketeers chocolate bar and half a hot dog, each courtesy of our American friends in Peshawar, a gesture that doubtless broke every U.S. government law on the separation of church and state. I traded part of my chocolate bar for a quarter portion of someone else's frankfurter, taking special delight in savoring the last mouthful. Tasting pork was a rare treat in Pakistan.

The disbanding of the Peshawar air base also resulted in a major furniture donation to Murree Christian School, of bunk beds primarily but also of chairs and formica-topped dining room tables. Perhaps they were bought at auction or unloaded onto us as scrap. In any event, it was astonishing to watch the stacks of furniture carried off the truck late one night, a seemingly endless display of the wealth of America benefiting our tiny school, lost in the vastness of the Himalayas.

There was something peculiar and barrackslike about the design of the furniture received from the Peshawar air base, especially the bunk beds, which were painted military gray and made of hollow steel tubes. Not long afterward, my brother David could not resist peeing down one of the tubes, an almost superhuman feat that would have been hard for anybody else to duplicate. Our housefather was not amused, ascribing vague sexual connotations that at that time none of us could fathom. He took David aside and whipped him with a belt, growing angry and stepping into the swing because David refused to cry. My brother's other punishment included several hours' work in a garden maintained especially for such disciplining in back of Sandes Home. I admired David for his obstinacy; he could rebel and resist authority in a way that I could not. As for the garden, it may have been acceptable as a form of punishment but was virtually useless when it came to teaching anything about horticulture. As far as I can remember, there was only one viable crop ever, at the end of one spring term when six turnips somehow grew big enough to be pulled from the ground.

More successful gardening techniques might have made a difference in our daily diet, which generated regular complaints. Breakfast was fairly basic, consisting of *suji* porridge followed by tea and toast. Lunch tended toward soups or basic variations on ground beef. Supper was more varied, ranging from curry and rice to roast beef and boiled potatoes. Like boarding students everywhere, we developed our own names for some of the more common dishes—elephant turd for Scotch eggs, apple crapple for apple crumble, monkey grits for elongated hamburger patties, and so forth. For years, boarding staff tried to encourage us to refer to our occasional stomach upsets as the *Murree Miseries* rather than the more familiar phrase *KZ*, incorporating as it did the initials of the head cook. Much later, I realized that institutional cooking is always a thankless task, that even if Khan Zaman had been a gourmet chef we still would not have been satisfied.

Mealtimes always began with a blessing, frequently in song. Even now, I cannot eat without recalling some of the more familiar verses:

Come and dine,
The Master calleth,
Come and dine:
You may feast at Jesus' table
Any time;
He who fed the multitude,
Turned the water into wine:
To the hungry now He calleth,
Come and dine.

or:

The lion's young may hungry be
And they may lack their food:
But they that wait upon the Lord
Shall not lack any good.

In a similar vein, the day began at six in the morning with fifteen minutes of "quiet time," spent alone and on our beds reading the Bible or related devotional material. Longer devotions were held each evening and included further Bible readings, prayers, and usually a chorus or two from the *Golden Bells* hymnal, a small volume published in England and bound in red cloth. Many of our favorites, including the dirgelike "There Were Ninety and Nine," seemed to date from the nineteenth century or come from the Moody-Sankey evangelistic crusades. Prayer request time often turned into a recital of the latest missionary projects involving our parents or, more commonly, a listing of family illnesses or the names of unsaved aunts and uncles who stood in need of salvation. It was especially tragic to hear of unsaved relatives suffering from terminal illness. On occasion, classmates related gripping stories of miraculous healings and deathbed conversions.

Much of our life was surprisingly insular, despite the sizeable Pakistani community that surrounded us. Attempts were made to teach us Urdu in grade school and, on one occasion, President Ayub Khan's daughter visited an art class. Several "Introduction to Islam" classes were organized for various grades, drawing the inevitable comparisons between the Bible and the Koran. I was especially struck with the information from the Koran that "God was as close as the jugular vein" and that He had "created us out of a blood clot," expressions that sounded strange and even threatening at the time but seem much more comprehensible now. On another occasion, as part of a comparative religion class, we were taken into the Catholic Church in Murree to observe a Sunday morning mass. The contrast between the simple whitewashed mosques that dotted the hillside and the ornate British-built church with its stained-glass windows and images of Jesus and Mary could not have been more stark. Like our Muslim neighbors, we too tended to think of the manmade human images on display in a place of worship as little more than idols.

Direct contact with Pakistanis came largely through encounters with the service staff, with those who drove the school bus, washed clothes, and made meals. Once a year, at the end of the fall term, there was a special dinner at which we waited on tables while local employees feasted on mutton curry and peas pilau especially made for the occasion. One of the drivers, an old hill man called Allah Dad, had served in Italy with the British army during World War II. He had a kindly disposition and a large white moustache that we all admired. One of the younger bearers was called Jerry Lewis, because he looked just like the film star; another we called Swoopie because of the dramatic way he delivered dishes to the table. In the early years of grade school, an ayah washed us every Tuesday afternoon. A Kashmiri barber came from Murree on the first Saturday of every month, toting a small brown plastic satchel with rusty clippers that seemed specifically designed to pinch pink skin. We lined up like convicts at the beginning of each cutting session and, in a matter of minutes, were quickly sheared as bald as tennis balls. In later years, we played soccer and basketball with teams from neighboring Pakistani schools, ranging from the elite at Lawrence College to the middle-class Government High School to the more working-class Potha High. I am not sure where we fit in the broader social hierarchy of the Murree Hills, but I suspect we were thought of as little more than an alien presence that somehow managed to survive British rule.

Only a very small number of Pakistani students ever attended Murree Christian School, in most cases the children of Christian Pakistani medical doctors who worked at the various mission hospitals dotted around the country. They later faced a difficult choice, between the westernized school environment in which they were educated and the limited opportunities available to any member of the small Christian minority in the Islamic Republic of Pakistan. Yet, in another sense, their private anguish only echoed in exaggerated form the same dilemma that all of us, children of one culture raised in another, eventually faced. We could never wholly embrace Pakistan as our own, even if we had wanted to. Similarly, because of our vastly different upbringings, it was hard to ever feel totally at home in the societies in which our parents had been raised and to which we ostensibly belonged. In the end, we tended to fall back on each other, creating our own micro-universe, complete with its own unique vocabulary, private jokes, and special cultural symbols. At times, it felt like being a member of one of the tiniest and most lonely minorities on earth.

Jhika Gali, the small village at the foot of the hill where Sandes Home had been built, represented the closest connection with the real Pakistan. As grade school students, we shopped there each Saturday, trading our ten-paisa and four-anna coins for large helpings of deep-fried *pakoras* or *jalabis* wrapped in old newspapers. Later on, in high school, the local tea shops became the focal point for a social existence measured out by the number of cups of tea we consumed. Two tea shop owners, one called Charlie and the other Joe, became specialists in curried omelettes; another was called Toes because of his skill in picking up chapatis off the floor with his bare feet; a third was called Nose for even more obvious reasons. Farther on, in the Murree bazaar, we each had our own favorite alley for ordering chicken *tikka* or mutton kebabs.

It is hard now to recreate the feeling of those late fall evenings when we sat outside the Jhika Gali tea shops, discussing the trivialities of the day, the foibles of the adults who surrounded us, and the fate of the universe that encompassed us. In one direction, in the valley below, small wood fires marking hundreds of separate households seemed to go on forever; in the other direction, the stars stretched out into infinity. Only the wind and the occasional high-pitched yammerings of a jackal broke the evening silence. It was astounding to reflect that the flickers of light above us represented a journey of thousands, even millions of light years. Some of the stars might even now be imploding into nothingness, whole solar systems and even galaxies slipping back into black holes. We would be long dead before news of such catastrophes ever reached planet earth.

More usually, musings on the fate of the universe were replaced by the routine, even the monotony, of boarding school life, dictated as it was by a regular schedule punctuated by the ringing of bells and the sound of human voices. For years, I woke up to the loud voice of Paul Davidson, our New Zealand housefather who later became an Anglican priest. "Wakey, wakey boys, rise and shine—give God the Glory, rise and shine." John Unreau, another houseparent who later became a Mennonite minister in the prairie provinces of western Canada, was more low key, usually opening the day with the simple announcement that it was time to get up. The morning routine included quiet time, breakfast, and a work assignment such as sweeping the verandah or cleaning the toilets. This was followed by the walk to school, eight hours of classes, an hour of free time, supper, study hall, another hour of free time, devotions, and then bed.

Weekends offered some relief, including a mix of American and British field games such as Capture the Flag, British Bulldog, and Red Rover. Sports included soccer, basketball, and field hockey. In the spring of 1968, the Pakistan national men's field hockey team practiced for weeks on end in the field across from school, in anticipation of the high-altitude Mexico City Olympic games. We were at nearly eight thousand feet and the training must have helped. They came back with the first of several gold medals for hockey, and we cheered along with the rest of Pakistan. Other leisure activities included camping on some of the nearby ridges with names like Patriata, Nathia Gali, and Monkey Hill. At other times, we travelled to Rawalpindi for the day or, closer to home, walked to Murree, wandered around some of the old

British cemeteries on nearby ridges, or explored the remains of the old Parsi-owned Murree Brewery at Ghora Gali, which had been burned down at independence in 1947.

In later years, attempts were made at Murree Christian School to allow siblings to spend time together. During the years I was a student, it was more difficult; when I was in the "middle boys" boarding department, Nancy was in "little girls" and David was already numbered among the "big boys." Contact between the various departments was usually slight; we did not eat together, we rarely played together, and we did not even sit on the same pew for church or chapel. From a distance, I admired my brother and had a deep affection for my sister. To some extent, I grew up in the shadow of my brother, even as my sister grew up in mine.

David was stubborn and articulate and would not let an argument end without making sure he had the last word. My mother at times thought he might make a good preacher—either that, or a lawyer, the profession he eventually adopted. Like me, David was a voracious reader, out-doing me in the hard sciences and philosophy while I tended to gravitate toward history and literature. He picked Will Durant's *Story of Philosophy* off my father's bookshelf early on and, as a high school student, lobbied successfully for the school to offer an Introduction to Philosophy course, an unusual item on any high school curriculum. He played a solid soccer fullback but never broke into the basketball lineup and eventually gave up the sport. He stood up against punishment, whether from staff or as part of the inevitable hazing rituals carried out by upperclassmen. Once, when locked in the bathroom as a joke, he responded by breaking the door down. He was generally well-liked and elected as school president during his senior year. At one time or another, he dated Leslie and Carmenia, two of the prettiest girls in high school. David was also asked to room with a "problem student" who had been expelled the previous year for drug use. He went on to establish a lasting friendship with the individual concerned, one that I, in truth, resented. David was forming emotional attachments that, in a selfish sibling way, I thought should be reserved for family members only. Drawing on biblical analogies, I imagined that our very names were given for a purpose, that brothers named David and Jonathan should be able to forge a friendship that would last a lifetime.

My first distinct memories of Nancy are of when I returned following boarding school and saw her outside the train window, standing on the platform at Rohri Junction and waving while she awaited our arrival. She had dark hair and big brown eyes. I was seven and she was five and I suppose it was at that moment that I had the first real inklings of familial love extending beyond my parents—she was beautiful, she was my sister, and I was immensely proud of the fact. I felt similarly protective when she started boarding school, though the boarding structure did not provide many opportunities for these feelings to be played out. Oddly, I also recall with special pride her exuberant part in a second grade production of "The Muffin Man" and, years later, on stage in a Chekhov play, the title of which escapes me. She seemed confident on stage, sure of herself in a way that I was not. When she left Murree in 1976 at the end of the her junior year, she seemed to shake the dust of Pakistan off her feet, more quickly and with fewer regrets than the rest of us. The world of a girl growing up in Pakistan was in many ways different than that of a boy, especially in adolescence when dress codes were enforced and outside travel often proved difficult. Her memories are doubtless much different than mine, emphasizing the constraints and impositions rather than the endless freedom and opportunity to travel and explore that I experienced. When Nancy was a teenager, a couple of Pakistani gentlemen approached my parents in apparent seriousness to ask if a marriage proposal might be worked out. She was the only one of us to acquire a southern accent on her return to Georgia, forging a successful career in the public relations and management side of the health care industry. Even now, I marvel at her control, business presence, organizational skill, and endless capacity for hard work. Perhaps in some respects she is having the kind of career my mother might have enjoyed, had she been born a generation later.

Boarding report cards for all three of us were mailed to our parents at regular intervals. In contrast to the more usual school reports concentrating on academic achievement, the grading categories for boarding tended to emphasize less tangible things. The list of character traits that our houseparents regularly commented on included politeness, self-control, sense of justice, ability to make friends, reaction to parents' visits, reaction to disappointment, consideration of the feelings of others, and respect for authority. I scored "satisfactory" on most items, along with the occasional "good"; on a couple of occasions, I rated an "outstanding," for truthfulness and for moral consciousness. During another term, the notation read "needs to improve" in areas such as personal tidiness and thoroughness in work.

On at least one occasion, in fourth grade, I was too truthful for my own good. The bus was loading for a day trip to the river, halfway between Murree and Rawalpindi. My best friend Tom Brown and I shared one seat; a classmate, David Hover, was trying to save a place for somebody else in the row behind us. Suddenly, the then-housemother for senior high girls (unkindly known to some as Ma Hag) walked up the aisle and sat beside him. I could hardly contain myself, breaking into a singsong screech that came out sounding something like "look at the hag that Hover has to sit beside." She did not think much of the alliteration and, alternating between tears and anger, slapped me for several minutes, until my cheeks became even redder than usual. Ordinarily, I was quick to cry at the slightest provocation; in this instance, I somehow kept my composure and simply stared ahead in stunned silence. Later that day, sitting like a small garden gnome on one of the rocks beside the river, I turned to the housemother and said that I was sorry. She looked pleased and gave me a hug. "I forgive you," she said. "And I want you to know that Jesus forgives you too." In later years, I came to understand that the Murree Christian School Board had been less forgiving. The incident was discussed at the board meetings that winter in Lahore. At the end of the meeting, it was decided that her contract would not be renewed.

•    •    •

The spiritual concerns of boarding life spilled over into school. Our flimsy green and pink notebooks, bought for three rupees each at the school bookstore and printed by Feroz & Sons in Rawalpindi, bore an inscription from the Second Epistle of Timothy, "Study to show thyself approved unto God." The same themes were emphasized in the school hymn, sung at chapel every Friday morning and written by Ralph Brown, the father of one of my classmates and the same Baptist missionary who had been there to meet my parents when they first arrived in Pakistan:

Nestled neath the great Himalayas, far above the plain,
Stands the school we love and cherish, more than earthly gain.

Built upon a firm foundation in God's hands a tool;
Shaping lives of dedication, Murree Christian School.

There within her halls of learning, Wisdom's torch burns bright;
Where indeed her students grasp the Good and True and Right.

Teachers, students work united towards the common goal;
Christ to serve with consecrated body, mind and soul.

Lord, with thanks and praise we honor Murree Christian School
May her life and fame and service for Thee ever rule.

In a few verses, the hymn captured almost all the metaphors of my early childhood—the mighty Himalayas that we looked out at every morning; the distant plains where our parents lived and worked; the school that shaped our lives; the importance of goodness and truth; the consecration of body, mind, and soul; and, above all, the reality of the Living God revealed in Jesus Christ, the God in whom we lived and moved and had our being.

It is strange now to read the comments in the early school reports and letters sent to my parents, written by adults whose own faith played such a decisive role in determining the shape of the lives of those who studied under them. Auntie Rosie—Rosie Stewart, the kindergarten teacher from Pennsylvania who later gave me piano lessons and also taught Latin—referred to my alertness and enthusiasm, my "love of talking" and my "happy disposition." Eunice Hill, my first grade teacher who arrived right out of Westmont College in California and whose brother, Arthur Hill, starred in several Hollywood films and a number of television series, described me as "a good little worker, anxious to get ahead." Miss G., my second grade teacher from England, was more circumspect, commenting that I was "quiet but responsive." In fact, almost all the class was quiet and responsive, largely because we feared her and the inevitable rap across the knuckles whenever we stumbled in any of our oral reading or math assignments. The only funny thing about her was that her birthday fell on April Fool's Day. It was the one time of year when we could do almost anything and get away with it. On one occasion, one brave but anonymous soul gave her a matchbox with a live scorpion inside.

Some teachers remained at Murree Christian School for decades; others stayed for briefer periods, looking at the experience as a stepping-stone to something else. Miss Blackstone, a teacher in grade school, married an American airman working in Peshawar named Mr. Anguish, taking on a new last name that even now strikes me as odd. Miss Steves married a Mr. Fairchild and became a missionary in Iran. Miss Cunningham, probably my favorite teacher despite her sometimes severe manner, seemed like she would remain single forever until a Mr. Mitchell, reportedly a press photographer who covered the Vietnam War, breezed through the Murree Hills, swept her off her feet, and convinced her to return with him to southern California, where they later jointly founded an organization for "Christians Working in Government." From the vantage point of an eight-year-old, all three teachers seemed much too old to ever contemplate marriage. More incredible still was the story of Bob M., the sometime maintenance man, a World War II veteran who, according to rumor, suffered from shell shock. Not long after arriving in Pakistan in the 1950s, he had proposed to Taj, a Pakistani Christian girl. Her father had hoped for better things, only relenting after sixteen years of trying without success to have her married off to someone else. Despite the late start, they went on to have several children. Taj Bibi herself became locally famous for the jams and pickles she contributed to summer bake sales. Later on, they emigrated to America.

There were doubtless times when the school administration had no idea of what was going on behind closed classroom doors. In fifth grade, one teacher, a single woman from Illinois who must have been among the last to teach writing using the Palmer Penmanship Method, made a concerted effort to convince us of the reality of UFOs. The

Bible was used as a starting point. After all, Jesus Christ had once referred to "other sheep" in need of salvation; these other sheep might
as well reside on other planets. More graphically, there were the
intriguing events described in the first chapter of Ezekiel used, as I
later discovered, by UFO buffs everywhere: wheels within wheels
moving in four different directions at once; the rims of wheels full of
eyes all around; the hubs projecting the power of sight. It sounded like
a convincing description of a visit by Martians, especially when this
was followed by readings from a much more recent book detailing
the abduction of a New Hampshire couple who later, under hypnosis,
described how they had been whisked to another planet for further
analysis. Samples had been taken of their skin and hair and yet they
were eventually returned in one piece to planet earth. Nowadays such
"New Age" thinking would not be tolerated in evangelical church
schools. At the time, it seemed like little more than a harmless di-
version.

Mr. K. represented another problematic case. Tall, with thin lips
and a narrow face, he was one of the few Pakistanis on the Murree
Christian School staff and was extremely popular among the student
population, especially high school boys. According to his title, he
served as office clerk; in fact he was widely known as the school fix-it
man, the one who dealt with the local bureaucracy, helping to ensure
that we got train tickets when seemingly none were available, or water
when the municipal reservoirs had ostensibly run dry. By the time I
reached high school, rumors abounded that his skills and contacts extended into other areas. He reportedly had ready access to cigarettes,
Murree beer, even Johnny Walker whiskey. According to at least some
sources, he was also emerging as a chief contributor to one of several
drug scandals that from time to time caused upset and concern. He was
asked to leave not long after I graduated. Somehow, he managed to
obtain a visa for the United States. Now he works in Philadelphia.

Numerous other staff passed in and out of our lives, some briefly
and others for a longer period of time. There was Bill Robb, the art
teacher from Britain who had grown up in the Salvation Army and
then married a Dane whose father was a Lutheran minister. There was
Lea Virtanen, the houseparent who reportedly had won a place on the

Finnish national women's volleyball team and who later married Derek Tovey, a teacher from New Zealand. There was Ellen Brell from one of the prairie provinces in Canada, short in stature and with a rare gift for teaching math. There were the English teachers, Glennis Brown and Elizabeth Leggett, from Maine and Scotland respectively, stout and at times emotional, but nonetheless capable of instilling a glimmer of respect for the likes of T. S. Eliot and William Shakespeare. There was Islay Harmsworth, the French teacher from Scotland whose poetic first name, I later learned, came from one of the islands of the Hebrides. I recall most of the names with thanks and gratitude—and I want to list them, each and every one, realizing all the while that names will mean nothing to those who never were part of that small and distant community of the Murree Christian School.

Looking back, I marvel at the many and vastly different personalities that somehow came to be recruited to an institution that even at the time seemed so tiny and inconspicuous. There were several retirees filling positions ranging from school librarian to school nurse to hostel manager. There was a series of young college graduates, usually filling houseparent roles. Somehow, it was thought that recent graduates would be more energetic and could relate better to students in a hostel situation. With the passage of time, former students began gravitating back to Murree Christian School and were occasionally used to help meet short-term needs. I am only dimly aware of some of the conflicts that must have taken place within the staff, a predictable occurrence given the broad range of nationalities and beliefs represented. A few of the recruits were clearly disastrous, arriving to meet a need that seemed desperate at the time, only to be eased out just as quickly when it became apparent that they could not cope with the stresses and strains of living at close quarters in a highly spiritual environment in which both missionary children and their parents often failed to live up to the high expectations ordinarily assigned to them by churchgoers in other parts of the English-speaking world.

The several French teachers who passed through the doors of Murree Christian School had an especially hard time, possibly because French always struck us as a useless language and France always seemed to have such a remote and tenuous connection to both our present circumstances and any conceivable future life. One teacher, a French Canadian, once broke into tears in frustration and slammed the door as she stormed out of the classroom. The windowpane promptly broke amid gales of laughter. It is much less amusing in retrospect. If some of us occasionally experienced unwarranted cruelty at the hands of the adults who were charged with caring for us, it is just as true that we occasionally visited unwarranted pain and sorrow on some of those whom we should have honored and respected.

High school biology offered a different challenge. I stayed as far away from the frog dissections as possible. Cutting open the carcasses of dead rabbits was even worse, especially when it was decided to celebrate the following evening with rabbit stew. Inevitably, late in the school year, there had to be a discussion on the "facts of life." We were a long time in coming to it. First there were presentations on single-cell animals, then several lectures on the reproductive patterns of plants. Gradually we moved up the chain until we were drawing diagrams and using words that began to cause a vague discomfort. In the end, the single hour devoted to the reproductive systems of homo sapiens proved to be quite graphic. None of it was news to us by this time, but we nonetheless listened in almost complete silence. It was as if we felt a deep embarrassment for the awkward gestures of our shy teacher, Mark Jones from New Zealand, in having to state the obvious.

At one point, describing "sexual urges," he commented that in a culture such as Pakistan, where most women covered themselves in the veil, a female student from Murree Christian School walking through Jhika Gali in a short skirt had the same effect as a naked woman would have on the boys in the class right now. He might as well have added that when Nancy or Linda or Rebecca or any of the tenth grade girls walked out of the class that afternoon, we would all be secretly lusting after just such an event. The passages about the scent of perfume and the attractiveness of small white breasts that we read in the Song of Solomon were fine for a while, but in the end narrative descriptions could never take the place of the real experience.

It was an experience that almost all of us left high school never having had. There was of course hand-holding and kissing and furtive embraces, especially on weekend nights when "walks" became something of an institution. The thirty or so high school students would be stretched out along the road for half a mile or more, looking for privacy and trying to make small talk. According to tradition, if a car with one headlight passed by, we could kiss the person closest to us. The palms of one's hand grew sweaty just thinking about it, hoping against hope that a one-eyed taxi from Jhika Gali might be coming around the next corner. Some relationships grew quite intense. A classmate went out for some time with a new girl from Germany whose father managed the glass factory at Wah and purportedly made it all the way to "third base." Shy and awkward as I was, I ordinarily had to content myself with the purple prose of James Michener in *The Source* and *Caravans*, occasional photographs ripped out of *Life* or *Sports Illustrated*, and the lingerie advertisements from a Sears catalog. One term, I fell in love with the pictures of a dark and long-legged Israeli track star named Esther somebody or other, no doubt associating her and her biblical name with the sultry images I had already gleaned from my feverish quiet time readings of some of the more erotic passages of Solomon's Song. I never was able to accept the interpretation, offered up by some, that Solomon had simply been inspired to write it as an allegory describing the equally intense relationship that Christ would enjoy with His church.

•    •    •

My time at Murree Christian School spanned almost half the career of Chuck Roub, the Conservative Baptist missionary from Minnesota who served as principal there for more than twenty years. Like my parents, his missionary career had started in Upper Sind, in the middle 1950s, near Shikarpur in a town called Jacobabad. After a single four-year term of evangelistic work in Sind, he and his wife Eloise were transferred to Murree, where he was asked to spearhead the effort to establish and sustain a viable school for missionary children in the mountains. It could not have been an easy assignment. The disparate views of the various strong personalities serving on a school board that represented a broad band of Christian missionary endeavor running from the extreme right to broad middle must have presented enormous challenges, especially when arguments were almost always cloaked with spiritual concern and linked to specific biblical passages.

Chuck Roub, large and imposing, was ideally suited for an almost impossible job. His loud laugh and jocular manner undoubtedly got him through many difficult circumstances, with students as well as with the school board. Parents were forever writing him, usually with complaints and suggestions. I suspect my parents wrote as well, though I have never seen any proof of this. One parent wrote a public letter criticizing the school administration for allowing a play such as J. B. Priestley's *An Inspector Calls* to be staged by students. The play touched on themes such as adultery, suicide, and the shallowness of Edwardian middle-class life in turn-of-the-century Britain. To his credit, Chuck Roub responded that the play raised vital questions that students would have to face sooner or later. Over the years, he grew to command great respect if not always affection. I suspect he used some of his favorite jokes at least a thousand times. When he finally retired in the middle 1980s, the main recreation room at Sandes Home was named Roub Lounge in his honor.

Three other staff families stand out, the three who arrived in Pakistan at about the same time in the 1960s and then spent most of the rest of their working lives in the smallness of Murree Christian School, dedicated to a ministry that was necessary if our own parents were to live out their lives in Pakistan—Don and Evelyn Calderwood, from Kansas, representing the United Presbyterians; Ian and Isabel Murray, from Edinburgh, representing the Church of Scotland; and Irv and Liz Nygren, from Washington state, representing the Evangelical Alliance Mission. Invariably, it was the husbands whom we got to know better than the wives.

Don Calderwood served as basketball coach, guidance counsellor, Bible teacher, and odd-job man. All our teachers were earnest, but he was even more earnest than most; he had a Tom Landry kind of disposition and only barely ever cracked a smile. Once he publicly reprimanded my sister Nancy in a Sunday morning worship service, a humiliation that embarrassed me and could have devastated her. She survived. It was Don Calderwood who maintained our transcripts and wrote letters of recommendation when it came time to apply for university. He also maintained a shelf of college catalogs, mostly representing small Christian schools but also a few from some of the state universities and more secular private colleges. I ranked in the middle of my high school graduating class and, looking back, can only imagine that he must have written a wonderful recommendation letter, enough to ensure not only that I was accepted at Northwestern University in Evanston, Illinois, for the class of 1979, but that I received a sizeable scholarship as well.

Ian Murray, a small Scot with tiny legs, a bushy beard, and a loud voice, over time became one of the most popular teachers in the history of the school. He coached soccer and taught the hardest subjects—physics, chemistry, calculus, and British history. He arrived in the middle 1960s with a fiery temper that, over the years, he actively—and successfully—learned to control. Once, during a sixth grade geology lesson, he passed around a large rock that he described as "really heavy" (actually, it weighed almost nothing). I reached for it in eager anticipation and then accidently let it drop. He glared in my direction, gritted his teeth, and hissed "grabbers don't get," a lesson in the getting of wisdom that I still remember well. Among the high schoolers, he was known as something of a flirt; black and white pictures of his favorite female students hung on a door in his chemistry lab, long after they had graduated. At soccer games, Ian Murray's voice echoed long and loud across the mountains. "Mur-ree, Mur-ree." "Long Cross, Long Cross." "Foul, Foul." "Hand Ball, Hand Ball." A visitor from the American School in Kabul once wondered aloud if perhaps "Murray Christian School" was not in fact named after him.

Irv Nygren, the onetime mayor of a small Pacific Northwest town whose brother was an editor at Moody Bible Institute Press in Chicago, taught history, speech, government, journalism, and Bible. It was easy to tell when he was about to lose his temper because the tip of his ears started to grow red first. He was imminently flappable and sometimes seemed to become flustered at the slightest provocation. Over time, I learned to share his quirky sense of humor and occasional bouts of cynicism. He too taught with an obvious earnestness, though I sometimes thought he was beginning to imagine that his role as teacher might be too confining, that he felt he might be missing his true calling. I still remember a sermon he preached, under the title "If These Walls Could Talk." At one point in the sermon, he looked around at the enormous edifice of Murree Christian School and wondered aloud what the eight young British soldiers who had died of cholera and whose memorial plaque hung on the English Literature room wall had been like. "If these walls could talk," he said, "what stories they might tell."

In my sentimental fashion, I loved Irv for that expression; it was a question I often asked myself, and not only about the past. If these walls could talk, what might they say, about previous decades perhaps, but also about our own life and times, to those who lived in centuries hence, to those who followed after us and yet would have no sense for the borders of our days, the pattern of our lives. I long imagined that even if the old garrison church at Gharial was eventually torn down, the stones at least would survive, as building material for new structures that those of us who lived in the here and now could not begin to imagine. The prospect of physically inanimate objects surviving long after we who had touched them had passed away even inspired a few lines of doggerel verse, a reflection of my own lifelong inability to properly express feelings that I somehow knew to be true:

> Voices from another time,
> Sing softly through the night:
> From houses made of stone,
> From houses made of stone.
>
> Call the voices quiet,
> Call the darkness night,
> The houses still won't move,
> For they are made of stone.

Soppy sentiment aside, the discovery of time also signalled in me the start of a thinking and reflective life, one in which questions mattered more than answers, in which the seemingly permanent structures of a particular time and place were in the end little more than dust in the wind. It is an evangelical kind of stoicism, almost. I respected what my elders taught, what they strived for even if they were never able to reach it. Life taken in its entirety was a serious business, but momentary humiliations or successes meant almost nothing; they were like the leaves of autumn, vivid for a few days and then gone forever. All things were transient. And yet all things and all manner of things would somehow and eventually be made well. There was a natural tension between particular events that seemed so important on any given day and the view of them as seen through a longer lens, from the perspective of eternity. It demanded an attitude of awe mixed with ambiguity, faith combined with uncertainty and, above all, a humbler and less ambitious view of life, one that accepted the failings of others, all the time hoping that others too would reciprocate and accept in the same way the failings in oneself.

I doubt if I will ever be able to take my own children back to the school where I grew up, to the hills that I loved, to the place where I was born. Murree Christian School may not even survive into the next century. At times, I imagine that it will one day be taken over by the Pakistan Army and used for intelligence training or artillery drills. There are already military installations on every side and the Army School of Education is located just up the hill. I expect that, for years, they have looked covetously in our direction. And yet, for my part, I can finally see that the seemingly circumscribed life I led for twelve years in the Murree Hills was no dress rehearsal, no mere preparation for adulthood. On the contrary, it was the first act of all that followed, introducing in a strange and wonderful way aspects of almost all that I would later experience. Most of what I have seen since is simply a variation on what I observed at school in the years before I reached my eighteenth birthday. It is remembering the events of childhood that finally gives them meaning. In my imagination, remembering Murree Christian School is like returning home after a long absence; how long, it is impossible to say. Only now can I start to recognize the familiar landscape, only now can I start to call it home.

# FIVE

# I Am Born Again

God talk came easily to us, from an early age.

We breathed the Bible. Jesus Christ was a living

presence, not some shadowy figure who walked the

earth centuries ago. Spiritual interpretations applied

to every aspect of our lives. No matter was so trivial

that God would not be interested, no event so small

that His hand was not somehow upon it. His power

held the universe together, His love extended to the

smallest of His creatures, His grace was sufficient

for seeing us safely through our own brief sojourn

upon this earth. In the end, our religion became as

all-embracing as Islam. "Not a religion at all," as Pakistani Muslims so frequently told us, supremely confident in their own faith. "A way of life."

At both home and school, the day began and ended with prayer and song: "When morning gilds the skies"; "Until the setting of the sun"; "Safely through another week, God has brought us on our way." It was almost as if we had a prayer for every event, a hymn for every occasion. Even casual browsing through a songbook offered special assurance, tangible evidence of the cloud of invisible witnesses who had completed their own disparate journeys through this vale of tears and now stood round about us, viewing our predicament from the vantage point of eternity. Some hymns were attributed to the ancients, Bernard of Clairvaux, Francis of Assisi, John of Damascus. Others were simply designated as "Ancient Irish" or "Scandinavian Melody." Still others were written by more familiar and recent Protestant figures such as Charles Wesley, Amy Carmichael, or Fanny Crosby. In the hymnbook, at least, time finally stood still. Ancient saints rubbed shoulders with recent revivalists. Beethoven and Mozart appeared next to folk tunes and modern choruses. It was as if the wisdom of the centuries had been fixed permanently within the bounds of a single book, like a volume of poetry, almost. Singing gave great pleasure from an early age, despite the fact that I had almost no musical talent.

Even before I began school, my father started each day with a chorus from a foldout music book for children. We would sit quietly at the breakfast table, before our plastic bowls filled with corn flakes (manufactured outside Rawalpindi by the Fauji Foundation) or puffed wheat (introduced into Pakistan by the Seventh-Day Adventists), and my father would turn the cardboard pages as David, Nancy, and I joined together in pleasant song:

How happy are the children
Who trust in the Lord:
Peace have they,
Joy have they,
Rest in salvation;
How happy are the children
Who trust in the Lord.

At night, we settled down for longer devotions before what was some-times called "the family altar." My mother usually started devotions by playing two or three songs on our old, off-key portable organ, the bellows wheezing away each time she pumped the pedals. "His Eye Is on the Sparrow" was one of her favorites. I hated the high notes and sometimes felt she was trying too hard, as if she was secretly in-timating that she was every bit as talented as Ethel Waters and that Carnegie Hall, not Shikarpur, should have been her true calling.

Actually, my mother was usually more rooted in the ways of the world than my father. She aspired to great things, for her children if not always for herself. She was sometimes critical of other families who "looked too much like missionaries." To her mind, this included dowdy, long-suffering wives with their hair pulled straight back and ill-behaved, slightly unkempt children on the look-out for free hand-outs. She did her best to break stereotypes, partly through her interior decorating skills and partly through her gracious Southern hospitality. Our house always had to be in perfect order, and she regularly wrought miracles in interior design using inexpensive local fabrics and furniture. The quest for perfection was also evident when it came to bringing up children and there was at times a tendency to be too demanding, too concerned about what others might think. She was determined that the difficulties of her own childhood would not be visited upon her children and she had strong views about how to bring this about, to the extent of taking responsibility for most areas of family discipline. She and David, as the eldest son, clashed on occa-sion, especially in the early 1970s when long hair, loud music and di-sheveled clothing became the order of the day. As the middle child, I tended toward the mediating role, looking for ways to avoid open conflict even when it may have been warranted and could well have been healthy. Unlike my father, my mother always maintained a very strong southern accent. After three months of boarding school, the first family conversations sometimes had a strangeness about them, re-minding me once again that we were a southern family, that we were held to certain standards, and that we ought always to be striving for greater things in the future.

Family devotions were designed to emphasize the spiritual side of these strivings. Singing and Scripture reading were always followed by prayer, each of us offering up our own thoughts and concerns in turn. My father ensured there was some order by carefully typing up prayer cards, one for each day of the week, as if to remind us of the needs of the world and our own responsibilities in it. The prayer list started with grandparents as well as aunts and uncles in America— twenty-four on my father's side, fourteen on my mother's side, not including those who married twice. There were cousins by the dozens. The prayer list also included our many supporting churches, those that gave sacrificially that we might spread the Gospel in Pakistan, small country or suburban churches mostly, spread from Pennsylvania to California. Fellow missionaries serving elsewhere in Pakistan were also listed by name. Finally we prayed for whole continents, for the advance of the Gospel in Australia, in Asia, in Africa, in Europe, and in the Americas.

My father always concluded the evening with a final prayer in which he carefully mentioned anything that we may have forgotten, especially as it related to the world outside Shikarpur. God's blessings were sought for stability in Pakistan, for peace in Vietnam, for prosperity in the latest recession; wisdom and guidance were requested for the leaders of Pakistan and, more broadly, for the leaders of the world. It seemed natural to pray for family concerns with one breath and for the victims of a natural calamity in the next, as natural as getting up in the morning and putting on a clean pair of trousers.

Our neighbors, pious Muslims all, seemed even more dedicated. After all, they prayed five times a day, not just twice, rising first at dawn, prostrating themselves at intervals throughout the day, and then bowing toward Mecca once again for a final evening prayer. Loud-speakers blared from mosques on every side. We were often awakened as early as four in the morning by the noise of sharp breathing into the microphone, a rasping cough, and then the verses from the Koran, verses that had echoed unchanged throughout the centuries. Some of the novice *maulvis* were my age, trained in the rites of their religion even as I was being trained in the rituals of my own. Although the mosque lacked congregational singing, I nonetheless felt there was something musical in the Koranic cadences, something almost holy in the tones. In later years, when I heard the call to prayer in Arab capitals, I came to think that the religious leaders there were less tuneful, that wake-up calls in the Arab world lacked the melodic instincts of South Asian Islam. Perhaps it was due to the Wahabi influence from Saudi Arabia, the view that even music was somehow too frivolous a medium by which to approach Almighty God.

Beyond the regular prayers, our Muslim neighbors fasted for one month out of every year, each day from dawn until sunset. Neighboring families woke before dawn to eat and drink in anticipation of the long fast. We were often awakened by occasional shouts and the banging of pots and pans. Later, after the sun had set, neighbors gathered for an *iftar* meal marking the breaking of the fast. It was almost as if a universal sigh emanated from the whole of Shikarpur at dusk each day during the holy month of Ramadan, when the wail of the siren from the fire department announced that the sun had finally slipped beyond the horizon. At the end of the lunar month, we joined everyone else in town in looking for the new moon from the nearest rooftop, for the slight sliver of white that announced the end of Ramadan, the ninth month in the Islamic calendar.

The closing days of Ramadan carried with them a special sanctity. One, the Night of Destiny, celebrated the handing over of God's Koranic revelation to the Prophet Mohammed, On Whom Be Peace. Unlike our biblical revelation, which had been written down by inspired prophets and apostles over several centuries, the Koran had been compiled within the lifetime of a single individual, passed down almost like tablets from heaven. On the Night of Destiny, all prayers were reportedly heard, all spiritual petitions properly answered. With the end of Ramadan came Eid al-Fitr, the festival of the breaking of the fast, celebrated in much the same way as Christians celebrated Christmas. Local families paraded about the streets in new clothes and children delighted in gifts of trinkets and candy. It was usually also on Eid al-Fitr that the circus came to town.

Eid al-Adha, the festival of sacrifice, was the second big celebration observed by our Muslim neighbors. It occurred during the twelfth month of the Islamic calendar, in connection with the pilgrimage to Mecca that tens of thousands of Pakistanis completed each year. The older men who participated often dyed their beards red with henna and were known forever afterward as Hajis. The details of the celebration always had an Old Testament ring, recalling as they did the story of Abraham and the near-sacrifice of his beloved son—Isaac for Christians and Jews, Ishmael for Muslims. In the Koranic version, Abraham blindfolded himself, cried out to God, and then slit what he thought was the throat of Ishmael; when he removed the blindfold, he discovered that a sheep had instead been slain.

In Shikarpur, unblemished sheep and goats began to be fattened weeks ahead of time in anticipation of the big event. At first, the animals seemed to enjoy the attention, basking in special feeds and in the green and purple dye that marked those about to be slaughtered. I sometimes thought I detected an inane note of self-satisfaction on the part of the larger fat-tailed sheep, munching away contentedly as if they would while away the rest of eternity in fields of four-leaf clover. It was only in the last days before Eid al-Adha that their demeanor suddenly changed, that they finally seemed to acquire a grim inkling of what might lie ahead. Perhaps it was the excitement in the household, the shrillness of children anticipating the coming events. The noise the night before the sacrifice took on special poignancy for me, and I often imagined that any bleatings after midnight were those of animals that had somehow become aware of their impending doom. After it was all over, the meat was divided into three parts—one-third for the poor, one-third for the family, and one-third for relatives and friends. We often shared in the final third, feasting happily on warm chunks of recently living flesh. Some portions came from a local landlord, others from the postman, others from the chief of the local fire brigade, and still others from the Brohis, relatives of one of the most prominent lawyers in Pakistan who happened to live in Shikarpur and became close friends of my parents.

The last month on the Islamic calendar gave way to an even more somber one, that of Moharram, the sacred month. Shia Muslims attached special significance to the month because it was on the tenth of Moharram that Hussein, the grandson of the Prophet Mohammed, had been cruelly killed at Karbala in present-day Iraq. His passion was played out in excruciating detail, the death of a martyr at the hands of a powerful foe, ostensibly Muslim but viewed by some Shias as the hand of an oppressive Sunni Islam. Each evening, local Shias held gatherings in their homes to listen to funeral elegies commemorating the terrible event at which Hussein, his family, and his small band of followers were first deprived of water and then cruelly killed in a final battle. "Cold was the wind and chilly the desert," ran one typical elegy, recreating the scene on the eve of battle. "Trees were swinging like men intoxicated." It was the closest that our neighbors ever came to understanding what animated us during the week before Easter, when we sang hymns remembering the crucifixion of our Lord. In the end, Hussein's head had been returned to Baghdad atop a javelin pole. According to one story, the head had miraculously responded to the ridicule of the crowds by reciting verses from the Koran.

On occasion, I witnessed the gigantic processions that marked the tenth of Moharram—the green banners, the crowds of mourners dressed in black, the wood and paper structures representing Hussein's tomb at Karbala. Oftentimes a white charger was included in the procession, representing the white bridal horse that Hussein's son should have ridden at his wedding just before the battle started. At various points along the way, the procession stopped and the mourners gathered for a public display of grief. The few women, usually elderly, beat their breasts in lamentation while young men stripped to the waist, thrashing themselves continuously with knives and whips and chains until the blood streamed down their shredded backs. In events such as this, it was as if blood was used to measure piety. I was fascinated by the emotions unleashed, by the power of faith, by the strength of their devotion.

In popular Islamic tradition, the tenth of Moharram also marked Ashura—the day on which God had created Adam and Eve, life and death, heaven and hell, the tablet and the pen. In this, we parted ways with the religious feelings of our Muslim neighbors. For us, the tablet and the pen was not created at a certain point in time—it was there before Creation, before even the beginning of time. In the beginning was the Word: the Word was with God and the Word was God. The same was in the beginning with God: all things were created by Him and without Him was not anything made that was made. It was the Word that animated us, that gave meaning to our lives. Sometimes I took this literally, imagining that God was writing several billion novels at once—trillions of words, billions of customized volumes, one for each person who walked this earth. We were an open book to God, who knew the story of our lives before we were even born. Somehow, for reasons that I could not begin to fathom, my novel was turning out to be more quirky than most.

· · ·

The Word manifested itself to me in three physical locations, in Sind first, then in Murree, and finally in the United States. The spiritual feeling in each place was different. In Sind, we experienced a close family life but were conscious of our position as a tiny minority enveloped by the enormity and occasional hostility of Islam. In Murree, we were part of a larger religious community, broadly Christian, but sometimes diverging on important questions of faith and practice. Even as children, it was apparent that being a Christian meant one thing to certain adults and something quite different to others. The American experience was strangest of all. From a distance, we imagined the United States as a promised land, a place flowing with milk and honey. On arrival, we had a hard time making sense of it all.

In Sind, the Baptist heritage of our parents was broadened by contact with Anglicans from England. Each winter, Church Missionary Society doctors, based in Quetta, came to Shikarpur to run an "eye camp" that specialized in cataract operations. Thousands of blind men and women from all over Sind, Baluchistan, and even southern Punjab came to be healed in a simple operation that took less than five minutes to complete. The English Anglicans provided the medical services; the American Baptists specialized in evangelism. "We have warm Christian fellowship with CMS missionaries, all from England," my father wrote in his diary in the late 1950s, surprised at the humble spirit in a group that at one time had seemed almost as idolatrous as the Catholics. "They are so consecrated to the Lord as well as dedicated to their work. Their love and zeal for the lost is a challenge to me and changes my opinion that all Anglicans are formal and liberal."

In high school, I came to better understand my father's feelings. The quiet spirituality of Ross Tully, the Anglican padre for the Shikarpur eye camps, did seem like something out of Little Gidding, reminiscent even of George Herbert or John Donne. He was tall, slow of speech, and heavily built, with large hands and the kind of deliberate mannerisms that might have qualified him to play the part of a butler in a BBC special on family life in aristocratic England. There were rumors that he had in fact been born into a wealthy family but had given it all up for the mission fields of Pakistan. His wife, Kay, was some years older and, when she turned sixty-five, they returned to England where he became chaplain in a mental hospital outside London, near Southall, a place where more Pakistanis now lived than in all of Shikarpur. England changed dramatically in his absence, even as America changed so completely in the years my parents were away.

There were others, too. Dr. Ronnie Holland and his wife Joan became larger-than-life figures for a generation of Baptist missionary children living in Shikarpur, symbols of a deep commitment that left a lasting impression on all whose lives they touched. In some ways, perhaps, Dr. Holland became the last hero in a heroic missionary past that has now been reduced to stereotype. His father, Sir Henry Holland, had founded the Quetta Mission Hospital and the Shikarpur Eye Camp. One son, Harry, became a missionary doctor in Peshawar, near the Afghan frontier; Ronnie followed in his father's footsteps by spending his working life in Baluchistan and Sind. He raised bees outside his house in Quetta, built a cottage in the juniper forests at Ziarat, translated the gospels into the Brahui tongue—and, in his lifetime, restored the gift of sight to at least one hundred thousand souls. His wife Joan had lost the use of her legs and arms while still in her early twenties, while on a visit to the mountains of Kashmir not long after they were married. She contracted polio there and the only heart-lung machine at the Civil Hospital in Srinagar no longer worked. Somehow, Dr. Holland managed to fix the machine himself, saving her life. They went on to have three children. When we knew them, they were in their sixties and nearing retirement. Joan seemed so frail as Ronnie picked her up, guiding her across the room, swinging her lifeless legs back and forth, the thin veins showing blue beneath her fragile skin. My parents often commented about the love demonstrated in their every gesture.

During the six weeks when the Anglican medical missionaries worked in Shikarpur, we went to their temporary quarters on the edge of town each Sunday for evensong, at what we referred to as the Holland bungalow. Services began promptly at seven. The occasional visiting doctor from America, sometimes Jewish, anxious to perform as many cataract operations in six weeks as could normally be performed in a lifetime of medical practice in California or Florida, also attended. A log burned on the fireplace and large enamel teapots, yellow trimmed with green, rested atop a heavy charcoal-burning stove. We Baptist children became almost lost in the large springless sofas scattered about the sitting room, sofas that must have been at least half a century old. The Baptist men took turns speaking, but the rest of the service came straight out of the Book of Common Prayer, Elizabethan English, distant and somehow deeply holy, in the manner of the King James Bible. It was in these services that my father first heard the words of John Bunyan's "To Be a Pilgrim," a hymn that quickly became his favorite. He once told me, in one of those rare moments that happen too infrequently between fathers and sons, that he hoped it would be sung at his funeral.

Not that it was all serious or that all English Anglicans lacked a sense of humor. One Sunday evening, after an especially long Baptist sermon preached by Uncle Larry—L. P. Johnson, referred to by local Pakistani Christians as "Long Play" Johnson, because of his ability to turn a one-hour service into two hours—the Anglicans were asked to say a grace before dinner. With a touch of impatience, Dr. Holland bowed his head and prayed. "For every cup and plateful," he intoned, "make us truly grateful." It was the shortest grace I ever heard until I attended a Christian camp in America several years later and was told about "Rub a-dub, dub, thank God for the grub."

Dr. Holland also played a critical role in the life of my father, during his own dark night of the soul when all seemed futile and my father despaired of the calling that had once seemed so real and had first brought him to Pakistan. Malaria was also involved. In retrospect, some might say it was malaria that brought on the depression; for my father, it was a terrible and very real spiritual battle between the forces of good and evil. "Yesterday I went again into the depths of depression and despair," he wrote in his diary in the fall of 1963. "He who never fails His children allowed Dr. Holland to be passing through Shikarpur at this time of year. I talked it over with him. He assured me that this is the sort of thing a great many people experience and it will pass away with a little help. He is giving me a drug for relaxing and sleeping. Although I would rather not depend on drugs, it must be the Lord's way of escape for me at this time. Already, before starting the medicines I felt much better. The talk with Dr. Holland helped a lot."

Dr. Holland proceeded by train to Karachi and my parents followed him there. "I feel like Jonah," my father wrote a few days later, despairing again. "I told Bettie that I have now come to the end of the rope. I felt that I was sinking down and could not pull myself back out again." And, three days later, "These have been dark days. I hardly know what to record. I have been filled with deep, pressing anxiety. It was a feeling of great inferiority in a world that is so much more superior to me. It is a sense of deep unworthiness. Through it all, I believe that God has a rich blessing for me. I can only cling to the fact that He called me to this place of service. Yesterday, when the world was so black, when I felt I had come to the end of my rope, I began to plan what I should do in the future. You would be surprised at what I had planned!" The depression continued for several more days. "Meet my need, Lord, that my life in Pakistan may not be in vain," he wrote. And, again, "I felt discouraged as all the failures of the past many years paraded before me." Still later, he continued to despair. "I ought to be improving. David is coming before long. I must be a husband and daddy to my precious family. What has caused all this?"

Nancy and I, accompanying our parents to Karachi, knew almost nothing about what was going on. It happened in November 1963, when I was six and she was four. My only recollection is of a missionary wife, Grace Pittman, running into the living room, waving a newspaper. "The kitten is dead, the kitten is dead," I thought I heard her say. Only later did I realize that this was the moment when I first learned that President Kennedy had been assassinated.

•     •     •

The weeks in Karachi struggling with depression were a significant event in my father's life, one I came to appreciate only as an adult, when he showed me the pages of his diary that detailed the episode. In a strange way, it also seemed to deepen his faith while at the same time permitting a more realistic sense of what might be accomplished on the spiritual battlefields of Pakistan. "We must be honest," he wrote in his diary sometime later, reflecting on the recent departure of a missionary who was wondering what to tell supporting churches back in America in the face of so few conversions. "If we are completely truthful, we would say that converts to Christ are few and from the Muslims even fewer. Most converts from Islam return to Islam. People in Pakistan are not crying out for the Bread of Life as promotion and publicity pamphlets would have us think. There is little interest or hunger for the Gospel. Having said this, I am certain that God wants His witness here—even if to be the watchman on the wall, crying out for the people to repent."

Several years later, on the resignation and departure of Sam and Grace Pittman, the Baptist missionary couple who had sailed with my parents on the *Steel King* when they first travelled to Pakistan, he reflected still more deeply on the difference between the expectations that had originally animated their missionary endeavor and the reality after nearly two decades of work in Pakistan. "It is sad that Sam has not found challenge and fulfillment," he wrote. "He came out the first time with expectations but I guess they were not fulfilled. It is certainly true that we have not turned the world upside down as we thought we might. Islam has remained unyielding. We do seem to have accomplished very little. Is Sam being more honest than we? Are we wasting our home church's tithes and offerings by staying on? I feel that God wants some of us to remain on barren outposts like this, as voices crying in the wilderness. Otherwise, there will be silence and hopelessness, just Islam which so much wants to bring silence to all other voices but its own. But why did God choose us to man this lonesome outpost? I won't try to figure that out—I am just lonesome right now so that's why my thoughts run in this vein tonight. Bettie and the children are in Murree."

Returning from Sunday evensong at the Holland bungalow was also connected with one of the more dramatic events in our spiritual battle in Shikarpur, a visible manifestation of the disdain and even hatred with which we were on occasion viewed by at least some in the local community. My mother commented on the seeming appearance of smoke above my father's book room as we climbed out of the Land Rover. My father said it was probably only dust, stirred up by passing trucks and donkey carts. But, opening the courtyard door, we were greeted by a cloud of smoke and the eerie glow of flames. Someone had climbed over the wall, swept the pile of religious books and tracts off the shelves, doused the carpet with gasoline, and then torched the room. The wooden ceiling was just about to catch fire when we arrived. We formed a bucket brigade and, by the time the fire engine arrived, had almost put the fire out. My father estimated that a thousand rupees worth of religious literature had been destroyed. For the next several years, he carried a charred Sindhi New Testament about with him, visible evidence of the opposition we sometimes encountered for the sake of the Gospel.

Most of our neighbors were deeply embarrassed by the event and offered profuse apologies, which my parents gladly accepted. And yet, to me, it symbolized something of the alienness of our presence, of the danger lurking beneath the surface of the seeming placidity of our Shikarpur home. I had several nightmares afterward, of a train attacked by bandits, of a school bus torched by outlaws. I sometimes imagined our walled house as a kind of Alamo, with a few of us given rifles to fend off a mob numbering in the thousands. It was almost like what happened at the British residency in Kabul, an incident nearly a century earlier in which a contingent of British Indian soldiers under Lieutenant Hamilton, VC posthumous, had been wiped out, provoking the Second Afghan War. We would man our posts bravely and, in the end, die there. There would be no survivors.

There were other moments, too, that forcefully reminded us of our continuing strangeness in a foreign land. Sometimes my brother and I would be greeted by cries of "Angrez, Angrez" (English, English) as we cycled about town; or, at other times, "Gora, Gora," a much cruder expression that I imagined was the local equivalent of "white boy." On occasion, rocks or clods of dirt were thrown. Once I jumped off my bicycle in anger and chased a group of schoolchildren who were tormenting me. I in turn was chased into a house where an old woman suddenly emerged as my benefactor, holding me in her arms and stroking my hair with her rough hands. She told the crowd off as if she were my grandmother, then offered apologies for their unseemly behavior. I never told my parents about the incident.

For the most part, they in turn kept us insulated from their feelings about the opposition they experienced in the early years. I only found out about it when I had opportunity to read pages from my father's diary dating to the late 1950s. There were near-riots in the Sukkur bazaar following a literature distribution campaign; in the end, the police had to come to their rescue and used bamboo canes to mount a *lathi* charge. There was the night in a village in Larkana district when a slide projector was being used and the axes of the local farmers flashed briefly in the moonlit sky. "They had better not say anything insulting about the Prophet," one of the villagers had said in Sindhi, loud enough for my father to hear. There were the shredded gospels left outside our door in Ratodero and more confrontational encounters in the marketplace. "Ralph and I went to the bazaar to show film-strips. By the time we were set up we had a very large crowd. As I began to speak on the prodigal son, the crowd became very noisy. It was impossible to keep them quiet so we began to fold up to go home. My screen was nearly torn up. I was kicked and pushed. Someone snatched away my flashlight. I was hit by cow manure all the way home." In the end, my father and mother both believed that confrontation was the wrong approach, that Christian missionaries spending their lives in Islamic lands were left with little choice but to either burn out in a blaze of glory or bear witness through the actions of a lifetime, incarnating faith in places where direct confrontation or theological argument had no chance of success.

We lived at the fringes of my father's ministry, and neither my mother nor my father ever actively urged us to follow closely in their footsteps, to devote our own lives to the service of God in a foreign land. They were acutely aware of the dilemmas missionary children would inevitably face when they finally returned home. "Occasionally, you hear of missionary children growing bitter against their parents' work and against the country in which they live," my father wrote to our financial supporters, when we were still quite young. "We can understand how this can happen. Missionary children need your prayers as they face life in a country so different than the United States." Later on, my father was more explicit about his hopes for our future. "We do not covet our children becoming missionaries," he wrote. "But we do want them to walk with Christ in whatever vocation the Lord may call them to."

During vacations, I sometimes accompanied my father on his village trips. Later, when he became more actively involved in a translation and publishing ministry, I often went with him to local printers to review proofs of his latest Sindhi publication. English type was on occasion still set by hand; for Sindhi manuscripts, the printed text was first written out in longhand by a scribe. I was fascinated by the noise of the printing presses, the newest of which dated to the turn of the century. I was also impressed with the page proofs for a new Sindhi edition of John Bunyan's *Pilgrim's Progress*, always a popular item. It featured line drawings with characters shown in Sindhi costume, landscapes incorporating date palms and desert. We were immensely proud of the final product. There was something seemingly permanent about a printed page, something to which both my father and I kept gravitating.

More memorable still were the few times when I helped staff the Baptist bookstall at local fairs. In many cases, these fairs were centered around the death anniversaries of Sindhi saints, a local practice condemned by orthodox Muslims but nonetheless having a strong influence in both urban and rural Sind. The shrines at Bhit Shah and Sehwan were especially well known, but dozens of others also dotted the Sindhi landscape. My father referred to an evil presence at these places, a feeling I was unable ever to fully share. I never viewed the strong

Hindu influence at these ostensibly Muslim gatherings quite so malignantly. The Islam of the mosque tended toward orthodoxy, even fundamentalism; the Islam of the shrine was more expansive and all-embracing, more accepting of others, more representative of the syncretic way in which the Hindu-Muslim encounter had at times been worked out on the Indian Subcontinent over the past many centuries.

The importance of shrines and holy places was often viewed as a unique feature of Sindhi Islam, one even the government recognized. Officials sometimes participated in the ceremonies. Heavy drums were constantly beaten and dancing continued late into the night. Some of the dancers were intoxicated, whether with opium or spiritual bliss it was never entirely clear. The shouts of "ya Allah, ya Mohammed" echoed into the dark with all the intensity of a Pentecostal revival meeting. Pilgrims came from throughout the province and it was not uncommon to meet professional Pakistanis—airline pilots, bankers, government bureaucrats, and so forth—visiting the shrines of their *pirs* or spiritual guides, hoping for some fleeting contact with the divine presence. The keepers of the shrines were described as Sufis, spiritual mystics. They were rarely hostile and at times quite generous. We were people of the book, after all, followers of God's revelation. They seemed to view us as little more than fellow pilgrims, stumbling down the same path in search of our salvation.

We also exhibited Christian literature at a more secular festival, the annual Horse and Cattle Show in nearby Jacobabad. The British had first introduced the event as a kind of county fair. Local landowners exhibited prizewinning cattle. There were camel and oxcart races along with tent pegging and mass displays by local schoolchildren. Commercial companies exhibited their wares along with representatives from local family planning clinics. The United States Information Service also arrived, passing out free literature in Urdu on the American Constitution and showing continuous films featuring washing machines, television sets, and suburban houses, suggestive of the material benefits accruing to those who chose a capitalistic way of life. The Chinese and Russians set up stalls of their own, as if to underscore the battle going on for the soul of Sind. They specialized in displays featuring steel mills and transmission pylons.

Our Baptist bookstall was usually off in a corner, in one of the less expensive sections of the show. We nonetheless drew crowds and I was always happy to help out, selling Gospel portions and passing out free applications for training courses offered by the Bible Correspondence School in Hyderabad. Helping at the Jacobabad Horse and Cattle Show also gave ample opportunity to see the races and visit the midway with its wooden, hand-operated ferris wheels and the inevitable "wall of death" featuring fearless motorcycle riders on ancient Triumphs and Harley Davidsons left over from World War II, defying gravity as they spun around a makeshift wooden pit at high speeds.

Dancing women, fully clad but nonetheless gyrating seductively, were on display in the wall of death during intermission; the audience stood on a ledge above the pit, throwing rupee notes into their outstretched arms. My father told me that the "women" with the painted lips and heaving bosoms were not actually women; they were female impersonators. I had a hard time believing him. They were in fact *hijras,* eunuchs castrated in childhood or hermaphrodites with underdeveloped sexual organs. Some even married, in a bizarre ceremony in which the Koran was ostensibly read backward. According to local belief, their sexual ambiguity and neutered status gave them special powers and special access to the divine. They were much in demand at local weddings, dancing late into the night before crowds of gawking men, until sweat drenched their *dupattas* and their faces became streaked with dissolving lipstick and kohl.

Other stalls were equally strange. One tent featured a lady attached to the body of a snake, a visual illusion using mirrors that even I, as a ten-year-old, managed to understand. Another tent displayed an assortment of jars containing pickled fetuses, freaks of nature, not all of them human—aborted Siamese twins, a calf with six legs, a lamb with two heads, and so forth. Cockfighting was hugely popular. On still other occasions, several ferocious hounds, white with pink eyes and mangled ears, were loosed against a solitary, moth-eaten Himalayan black bear with a heavy metal ring through his nostrils. The chained bear pawed the air angrily, looking bewildered as he tried to protect himself from the snapping dogs and jeering crowds. Once I thought I detected a deep sense of loneliness in the bear's expression, as if he too wondered how it was that, as a cub, he had been kidnapped in the mountains of Kashmir and forced to wander forever across the bleak plains of Punjab and Sind.

The bizarre and sometimes cruel displays both fascinated and repelled me. At the worst of times, I imagined that I was part of a larger circus, that we missionary children were also on display, whether living as foreigners with our parents in Pakistan or accompanying them on their occasional visits to raise financial support in churches back in America. It was almost like being one of the mouse-like cretins who frequented fairs and circuses in many parts of Pakistan, stunted humans with small heads and simian features who were led around on leashes, distorted creatures with a bewildered and forlorn look that haunts me still. At Lakhi, only a few miles from Shikarpur, the insane were chained to trees outside the shrine of a local *pir*. Twenty years on, they were still being kept there—even as the brother of the holy man who managed the shrine was winning an election to represent the area in the National Assembly.

It was hard to comprehend the cretins, where they had come from, what they thought and felt, how they lived, why they lived at all. Some said that they had been born deficient, others that they were shaped into imbecility because they had been forced to wear steel caps from an early age. It was hard to know for sure and, in the end, it did not make that much difference. They were few in number and their main justification for living seemed to be to challenge all notions of normality, to blur the line between humankind and the rest of the animal kingdom. Like the *hijras* dancing frenetically beneath the wall of death, it was if they hid deep within themselves, in ways that others could only vaguely comprehend, the hidden purpose of minorities everywhere—to at once be abused by those around them and, at the same time, undermine the complacency of an existing social order, of a majority population who were convinced that there was only one plausible way in which to organize an entire society. According to the 1961 census, Christians in Sukkur district, which at that time included Shikarpur, numbered 739 out of a total population of more than one million. At times, it was almost as if we really were freaks, members of a small and insignificant minority that some might well have wanted to wish off the face of the earth.

• • •

It was different in Murree. We remained isolated, but the structure of boarding and school brought with it the feeling that we were part of a larger body, with branches that spanned the globe. Teachers and fellow students came from several continents and represented many churches. From a distance, it was as if our parents were part of a bigger, more heroic endeavor.

Weekly letters from home helped keep us informed. One fall, there was a long letter about the week that my mother, father, and Nancy, then only five, spent in a village north of Sukkur, among a group of Hindu tribals who had expressed an interest in learning more about the Gospel. There were also occasional references to J. K. Durrani, a personal friend of my father who was an orphan and seemed possessed of a restless spiritual longing. The turning point in his life was a passage in Peter's First Letter, about "casting all your cares upon Him, for He careth for you." That God cares became the theme of his life, a touchstone in a heartless world. Mohammad Hussain Hafiz, the tailor, was another such man who occasionally figured in my father's letters. Unlike Durrani, he never went public with a confession of faith. He had been given the title *Hafiz* because, as a boy, he memorized the entire Koran. My father sometimes visited him at the tuberculosis sanatorium at Kotri, where he was by then a patient. Not long afterward, on one of my winter vacations in Shikarpur, I was cycling near Lakhi Gate. An enormous crowd was spilling out of a nearby mosque. I asked a bystander what was going on. "It is Mohammad Hussain's funeral," came the reply. "He died early this morning. He was a Hafiz and it is only natural that so many people should show him respect."

Over time, my own letters home began to betray something of the beginnings of an interior life, of a questioning attitude that sometimes had difficulty moving between the heroic spiritual imagery on which I was raised and the reality of the here and now. "I am reading the devotional books which you gave me," I wrote to my parents on one occasion, shortly after beginning second grade, just after turning seven. "It says you can make pills with moldy bread." Pills from moldy bread? It must have been a sermon illustration used in my Scripture Union booklet, a picture of how even the most miserable of God's creatures could be transformed into an agent for healing and salvation. On this particular occasion, the spiritual imagery completely passed me by. "I started reading from Genesis because I finished the devotional books," I wrote several weeks later. And, the following year, "I have finished the Book of Revelation." I did in fact read the entire Bible before I turned eight, straight through, mainly so I could say that I had done it.

Along with the Bible, I was reading an eclectic mix of history, biography, adventure, and science, the stepping-stones to a future known only to God. Early titles included *Robinson Crusoe* (gifted by Dr. Maybel Bruce), *Robin Hood and his Merry Foresters, Birth of Texas, Viking Tales, Battle of New Orleans, Barbary Pirates,* and *Genghis Khan and the Mongol Hordes.* I read *Adoniram Judson* and thought of dedicating my life to converting the heathen in Burma. I read *West Point Story* and pictured myself as a famous general, another George Patton or Robert E. Lee fighting for my country in its time of need. I read *Tom Swift and the Asteroid Pirates* and imagined life as an explorer in outer space. I read *What Bugs Are* and briefly thought of myself as a scientist, an occupation with few role models within the missionary ranks. I read *Teddy Roosevelt and the Rough Riders* and imagined that I might one day be president of the United States—until someone informed me that it would not be possible; according to the American Constitution, the president had to have physically been born in the United States. I would have to look into an alternate career.

In retrospect, it is strange to think how often we moved from spiritual sublimity to mundane ridiculousness. On the one hand, there were earnest devotions, lengthy prayers, and a deep concern for the unsaved. On the other, there was little sacred in the way in which we mimicked and on occasion even ridiculed the institutions in which we were raised. In popular grade school jargon, the United Presbyterians or UPs were known as the Under Pants Mission, even as the Conservative Baptists or CBs were known as the Cry Babies. So too, if someone was late for a meeting, it might provoke the comment that "maybe the Rapture has come and we've been left behind," a sort of gallows humor for young Christians, given our belief that Christ's imminent return to earth would be marked by our immediate rapture to heaven. The fact that our faith might not be complete, that we might be left behind when Christ came to claim His own, was so chilling that perhaps humor was the only way to deal with it. Similarly, hymns were fertile ground for budding poets. "Rescue the Perishing" became "Rex Chew the Paraffin." A more elaborate ritual surrounded our version of the chorus for "In the Sweet By and By," part of which I learned from my father:

> In the Sweet (Give me some Meat)
> By and By (Give me some Pie)
> We shall meet on that Beautiful Shore
> (Give me some more)

Hearing "When the Roll is Called Up Yonder" for the first time, I wondered if it meant we'd be served muffins and biscuits in heaven. "Here I raise my Ebenezer" was odder still. What on earth was an "Ebenezer"? In high school, reading the first volume of Bertrand Russell's autobiography, I realized he had laughed at the same joke. In a sense, we ourselves were actually living a Victorian childhood, more than half a century after Queen Victoria had passed away. On occasion, our response to it was as juvenile as those of the immediate post-Victorians.

We were constantly reminded that there was no such thing as a "second generation Christian"; every generation had to confront the reality of Jesus Christ independently and on its own. Those of us that did so and responded in the affirmative were born again and need no longer fear about our own ultimate salvation; we would spend eternity with Him. It was a momentous occasion when it finally happened, although, in truth, the event often turned out to be less awe-inspiring than one imagined beforehand. For me, it happened in second grade, in the late fall of 1964, on the top bunk after devotions led by Inger Gardner, a kindly grandmother of Norwegian stock who had left several grown children behind in Illinois to become a houseparent for missionary children in Pakistan. An old Victorian print hung on one wall in the cinder block building in which we then lived. There was Jesus standing outside on a cold winter day, holding a lantern glowing yellow in the dark, snow falling in every direction, nail holes piercing His soft and gentle hands. But there was no knocker on the door—that was up to us, we were often told; we had to open the door ourselves and let Him in. It was snowing outside that night, and Auntie Inger closed devotions by asking if we too wanted to open our hearts to Jesus. I briefly imagined the hinges of my own heart creaking open and then closing, just long enough to let Him in. It was enough to mark me for Christ for life. I could not escape from it, even if I had wanted to.

I was lucky. My entry into the kingdom was less traumatic than at least one fellow student, who made his momentous decision while on vacation. He approached his father and said he wanted to be born again. It was a busy day and his father said not now, Daddy has too much to do, let us schedule a meeting for later this afternoon. At least that was the way he remembered it. Imagine, wanting to make such a decision, with eternal consequences, with heaven and hell hanging in the balance, only to have your father say it had to fit somewhere else on his calendar. Years later, he was still trying to understand what made his father do it. On another occasion, in junior high, I stayed up all night with a classmate who repeatedly wondered if he really was saved, somehow fearing that he had been predestined to spend the whole of eternity damned and without God. I cannot say that the fear of hell figured prominently in my own decision, though I certainly had cause to take it into account. One visiting parent, taking evening devotions in the place of an absent housefather, looked over at the kerosene stove, pointed to the blue flame, and then remarked about how hot it was. "It is beautiful," he said. "But I can't hold my finger there for more than a second. I would hate to imagine spending a million years in such a place."

With the passage of time, the faith of childhood gave way to the spirituality of adolescence. In grade school, there was no real need to doubt the wisdom of our elders or the religious formulas on which we had been raised. In seventh grade and beyond, it was no longer enough to parrot the verses from Sunday School class or the spiritual maxims our parents had taught us. Genuine faith, to the extent it was possible, had to be internalized so that it became our own. One week, it was the intellect that needed convincing; the next week, intellectual arguments seemed as dry as burnt bread; God could only be real if we experienced Him for ourselves. Overlying everything was the fact that, by and large, it was in adolescence that our own parents had first been saved and acquired their missionary vision. In a sense, their experience was turned into something of a prototype for our own. On some occasions, we took that prototype farther than even they might ever have imagined.

I went through several revivals in my time. "There is not much going on except a revival is sweeping this place," I wrote to my parents at the beginning of seventh grade, briefly assuming a pose of guarded understatement. "A lot of people are getting closer to God and sometimes just a few people get together for a prayer meeting." Six months later, it was the ill-fated flight of Apollo 13 that provoked religious anxiety. The way we understood it, there had been an explosion aboard the spaceship that destroyed several oxygen tanks and damaged the navigation system. The three astronauts, having aborted their planned mission to the moon, would have to return to earth as quickly as possible. If they entered the atmosphere at the wrong angle, they would bounce back into outer space like a stone skipping across water and be lost forever. If the protection shield in the back of the spacecraft had been knocked loose, they would be charred into oblivion within seconds. The suspense and tension of the long journey back seemed almost unbearable. "We too were praying for the astronauts," I wrote, comparing spiritual notes with my parents. "One room had a prayer meeting Friday night. Praise the Lord, they made it."

Not long ago I discovered an account of one of the revivals I attended written by an adult. It makes interesting reading, if only to recall that the perceptions of the leader of a particular religious movement will rarely coincide with those of his followers. The description comes from Viggo Olson's *Daktar Diplomat in Bangladesh*. Olson was a kind of evangelical Dr. Schweitzer whose autobiography, published by Moody Bible Institute Press in Chicago, became a bestseller in the middle 1970s, sold hundreds of thousands of copies, and briefly entered even the secular marketplace. I simply reported home that "Mr. Olson preached last Sunday. It was really good." His book amplified on the event much more fully. "In the science classes I spoke throughout the week on Christian evidences. Biblical-inspirational subjects captured our attention during the evening meetings. Other hours I rapped and counseled with dozens of students. Day by day, as our meetings and discussions progressed, God's spirit began influencing and directing many. By the end of the week several dozen had responded to God's work in their lives by accepting Christ or dedicating their lives to him. Some gave themselves for full-time Christian service. My own heart was thrilled and refreshed to see God work deeply in many young lives." I was not one of those who walked the aisle on this occasion. Perhaps I was too young to appreciate the Christian evidences, though I do recall that, at the time, I found the appeal to intellectual reason refreshing, while the emotional part of the argument left me completely unmoved. I cringed when I heard the word *rap;* it had already gone out of adolescent fashion. I was not about to join the procession of emotionally wrought students marching to the front of the sanctuary to publicly commit their lives to God.

Two years later, I provided a more spiritually uplifting report back home. "I read and understand and am interested in the Bible like never before," I wrote this time, before launching into a more sanctimonious tirade. "After the revival here, it spread to the girls. Anyway, pray for it because some who claim to be Christians do not act like it." This revival, in ninth grade, just after I had turned thirteen, is the one I remember most, if only because those around me also seemed to experience it so vividly. I never felt very comfortable praying aloud but, for a brief time, I took my turn more often than usual, voicing spiritual longings more fervently than ever before. I tended to think of myself as something of a loner. On this occasion, I briefly felt it might be possible to lose myself within the warm and secure embrace of a larger group.

The fact that the school atheist, a fellow ninth grader, briefly got saved added to the momentum. He was incredibly intense and what convinced him in the end was Kierkegaard's "leap of faith," coupled with Pascal's "cosmic gamble," combined with a paragraph from Francis Schaeffer, the thinking man's evangelical who wrote books bearing such titles as *The Mark of a Christian* and *He Is There and He Is Not Silent.* One paragraph from Francis Schaeffer described a climber who had fallen onto a ledge in the Swiss Alps and compared his fate to that of contemporary humankind. Suddenly, out of the darkness, comes the voice of a local guide who knows every path on the mountain and who urges the man to jump in a certain direction, at which point he will be rescued. He does it in faith and is saved.

For as long as it lasted, my classmate lived out his faith to the extreme, intellectually, emotionally, with all his heart and mind and soul. For some reason, I held back. I was running a marathon, not a fifty-yard dash. I did not want to burn up all at once. I sometimes briefly danced into the circle where the crowds seemed to be gathering. But, more often, I hesitated, observing the spectacle as an outsider, wanting to join in but somehow lacking the courage of my convictions. I liked the image of the lonely climber, lost in the Alps; living in the Himalayas made the metaphor even more compelling. But articulating that faith in the grubbiness of day-to-day life always seemed much harder. We were taught that salvation was a single event, a personal response to the invitation of Christ that we need experience only once, in the quiet of our hearts. In contrast, Saint Paul had talked about the need to work out one's salvation "in fear and trembling," as if it were a more long-term process. It was a helpful turn of phrase, one that stayed with me long after I had finished high school. I had no quarrel with the idea that we had to come to the Father through the Son. But, without first experiencing the fear and trembling, we might never come to the Father at all.

.        .        .

In America, we had opportunity to relearn our religion all over again, in new and different ways. I visited the United States on three occasions before my eighteenth birthday, once at the age of three, a second time when I was eight, and a third time just after I turned thirteen. Each yearlong sojourn in America was known as "furlough," as if we had been handed extended leave passes in reward for faithful service at the battlefront. In fact, my earliest definite memories are of the United States, not Pakistan. They date from 1960 and involve two separate events that occurred in the months after my third birthday.

The first is Christmas 1960. The only thing that I remember about the event is following my father and brother into the woods outside Macon, near the place where my father had grown up, not far from the tree where he had committed his life to the service of God on a foreign mission field. We sized up several pine trees and, in the end, chopped one of them down. We dragged it to our red brick house on Joycliff Road and tried to raise it up, only to find that our judgment had been wrong, the tree had been too tall. We chopped off several more inches of trunk until we got it right. Early in the new year, when the needles had already begun to turn brown, we carried the tree to the garbage dump, where it would wither and rot away. It is almost as if, even then, I had begun to sense that impermanence would be one of the recurring features in my own life, that times of celebration would be followed so quickly by the sadness of separation and loss.

The second memory is of me trying to fall asleep on plastic seats in the back of a green '52 Plymouth we had bought from an uncle to see us through our travels across America. It is night and we must be coming home from a Sunday evening service or a Wednesday evening prayer meeting. We are always going places and I am trying to sleep, always trying to sleep. Perhaps I was also unconsciously living out some of my father's anxieties, his tiredness after thousands of miles on the road and his feelings of inadequacy after being on display before so many different audiences.

"We are enjoying our time, but feel the emptiness of life in America," my father had written, soon after returning in June 1960 to Macon, Georgia, where we had been met by more than a hundred family, friends, and well-wishers. "People have so many things, but their lives are so shallow. We are longing for Pakistan. We did not know until now how attached we are to that land."

It was this same message that he carried to dozens of churches across the country during the next twelve months. Contrary to the belief of our neighbors in Pakistan, missionaries were not paid for by the United States government; they had to raise their own support. Some missionaries attempted to live solely on faith, waiting expectantly for small and unexpected financial contributions to arrive by mail. My parent's support was somewhat more regularized, based as it was in part on faith and in part on their affiliation with the Conservative Baptist Foreign Mission Society. The society had been formed in the late 1940s, by a splinter group that had broken off from the much larger American Baptist Convention because of its liberal leanings. Like many Baptist groups, it emphasized a conservative theology as well as the independence of the local church.

The Conservative Baptists provided a structure and a network of interested churches, but not the funds. My parents still had to enlist financial pledges from dozens of individuals and churches, each of whom had to commit themselves to either a onetime gift or a monthly contribution, sometimes as little as five or ten dollars at a time. Returning to the United States in 1960 with two more children required another round of what was referred to as "deputation," the raising of funds for the next four years abroad. The mission board would not allow my parents to return to Pakistan until adequate funds had first been raised. My father's target was $1,800 for a new Land Rover, plus $420 a month for living expenses.

Between the end of June and Christmas 1960, my father preached at more than seventy services in a series of Baptist churches stretching across the country. Many were in the South, in cities as far afield as New Orleans, Natchez, Durham, and Chattanooga. He also visited more distant places, larger cities such as San Francisco, Denver, Houston, and Detroit and smaller towns such as Muscatine, Iowa, and Mariposa, California, not far from Yosemite National Park. Mr. Homer, one of the members of the Mariposa congregation, responded to my father's sermon by selling one of his steers and donating the proceeds—$183—to our Land Rover fund. "The Lord works in such unusual ways for us," my father wrote. "We are sometimes ashamed to accept His bounty."

At times, it was almost like a religious version of a presidential primary campaign: breakfast in one town, dinner in another, a never-ending sea of strange faces reflecting a mix of skepticism and interest, boredom and conviction, hostility and support. Slide shows, usually ending with a rural sunset scene and an appeal to the Lord of the Harvest to supply more laborers, provided a visual sense of what Pakistan was like. The missionary family, dressed in native costume, brought the image still closer to home. In those less complicated times, the sight of my mother veiled in a *burka* or *chador* brought chuckles, not alarm. All this was in the days before the Third World moved to America, when there was still something novel and even interesting about a seemingly normal family that had uprooted itself and travelled halfway around the world in response to a call from God. On many occasions, my father was interviewed by local radio stations about life in Pakistan. Once or twice, we were interviewed as a family on local television—including an appearance on the *Del Ward Show,* a local Macon talk program. Occasionally, too, my mother and father would be asked to speak in public schools, in morning assembly and Friday chapels. All this was at a time when rural schools in Georgia still held chapel services, when morning prayers and partisan public speaking on religious topics had not yet been banned.

Late in the year, in what now would probably be diagnosed as a combination of physical and mental exhaustion, my father suffered a collapse that threatened to end his missionary career, a precursor to what would happen three years later when he was suffering from malaria in Sind. It was familiar enough to anyone who had read the Bible closely, an affliction felt by Moses himself who claimed that he was a stutterer and hence incapable of public speech. My father came to this realization at the Mikado Baptist Missionary Conference in November 1960, just after Thanksgiving. "I am in an awful mental state about speaking in public," he confided in his diary. "I feel as if I cannot speak again." A few days later, "I could not sleep last night because I dreaded speaking this morning at Mikado. I became nervous and went dry." And again, "This has been a great trial and a time of deep soul searching. My ministry is a speaking ministry and it would seem that Satan would cripple me completely."

Time and prayer eventually provided healing and my father was after all able to return to the pulpit and, eventually, raise the funds required to ensure our successful return to Pakistan. Nonetheless, the experience left a lingering feeling of self-doubt, of uncertainty and even defeat. These feelings were accentuated when an invitation to conversion or the rededication of one's life to Christ was extended at the end of a service and no one would come forward. "I am disturbed at no response to the invitation," my father wrote at one point, expressing his anguish. It was disconcerting to preach a sermon and then go through all the verses of "Just As I Am, Without One Plea" and still see no results. Just as I am, without one plea, but that my God who died for me—I come, I come. The final refrain, echoing into a terrifyingly empty night, was hard to resist.

On one occasion, five years later, when we had returned to Georgia for a second furlough, I inexplicably responded to my father's invitation at the end of one of his sermons. It was after all the verses of "Just As I Am" had been sung, after all the pleas and prayers and heartfelt exhortations, and still no one had come forward to accept Christ's salvation. For reasons I still cannot fully understand, I suddenly slipped out of my seat during the final chorus and made my way quickly down the aisle, as if to assure my father that his message had after all touched the heart of at least one member of the congregation. My simple act seemed to have unleashed a flood of similar feelings for a number of others also made their way forward to the altar rail that night, some in tears. So many people came forward that all the verses of "Just As I Am" had to be sung once more, in their entirety.

This was the same year—1965—when I walked the aisle to ask for Believer's Baptism. It happened at Mikado Baptist Church, when I was in third grade, during one of the periodic revivals held there. My brother David followed soon after and we were both baptized together, in white robes, treading the dark, cold waters of the Mikado baptismal pool. There was a painted scene at the back showing the Jordan River, that distant body of water that all of us one day would have to cross alone. Pastor Carl Green from North Carolina baptized the both of us. A scholarly and kindly man, he had the misfortune to follow a popular minister into the pulpit and eventually had to leave following a split in the congregation. Friends and supporters of my parents were represented in both the dissident group and in that part of the congregation that stayed on. Somehow, they managed to remain on good terms with people on both sides of the quarrel. It was one of the ways in which Baptist congregations multiplied, like living cells almost, constantly splitting apart and then reorganizing themselves, only to split apart yet again a few years later. Scratch any Baptist church, and you will almost certainly find a schism somewhere in the past.

I always remembered Pastor Green, not only because he baptized my brother and me, but also because his second son, Sergeant Stanley Norris Green, 101st Airborne, 7th Squadron, 17th Cavalry, was killed during combat in Vietnam. He was awarded the Distinguished Flying Cross, Air Medal with first and second Oak Leaf Clusters, posthumously. We heard the news three years later, in November 1968, after we had returned to Pakistan. His helicopter had been struck by hostile fire, crashing and burning while on a search-and-destroy mission. The memorial service was held at Mikado Baptist Church. It was followed only two months later by another memorial service for someone else we knew, Marine Lance Corporal Terry Kent Jackson, killed during combat in Quang Tri Province, near the Laotian frontier. Friends sent us programs from both memorial services, suggestive of rituals that must have been taking place all across the state of Georgia at that time.

The band from Willingham High played the national anthem at both services. The congregation sang "My Country 'Tis of Thee" and "Onward Christian Soldiers" and there were pledges of allegiance to the American as well as the Christian flag. The memorial handout featured studio photographs of young soldiers in military uniform, taken by Olan Mills. Terry Jackson's program included an excerpt on "heroism," lifted from an essay he wrote while a student at the University of Georgia in Athens. Stanley Green's program included a poem written at Pleiku less than three months before he died. It was called "The Little Things" and consisted of a litany of items he longed for—a cold Pepsi, a hot bath, a dry place to sleep, a telephone call from a friend, a girlfriend's smile, all-night fishing. "We'd give a month's pay for a sure day of calm," he wrote. "And to have with us again all the buddies we've known." The poem ended with the heartfelt comment, "Oh, how we thank God for the little things."

Years later, having chosen to go to university outside the American South, I overheard a foreign student, from Israel as it happened, remark how strange it was that he had yet to meet a single American who knew anyone who had died in Vietnam, as if to say that it was only the poorest of the poor who had fought and died in that tragic and unpopular war. I was outraged but, as on so many other occasions, managed to keep my silence. If I had said something, I probably would have included a reference to the fact that in the South we were different. It was because we were the keepers of older traditions, respectful of soldierly ways, providers of cannon fodder in disproportionate numbers in all the nation's wars.

The fact is, I knew many who had fought and died—Stanley Green; the Jackson boy; a teacher's brother, shot down over Hanoi; the brother-in-law of our family dentist, missing in action for years and then eventually killed in captivity by the Vietcong. Perhaps this is why I wrote from boarding school and asked my father for the words of the "Ballad of the Green Beret," why I wrote away to West Point and asked for a college prospectus while I was still in grade school, why I dreamed of the time when I too might fight and possibly die in defense of my country. I was too young to appreciate the moral ambiguities of Vietnam. If I had been old enough, I almost certainly would have followed Stanley Green who, after all, had written to his parents that he "was still old-fashioned enough to believe in patriotism." I would have been that old-fashioned as well. If I had been born ten years earlier, it might as easily have been my memorial service.

After Stanley Green was killed, his mother sent us his stamp collection as a final gift. My brother and I went through the album, page by page, each choosing our own stamps in turn. It was like dismantling a creation from childhood, like dicing over old clothes immediately after a hanging—it never felt quite right. Twenty years later, I found my way to the Vietnam Memorial in Washington, D.C., and looked for Stanley Green's name among the tens of thousands of other names, arranged chronologically, in order of when the soldiers were killed. His name was there, somewhere near the middle. I could just barely imagine the grief and sadness of those around me, each looking for the names of those whom they too had once known and loved. Like them, I ran my fingers across the lettering set in dark stone, as if to acknowledge that the simple act of touching might yet bring back lost memories and somehow make them whole.

SIX

# Rumors of War

Pakistan's first major war with India passed me
by. The year was 1965 and we had just arrived in
Georgia for one year of furlough. I was eight
years old. I was about to enter third grade and I
was watching television for the first time. The
evening news became a family altar, Walter
Cronkite a secular prophet neatly packaging
events of the day in comprehensible form.
Each newscast ended with the same reassuring
statement: "And that's the way it is." As if all that
was significant and happened in the world in the

last twenty-four hours, to all three billion of us then living on planet earth, could be confined within the borders of a single half hour, edited in New York and broadcast as television film for the entire nation to see.

We watched the television news each evening with anticipation, looking for reporting from the Indian Subcontinent, fascinated by the images of our distant home, a country that had only rarely made television news before. Somehow, the moving images made it all seem real, more real even than if we had been there ourselves. The maps behind the newscasters located us on the planet, gave meaning to our travels, legitimized our lives, provoked interest among strangers who previously had only vague notions of where Pakistan might be located.

The vocabulary of war was exciting, especially to an eight-year-old who already harbored notions of going to West Point and embarking on a military career. History was being made before our eyes. As I understood it, it was a last attempt by Pakistan to right the wrongs of independence, when half of Kashmir, with a Muslim majority population, somehow became part of India instead. The long-awaited, UN-sponsored referendum on Kashmir's future never took place. Seventeen years later, Pakistan tried to force the issue by sending a few hundred lightly armed commandoes into Kashmir. Force Gibraltar, special forces trained at camps in Murree, near Murree Christian School, in fact, were ordered to infiltrate the land as spies and provoke rebellion among the Muslims living there. The Indians responded with a full-scale military offensive against Punjab, setting in motion the largest tank battles since the Second World War. From Pakistan's perspective, the greatest heroes of the war were the few dozen Air Force pilots in their American-built Sabre jets, fierce guardians of the Islamic sky, outnumbered two to one yet still performing magnificently.

We cheered for Pakistan every step of the way, knowing the chances of victory were slight but nonetheless hoping for a miracle. The United Nations Security Council met late into the night, trying to force a cease-fire. Both sides were angry at the Americans for arming the other and then imposing an arms embargo once war had broken out. For their part, the Americans had thought they were arming Pakistan against the Soviet Union and India against China; the two sides were not meant to start fighting each other. Seventeen days later, the headlines announced that it was all over, that there would be a cease-fire. Both India and Pakistan claimed victory, India because it had taken more square kilometers of Pakistani territory, Pakistan because it had avoided outright defeat in the land war against seemingly impossible odds. The Russians mediated the peace settlement that followed the war, resulting in the Tashkent Declaration that restored almost everything to the way it had been before the outbreak of fighting.

Back in Murree, my classmates were living the excitement of distant battles, experiencing the drama of war at close hand. Indian Air Force planes passed overhead on their way to Rawalpindi. Army convoys roared through Jhika Gali, on their way to Kohala, Muzzaffarabad, and the furthest reaches of Azad Kashmir. "Evacuation kits" were diligently inspected, small satchels containing passports, tinned fruit, clean underwear, a toothbrush, and a bar of Lux soap: the essentials in the event of a forced departure by chartered plane to Tehran or Beirut, places of refuge then, recommended safe havens in the event that the American embassy ever called for a general evacuation of American civilians from Pakistan. I too had always gone off to boarding school in Murree with an evacuation kit in hand, secretly hoping that it might one day be used.

Our chance finally came six years later, in December 1971. Throughout the fall there were repeated rumors of another impending war. Murree was quiet as ever but, a thousand miles away in East Pakistan, there were stories of death and destruction, of a civil war that threatened to tear the country apart. Classmates whose parents worked in East Pakistan told of atrocities involving the Pakistan army and were openly sympathetic to the idea of an independent Bangladesh. I could scarcely believe the stories of cruelty I heard and thought that perhaps the Pakistan government's own White Paper on the rebellion, prepared for international distribution but also available in local bookshops in Rawalpindi, just might be true. If the Pakistan army was brutal, it must be because Pakistani soldiers had themselves been brutally murdered in the streets of Dacca and Chittagong. A news photograph of a triumphant Bengali civilian waving the severed head of a Pakistani army officer was especially shocking. Few photographers got close enough to record the tens of thousands of Bengali civilians who were gunned down by Pakistani soldiers during the early days of fighting.

Months before the war began, there was an enormous tragedy of another kind—the once-in-a-generation cyclone, an act of God blowing in from the Bay of Bengal, provoking fifty-foot waves that spared no one, not even small children lashed to the branches of trees, tied there by frightened parents in a vain attempt to ensure that at least one family member survived. Some reports said a hundred thousand died, others talked of a million. "Many in America will turn on the television, view the pictures of the dead and say how horrible, then turn the dial," a missionary colleague in East Pakistan wrote to my father, describing some of the horror he had seen. "Some will pick up the newspaper, read reports of a hundred thousand dead and quickly turn to the comic page. But to the missionary in East Pakistan—well, I guess we'll never be quite the same."

Eventually the fallout from cyclone and war reached us in Pakistan. The feeble official relief effort convinced the Bengalis that the government in Islamabad cared little for them. Subsequent national elections—the first since independence in 1947—confirmed the Bengali desire for independence. The Pakistan military stepped in to suppress the independence movement and ten million Bengalis fled as refugees to India. The only question was if and when the Indians would intervene.

The announcement at Murree Christian School came on a chilly day in late November 1971, when all 140 students were called into the auditorium for a special meeting. Our principal, Chuck Roub, was unusually somber as he addressed the gathering. School was over. We had twenty-four hours to pack up and get out. The bus would depart for Rawalpindi at dawn the next day. We would board trains going south in sequence, turn by turn, as soon as seats became available. Students from East Pakistan, Sri Lanka, and Abu Dhabi would fly home on the next available plane. Telegrams were sent to parents across Pakistan, even as the brief meeting was breaking up. Our parents must have feared the worst, but for us it was all an enjoyable game. At fourteen, we were invulnerable. We would have been disappointed had war not broken out.

The Baptist group was the first to leave from Rawalpindi station. The train—the *Teẕ Gam,* if I remember rightly—headed south to Rohri, the major rail junction for all of Upper Sind. Some passengers would proceed from there to Quetta, capital of Baluchistan, the only city in all of Pakistan that was beyond the range of Indian military aircraft. We climbed into the crowded third-class compartment one by one, like anxious survivors of an ancient species clambering into Noah's Ark even as the first raindrops began to fall.

The journey across the length of Pakistan took eighteen hours. What I remember most about that long trip south was the darkened railway car, the pile of sleeping bodies shrouded in white, silent corpses almost, an image of things to come. I also remember the sound of the railway wheels clacking away into the night, counting off the kilometers—getting closer, almost home, getting closer, almost home. The distance we travelled was seven hundred miles. Lines of tanks were being loaded into flat railway cars at Jhelum and then again at Multan, their long green snouts pointing east. At some points we were almost within sight of the Indian frontier.

Half an hour before reaching Rohri, a classmate shouted that he had seen the massive suspension bridge across the Indus at Sukkur, silver cables glistening in the distance, bright against the early morning sun, a magnificent structure that was bound to figure high in the list of potential Indian bombing targets. I was disappointed; I always wanted to be first to see the bridge that announced we were almost home. There was another shout as we entered the station. Mothers and fathers crowded the platform, having waited there all night, scanning each train, not knowing for sure when their children would arrive.

The next week, Indian planes bombed Rohri Junction. Several Pakistanis were killed, including a local magistrate and his young wife, caught unawares in their small Volkswagen as they made their way across the Indus River on a bridge connecting Rohri and Sukkur. Some of the railway coolies, doubtless including those who had carried our baggage to the waiting Land Rovers, were also caught by shrapnel and killed. I thought about it for a long time, even years afterward. The bearded grandfather in the red uniform who slung my duffel bag so easily over his shoulder, was he the one? The young man with the moustache who pushed two other coolies out of the way to grab my trunk, was he too numbered among the final casualty count?

The morning newspapers—*Dawn, Morning News, Pakistan Times,* all published in Karachi—reached Shikarpur in the late afternoon. The headlines were always the same: Big Victories in Land War in East Pakistan; Indian Troops No Match for Our Brave Fighters; Pakistan Air Force Gains Superiority in the West; One Hundred Indian Planes Downed to a Loss of Ten of Our Own. On many occasions it was stated that Hindu India would wilt before the might of Pakistan, armed as it was with its all-consuming faith in the God of Islam, bolstered by a mighty army of unseen Islamic angels, armed with the Sword of Islam against which there was no human defense. The claim that one good Muslim soldier was equal to ten Hindus was often made.

Each evening we gathered around our heavy Zenith shortwave radio, tubes glowing in the dark, feeling faintly like a family in occupied Europe listening to illicit broadcasts from London during the Second World War. The familiar signature tune through a storm of static, the sound of Big Ben clapping—it came with the voice of authority, as if from heaven, with more authority even than Walter Cronkite on the CBS evening news back in America. Again I thought, this night and all other nights throughout the war—this is how it must have been for the French Resistance, huddled against an illegal wireless, waiting anxiously for coded messages on a forthcoming parachute drop, for word of the Normandy invasion, for information on the imminent liberation of France.

The news on BBC was different from what was being reported in the Pakistan press. The Indians were surrounding Dacca. Fearsome air raids were being launched against Karachi and Lahore. The Pakistan navy was trapped in Karachi harbor. The only Pakistani vessel that managed to escape, a submarine, had been sunk by Indian depth charges outside Bombay. Indian armored divisions were mounting major offenses, in Punjab, toward Rahim Yar Khan, against Umerkot in the south, capturing huge chunks of Pakistani territory, hundreds of square miles at a time. It sounded like a defeat of Himalayan proportions. As foreigners, we wondered what it would mean for those few of us left behind, especially as the propaganda campaign against the United States for once again "letting Pakistan down" increased.

Late in the war, a caravan of British and Canadian missionaries from Rahim Yar Khan, in southern Punjab, arrived unannounced on our doorstep just after daybreak. The situation there had gotten too bad. The Lever Brothers plant, a British-owned soap factory near the train station that we passed on our own trip south hardly two weeks before, had for some reason been turned into a major industrial target. Indian war planes buzzed the city repeatedly, and an Indian land offensive threatened to capture a nearby town. We found room for all of them and wondered when our own turn would come.

My father was field chairman at the time, responsible for the dozen or so Conservative Baptist missionary families in Sind province. Land Rovers were kept in garages, fuel tanks full, jerry cans at the ready, emergency rations packed, prepared for the day when we too might have to drive by night toward Afghanistan. The Pakistan army was confiscating trucks and jeeps from civilians for use in the war effort. Our Land Rover was painted olive green and could be drafted into war service at any time. I imagined what it would be like to have a gun mounted on the back of our jeep as we crossed the desert in a brave effort to recapture the whole of Thar Parkar. Perhaps the Pakistan Army would let me stay with the vehicle. The only reason it was not confiscated was because my father, on the advice of a local official, parked it in a garage for the duration of the war.

Finally, with Rahim Yar Khan and Umerkot threatened by land, with all civilian air flights cancelled, with the evacuation of most embassies and consulates from Karachi, Lahore, and Rawalpindi already complete, my father had to make the big decision for those of us holding out in the interior of Upper Sind. We had no faith in President Yahya, whiskey-imbibing, mistress-embracing Yahya Khan, blustery villain of the whole sorry episode, he with the heavy jowls and thick black eyebrows—ladies and gentlemen, may I present General Yahya Khan, president of Pakistan. We waited for his speech with mounting concern. My father had placed a fleece, like the prophets of ancient

Israel: a tempting of fate, a test to see in which direction God's hand would point. If Yahya Khan talked of peace, we would stay; if he talked of war, we would form our own small convoy and head by road toward Quetta, Kandahar, and the safety of Afghanistan.

We listened spellbound to the speech, delivered in slurred English on the evening of December 16, a language understood by only a small percentage of the Pakistani nation. Dacca had surrendered. The war in the east was over. But let a thousand years go by, let ten thousand years go by, and still there would never be peace. Until the last Muslim is shot dead in the streets, Pakistan will continue to fight against the enemy Indian nation. We will fight for all of Islam. A setback on one front does not mean the entire war has come to an end. It is like France in 1940. Our Chinese friends will help us in the end. The American aircraft carrier *Enterprise,* armed with nuclear weapons, is sailing into the Bay of Bengal. Have faith, have confidence, the war continues. Pakistan Zindabad, Long Live Pakistan.

After the broadcast, we looked toward my father, waiting for the word that we would load up the Land Rovers that night and head west toward Afghanistan. But the word never came. General Yahya was bluffing; we knew it along with the rest of Pakistan. He could never lead an armed struggle against India for a month, much less for a thousand years. Next day a cease-fire was declared. The entire nation was stunned into silence and then deep depression. Yahya Khan was out, free to spend the few remaining years of his life in the arms of an aging mistress, whiskey bottles in hand, countenance dark in defeat, as the general who brought shame and ridicule to his country. The war had lasted fourteen days.

Zulfikar Ali Bhutto—flamboyant, emotional, table-thumping Zulfikar Ali Bhutto—was coming home. According to some stories, he had ripped up his speech in front of the assembled delegates at the United Nations; according to others, he had taken off his shoe and angrily pounded it on the podium at the General Assembly, cursing the organization for its ineffectiveness while his country was being dismembered. Zulfikar Ali Bhutto was coming home, ready to take over leadership of a broken nation, dreams of Islamic unity shattered, its vision of a single homeland for all the Muslims of British India passing into ignominious defeat. Now there were more Muslims in India than in all of Pakistan, more Muslims there even than in the new nation of Bangladesh. Pakistan, the self-proclaimed homeland for the Muslims on the Indian Subcontinent, was no longer the single largest Islamic nation on earth. Zulfikar Ali Bhutto, son of a wealthy landowner in our own upper Sind, acquaintance from Ratodero days, the same Zulfikar Ali Bhutto whose family had once sold us a puppy named Prince, called by fate to revitalize Pakistan and restore it to its former glory as a beacon of hope for all the world. Zulfikar Ali Bhutto, Berkeley graduate, Islamic socialist, friend of the people, savior of Pakistan. Zulfikar Ali Bhutto, leader of the masses, writer of historic speeches, fated to hang by his neck until dead in Rawalpindi jail not seven years hence, fated to be buried alongside his ancestors near Ratodero, in his home village of Naundero, in the soil of our own Upper Sind.

The fact is, we admired Zulfikar Ali Bhutto's rhetoric from a distance, his gift for inspired speech, his ability to put down the bearded ones on the religious right who were constantly demanding our expulsion from Sind, the expulsion of all Christian missionaries from Pakistan. Once a religious opponent publicly denounced Zulfikar Ali Bhutto for drinking too much. "I may drink whiskey from time to time," he had retorted. "Unlike my opponent, I don't drink the blood of the people." Even to a fourteen-year-old, there was something captivating in the way in which Bhutto was able to mesmerize a nation. My father always said that Bhutto was the first Pakistani politician to give the common man a voice, to make them think that they might actually matter. My father could even claim to have known Zulfikar Ali Bhutto. In the early 1960s, in the early days of Bhutto's political career, he had heard him address a rally at the Shikarpur Boys College. He had also met him on several occasions in Larkana when he was a rising star in Pakistan's underpopulated political firmament, the youngest foreign minister in Pakistan's brief history, the boy wonder who everyone said would one day rule Pakistan with a velvet glove and an iron hand. According to legend, one of his own schoolteachers had predicted that Zulfikar Ali Bhutto would be president one day— either that, or hang from the gallows. Few imagined he would ever do both.

We had met the Bhutto family at a tea party in Larkana more than a decade before. Charming young Pinky was there, little Benazir, apple of her father's eye even then, the strong one in the family, the one who would outshine her brothers and make history on her own, becoming the first female head of state in the modern Muslim world, the first elected head of state in the entire world to ever bear children while holding high political office.

Shahnawaz was also there, a small boy then, dark hair and with a large nose and a precocious arrogance, like his father, whose impetuousness he inherited. Shahnawaz and I were the same age. We would meet once more, years later, on a football field in Islamabad. He had reportedly gotten in a fight with the German ambassador's son at the International School in Islamabad, which they both attended, following insults about Prussian military failures and the guilt of a Nazi past. The German boy was quick to retort, "It took the whole world six years to defeat us, yet your Pakistan could not stand against India for even two weeks." In a moment, the two were thrashing about on the ground, grabbing for each other's throats. Later, on the football field, a classmate of mine knocked Shahnawaz down, blocking him as he tried to make a tackle. The classmate returned to the sidelines amid great excitement and hilarity, shouting all the while in a singsong voice that might easily have come from *Lord of the Flies*, the book we were then reading in our English literature class. "I hit Bhutto's son, I hit Bhutto's son," he shouted, repeatedly and with great satisfaction. "I hit Bhutto's son."

Years later, there would be rumors that Shahnawaz was involved in a terrorist group aimed at avenging his father's death, that he had helped arrange the hijacking of a Pakistan International Airlines plane to Kabul, an incident in which a Pakistani diplomat was shot dead. Still later I would hear that Shahnawaz had also died, murdered or killed from drink or drugs. Like so much else in Pakistani politics, the cause of his death was never established. His estranged Afghan wife Rekha—astonishingly beautiful in photographs, though apparently with a heart of stone—was with him in the same hotel on the French Riviera. She had been in the next room and must have been aware of his slow dying, must have heard his death gurgles from a distance—

and yet she had seemingly refused to call for help until there was only quiet.

It was impossible to imagine all this in the fleeting happiness of our Larkana tea party in the late 1950s, underneath the neem trees inside a walled-off courtyard. Zulfikar Ali Bhutto and his young family, born to tragedy, destined for sorrow, acquainted with grief. Unbeknown to all of us, the shadow of the gallows was hanging over our china teacups, even in the stillness of that languid Sindhi evening when the burdens of political power seemed so long and far away. "Mr. Bhutto, the new President, is trying to pick up the pieces of a shattered dream," my father wrote to friends in America from our home in Shikarpur in early 1972, nearly fifteen years after that memorable tea party in the Larkana garden where we had shared ice cream with the Bhutto family. "Everyone is wondering how he will put them back together again."

•    •    •

The image of war lingered in my mind long after the fighting ended. We lived through the conflict with our next-door neighbors, Rita and Pasha, upper-class Bengalis from East Pakistan. Aliens like us, they waited for the town to turn on them in anger, to root out and destroy these foreigners whose compatriots had inflicted such grievous injury on the heroic Pakistani *jawans*, young soldiers sent to die in the cause of Islam. Even the Pakistani press acknowledged in the end that it had been a military disaster, the worst defeat ever inflicted on an Islamic army in a history that went back fourteen hundred years. Ninety thousand soldiers surrendered in a single afternoon. Tiger Niazi signed the shameful surrender documents for Pakistan at the Dacca Race Track in front of the world press, in front of General Jagjit Singh Aurora, one old soldier from British Indian Army days passing his pistol and sword to another. There were rumors of war crimes trials to follow.

Pasha, our Bengali neighbor, was the senior Pakistani official in town, the subdivisional magistrate, the workhorse of the civil service on whom the local civil administration depended. But even that offered scant protection. As the Pakistan army surrendered in East Pakistan, dozens of leading Bengali intellectuals were massacred on the streets of Dacca, their bodies thrown to rot in open drains and irrigation canals. Rita's father was vice chancellor at Rajshahi University in East Pakistan. She waited in fear that his name would show up on a list.

After the war, Pasha was transferred, to Sukkur first and then to Khairpur, an unwilling hostage in the final act of Bangladesh's war for independence. Sheikh Mujibur Rahman, father of Bangladesh independence, was also in Pakistani hands, first in a jail cell in the wilds of Baluchistan, west of Shikarpur, later in the great Moghul fort facing the Indus at Attock, halfway between Rawalpindi and Peshawar. Would there be war crimes for the thousands of Pakistani soldiers captured in the east? Would the prisoners of war ever return? What about the thousands of Bengali civilians still trapped in West Pakistan, like Pasha and Rita; would they ever go home?

One senior Bengali pilot in the Pakistan Air Force had tried to escape to India from the military airport in Karachi, flying desperately for the border in a two-seater training plane. The young pilot in the rear, an Air Force cadet in training not much older than I, fought back, forcing the plane down in the desert near Thar Parkar, close to the Indian border. There was an explosion just before the plane crashed. The trainee pilot was posthumously awarded Pakistan's highest medal for military valor. He was a seventeen-year-old hero whose memory was resurrected each Independence Day amid a resounding silence about past defeats. After all the killings in East Pakistan, he at least would be forever young, the winsome hero who rose above the bloody land war to find eternal glory in the skies above his beloved Pakistan, land of hope and glory, home of the pure and righteous. After this incident, Bengalis in government service were trusted even less than before.

One day, Rita arrived in Shikarpur, alone and unexpectedly, for a brief visit with my mother. She carried her gold wedding jewelry with her. She surprised us after supper by giving us the jewelry, and then departed quickly into the darkness of the night. "If the Pakistanis come, throw it in a canal," she told my mother. "Better that it should be buried than go to the Pakistan government. Better that it should be lost in the water than go to a Pakistani soldier."

It was months before we heard of them again, and then only through a cryptically written note that bore a Canadian postmark. Rita and Pasha had made it back to Bangladesh, smuggled out in the back of a Bedford truck with a number of other Bengali refugees, let off at the edge of the desert to walk alone toward the Afghan frontier. Afghanistan was a dozen miles to the west and they would arrive with little more than the clothes on their back. Kabul was another day's journey by bus. The jewelry was ours to keep—unless we could somehow figure out a way to get it back to Bangladesh in the coming years.

In the end, the jewelry was returned, piece by piece, rings, bracelets, nose ornaments, the heavy golden treasures of a young Bengali bride, restored at last to the rightful owner. By the time the last gold earring was sent, Rita and Pasha had two children and Pasha was rising quickly in the ranks of the Bangladeshi civil service. There had also been other cyclones and other wars, mutinies in the military and a series of bloody coups. Sheikh Mujibur Rahman, George Washington of his country, released because of the magnanimity of his archenemy Zulfikar Ali Bhutto, was himself killed in a bloody coup. He died violently at home, killed with most of the rest of the family in a shoot-out with disgruntled sections of his own military. Only a daughter survived to carry on the career of yet another South Asian political dynasty, from father to son, from father to daughter, until the tanks tread noisily into position, until the hangman arrives, until the bombs begin to fall. Another leader overtaken by the military, young corporals and old generals dreaming of fleeting fame and glory, driven by a death wish and a desire to save the country from disaster, again and again.

Rita and Pasha were not the only victims of the 1971 war with India. There were others, tens of thousands of others: perhaps a million people died in the bloody birth of Bangladesh. We knew one of them well, one of Pasha's civil servant predecessors, also a subdivisional magistrate in Shikarpur. His name was Qudrat Elahi and he lived there in the middle 1960s, a sophisticated and worldly intellectual by our lights, giving us children our first personal glimpses of the rapidly changing world beyond our little town. It was Qudrat who read to us from Tolkien's *Lord of the Rings,* played Joan Baez on his gramophone, and settled down with a bottle of Johnny Walker on lonely evenings, far from his native land. It was Qudrat, too, who introduced us to Bengali nationalism, to the poetry of Tagore, to the deep-seated frustrations and resentments harbored within the Bengali soul against their Punjabi masters in the west. "We're colonized by the Punjabis, just like my father's generation was colonized by the British," he said, not once but on many occasions. He talked a lot about colonialism, about the injustice of rule from Islamabad, about the beauty of Golden Bengal, about the prosperity that would follow when the West Pakistanis finally left forever.

We saw Qudrat several times after he was posted away from Shikarpur; it was a friendship my parents actively cultivated. The last time was in Hyderabad, in 1969, when he took our family out to eat at a small Chinese restaurant near the center of town just before taking up his new posting in East Pakistan. My father presented him with a Bible bound in leather, translated into Bengali, a parting gift, a small remembrance of our esteem and our friendship over the past many years. He urged Qudrat to read it carefully, to understand the Scripture on which our own lives and hopes for all eternity were based, the book that had brought my parents from rural middle Georgia to the heat and dust of Upper Sind, to the far-off land of Pakistan.

Qudrat, always talking, had something of his own to say. "Remember this," he told my father as we parted for the last time. "No matter what you hear or who talks to you, I am a Bengali patriot, first and last, until the day I die."

My father later remembered that last night when we gifted the Bengali Bible to the animated and courageous civil servant from East Pakistan who had briefly crossed our path, impressing us deeply. "Closing the gates as we left, I glanced up into the midnight sky," my father wrote, to friends and financial supporters in America. "It was one of those starry heavens that declare the glory of God and I whispered a prayer for my friend and for others whose lives we have tried to bring in contact with Christ here in this distant land."

Qudrat's brother, also a civil servant, eventually told us the rest of the story. He was attending Harvard University at the time, under a graduate fellowship program for Bengali government officials, the kind of course Qudrat himself would have taken and thrived on had he survived. The story was chilling. Qudrat had been one of the first casualties of the uprising and had died violently on a grassy field in his own native Bengal. It happened in the north of the country, when all East Pakistan was in flames. He was a local magistrate, the leading civil servant for a government that was ceasing to exist. The Mukti Bahini, the Bengali freedom fighters, were taking over and did not have much time for a civil servant, even a Bengali civil servant, "A Bengali nationalist first and last, till the day I die."

The Mukti Bahini irregulars rounded up several dozen Punjabi militia men, Razaaks dressed in gray uniforms and carrying World War I vintage Enfield rifles, hiding in bushes and outhouses on the outskirts of town. Their fate was clear. They sobbed, lifted copies of the Koran toward heaven, pleaded for their lives, cried for salvation, soiled their *shalwars* amid shouts for justice and mercy, and clung desperately to the rope of Allah, crying again and again for mercy, for compassion, knowing all the time that it was useless, that their time on earth was growing short. In the name of God, the merciful and compassionate, let us live, let us live. God, Qudrat tried, how hard he tried. He always had to be the hero, accomplished in the desperate gesture, skilled in all manner of courage. Uninvited, he threw himself into the melee, between the militia cowering on the green fields of Bengal and the Mukti Bahini detachment, rifles and machine guns in hand. He promised the Razaaks that he would see to it that their lives were spared. He argued with the Mukti Bahini for time, shouting loudly that the soldiers of Bengali nationalism were beyond this kind of revenge and should set a better example for the watching world. But of course there would be no more time. In a moment, Qudrat himself was cut down, killed by his own people, torn into pieces by machine-gun fire, to lie forever in the fertile earth of his own Golden Bengal.

We remembered, and grieved. "Some time ago we wrote that we had given a Bengali Bible to a friend, a government official stationed here from East Pakistan," my father reported to friends in America. "Soon after that he was transferred back to his home and we requested your prayer that the Holy Spirit would use the Word to lead him to the cross. We learned the other day that he was one of the countless numbers who perished in the holocaust there. Because of the Bible we gave and the prayers you offered we may yet see him on that day when, in a moment, in the twinkling of an eye, at the last trumpet, we shall be forever changed."

There were others too, mostly civil servants we had known from our Shikarpur days, caught up and forever changed in the tragedy and nightmare that became Bangladesh. Mr. K., from Kashmir, was yet another government official who served a couple of years in Shikarpur and then left for a new posting in East Pakistan. This time it involved the Pakistan army in Jessore, a critical military sector bordering India. The local military commander there asserted his authority immediately after the rebellion began. Names, names, he wanted names—a dozen Bengali nationalists each day, troublemakers worthy of summary execution, traitors guilty of high crimes against Islam and the state.

A fellow Baptist missionary, serving in East Pakistan in the same town in which K. was posted, met him on several occasions and wrote movingly on the obvious psychological stress that he experienced, pulled between loyalty to country on one side and loyalty to conscience on the other. According to one story, K. was unable to do what the government required of him and was sent home in disgrace, incapacitated by a mental breakdown. He arrived in Karachi on the eve of war with India, in one of the last planes to leave East Pakistan before the onset of fighting. We met him soon afterward, still recovering from the killing and war, still grieving for the loss of a dream. His father had left everything in 1947 for Pakistan, for the Islamic Republic, forsaking even Kashmir, beautiful Kashmir, the Garden of Eden, the place where Jesus Christ found rest, the place where Nanga Parbat could be seen, shining white against a moonlit sky. Nationalists all, till the day we die.

·     ·     ·

In spite of everything, I was disappointed in my meager allotted portion of the war. It was not enough to simply tape up our windows and observe a blackout each evening. I wanted to see real action. I wanted to dig an air-raid trench, even though my father said trenches would not be necessary in Shikarpur. I wanted to see an airplane go down in flames, a parachutist limply float toward earth. I wanted to hear the sound of distant guns, smell the smoke of battle, see the tracer bullets light up the darkness of night. Every afternoon, when the air-raid siren from the local fire brigade screamed throughout the town, I ran immediately for the roof, scanning the deep blue winter horizon for one of Pakistan's American-built Sabres or Chinese-built MIG jets defending our sacred land from the enemy across the border. It never happened. Only a single Pakistan Air Force squadron defended all of Sind north of Karachi. Air-raid sirens sounded whenever an Indian plane crossed the border into our province, yet no war planes ever reached Shikarpur.

Nothing ever happened. The closest we got to war were the several air raids on Sukkur and less successful bombing attacks on nearby Jacobabad and Larkana, both by single Indian Air Force jets that had probably gotten lost trying to find Hyderabad or Sukkur, dropping their bombs on whatever city they happened to be flying over at the time. Probably the Indian pilots could not have found Shikarpur even if they tried. Probably Shikarpur was not on their maps. Probably they did not even know where Shikarpur was.

But we did at least have one war story to tell, to expand on and exaggerate in the coming years when we recalled the glamour and excitement of our life in Pakistan. Toward the end of the war, our water carrier and general handyman Baroo came running into the kitchen with an unexpected burst of energy, joy scrawled large across his moon-shaped face. "Memsahib, I want to go," he said breathlessly. "An Indian plane has been shot down. There is an injured Indian pilot now being taken to Shikarpur jail."

Baroo and I walked up the dusty road toward the jail together with big, rapid strides, trying to get there before a large crowd of other townsfolk had gathered and obstructed the view. Several dozen people were already waiting outside the open jail cells when we arrived, all staring intently at a bewildered man huddled in the corner of an otherwise empty cell, hands manacled together, terror in his eyes, madness on his face. It was never exactly clear who he was. He may have been an escapee from the walled mental asylum, what we called the "Pagal Khana," the house for crazy people. He may have been a disoriented burglar. He was certainly no Air Force pilot and he could not have been from India. After a while the crowd sheepishly began to disperse. Baroo and I, disappointed, left too, walking in silence toward home.

That was my war. Blackened window panes, BBC broadcasts at midnight, tragedies among our Bengali friends, a desperate search for fighter planes in the lifeless Sindhi sky, a drunken radio speech from General of the Armies and President for Not Quite Life Yahya Khan, and a crazy man in a Shikarpur jail whom everyone in town wanted to believe was a captured Indian Air Force pilot. By March 1972, nearly three months after the war ended, nearly three months after Bangladesh won its independence, it all began to seem like little more than a distant memory. We headed north by train, back to boarding school in Murree as usual, along the same route that we had travelled amid such high drama in late November. We passed through Rahim Yar Khan, Multan, Lahore, Jhelum, and finally Rawalpindi. Some of the train stations and factories along the tracks were damaged by shrapnel, gunfire, or bombs. A trainload of damaged tanks had been placed on a railway siding outside Kharian Cantonment, north of Lahore. In one town a railway signal tower was bent double, almost broken in two, dangling uselessly in the wind, blackened by fire and smoke. On another wall someone had written in large green letters the favored slogan that had appeared throughout the length and breadth of Pakistan in the weeks leading up to war. The markings were already beginning to fade. "Crush India," it said. "Crush India." Nationalists all, till the day we die.

# SEVEN

# Wayfaring Strangers

During the 1960s, the flotsam of Europe began

making its weary way toward the mystical East.

Kathmandu and Goa were the usual destinations,

Shikarpur only a hot and dusty transit point along

the way. Some travellers ended up on our

doorstep. "One of your people," the locals would

say, introducing yet another bedraggled visitor

who almost always was skeptical about

missionaries but nonetheless welcomed a hot

shower and free room and board for the night. As

far as the Shikarpuris were concerned, anyone

with a pale face and a European or American passport had to be a Christian. Everyone was born into a society, whether they liked it or not. Everyone had a religious identity, whether they accepted it or not.

Our own concerns centered almost entirely around narcotics. An overdose, a death on our doorstep, a police raid that turned up the personal hashish supply of one of our short-term European or American guests—the position of a missionary in Pakistan was precarious enough without the added complications of an official inquiry. Expulsion would be almost certain, and the American embassy was unlikely to be in a position to offer much help. More probably, our embassy would respond with a list of local lawyers and wish us well in fighting the charges in court.

The government of Pakistan needed to be vigilant in enforcing its drug laws. Church workers, like anyone else, might choose to involve themselves in the lucrative narcotics trade. One British missionary spent several weeks in a crowded Karachi jail cell on dubious drug smuggling charges, yet received little sympathy from his embassy. A cloud of suspicion continued to hang over him, even after all charges were dropped. He eventually returned to London, his missionary career in Pakistan all but destroyed. Yet, even in this case, there was a kind of vindication. According to one account, while in prison he had converted three of his fellow prisoners to the Lord.

Spared such high drama, we too occasionally waged spiritual warfare against these dispirited refugees from a Europe that local Sindhis and the missionary community alike were convinced must be on its last legs, in the final stages of complete moral collapse. For our Muslim neighbors in Shikarpur, the occasional long-haired traveller—referred to with derision as "happies"—demonstrated the complete degradation of the Christian West. For us, they showed the dangers of a secular society that turned its back on the past and rejected entirely the authority of Scripture.

My father noted the first of our overland travellers in his diary as early as October 1961. "I saw the strangest sight in Shikarpur today," he wrote. "There were two English girls walking down the street. I found that they were among a group of young people stranded here because their car is broken down. They are going from London to New Delhi in the interests of some youth organization. I invited them to come to our place and get some fresh water." It was the first of many such invitations that would be extended over the years.

Later visitors were less interested in youth organizations, rarely had their own transport, and usually travelled alone. One English student argued late into the night with my parents about the use of drugs and the evils of addiction. "Can't you see what you are doing to your body, the temple of the Holy Spirit for which you alone are responsible?" my father asked. The student responded with pointed arguments of his own. "They have been smoking hashish here for centuries," he said, forgetting for a moment the nineteenth-century British promotion of—indeed, monopoly over—the world opium trade. "Who are you to impose your own values on this society?" When the visitor left town, we discovered a bundle of discarded hashish in the garbage can and a small clay pipe lying broken into small pieces beside his bed. The scattered pottery shards seemed to suggest that perhaps our witness had born fruit after all. The case of the broken hashish pipe was considered a minor victory, evidence that perhaps some spiritual counsel had after all penetrated into the fog of indifference and tiredness that seemed to characterize most of the poor wayfaring strangers wandering through our barren land.

On another occasion, we completely misread the motivations of one of our European guests, this time from Germany. He was quiet, with long hair and a wispy beard, and stayed with us for much longer than the usual single night. On Sunday, he shocked all of us by pulling out a small red concertina and participating in the afternoon worship services held for about two dozen Punjabi sweepers on the floor of our front verandah. Most of the church music—loud singing, occasional clapping, a tired harmonium, with clanking fire tongs providing percussion—was makeshift anyway. Additional contributions were always welcome. My notions of Europe being what they were, I could not help but imagine this particular visitor wearing leather shorts and long stockings, entertaining some peasant farm gathering in a remote and beautiful corner of the Bavarian Alps. Courting Heidi, no doubt. I wondered why he had ever left.

A less welcome Dutch guest ransacked my father's toiletry cupboard, borrowing his good razor and shaving brush and leaving the bathroom in disarray. My mother was outraged and vowed for several weeks afterward that foreign guests would no longer be welcome, not in our bathroom at least. From henceforth they could use the Eastern toilet, the *dessi* squat pot outside, the same one assigned to our water carrier and general handyman, Baroo.

Baroo later related another story, long after the Dutch traveller left town. He had entered the room of the young Dutchman that same afternoon with a teapot and a plate of English biscuits in hand. The Dutchman, stark naked, blond hair trailing down his sunburnt back above his sunburnt buttocks, was doing yoga exercises on a straw mat placed on the red brick floor. He looked beatifically in Baroo's direction, expecting perhaps a kindred spirit who might have meditation techniques of his own to share. Baroo looked bewildered for a moment, gaped in astonishment, and then without saying a word dropped the tea tray and fled into the safety of the courtyard.

On another occasion, a European couple travelling the world on a bicycle built for two stayed with our neighbors, Larry and Connie Johnson. Next day, Uncle Larry told us that he had been able to explain the way of salvation to the couple the night before. They had talked until well past midnight. "They were almost persuaded of the claims which I thrust upon them," he reported. I felt that perhaps we should be more bold in our own witness, as direct and forceful with our European visitors as the Johnsons had been with theirs. I also felt badly for the couple, for receiving a rare opportunity to believe only to reject the plan of salvation that had been offered up to them. It reminded me of the song we occasionally sang in our evening services, based on a New Testament incident and titled "Almost Persuaded." Almost persuaded to believe.

Their close encounter with the Word had a sort of poignancy for me, even at the age of twelve. We were driving the twenty miles to Sukkur the same day and later passed the young couple in our Land Rover as they cycled down the dusty pavement a few miles outside of Shikarpur. The man, with a beard and a long ponytail, was peddling furiously and barely looked up. The girlfriend, looking tired, waved wanly as we passed by. I wondered what ever became of them.

Fewer visitors from Europe ever made it to Murree. The Pakistani Himalayas were less well known than those in Nepal, and Murree itself was no longer on a direct route to anywhere now that the road to Srinagar and Indian-held Kashmir had been cut off. But one traveller did pass through town, an older German approaching fifty, dressed in brown trousers and a checked flannel shirt and carrying a canvas knapsack on his back. His silver hair was combed straight back and he had a round and wrinkled face. He wore thick plastic glasses, taped together at one corner where the frames had broken in two. He walked down the road from Jhika Gali one autumn afternoon in the early 1970s and must have seen the Murree Christian School sign. The sight of a group of European-looking schoolboys dressed in jeans and lounging outside a local tea shop must have astonished him even more. He launched immediately into a contentious conversation about comparative religion, about the fate of mankind, about the mysteries of the universe.

"What about your Muslim neighbors, are you condemning them all to hell?"

"Do you really believe that God created the universe in six days, that there was a literal Adam and Eve, a Cain and Abel, a Noah, even an Abraham?"

"You mean you haven't heard about the contradictions in Genesis, about the fact that there are two and not one creation stories?"

"You actually believe there was once a great flood and only two of every species were saved? How could they all have fitted on the ark?"

"Oh good, you have heard of Charles Darwin then."

"What about the crusades? What about the inquisition? I suppose these too were done in the name of the Lord?"

"If God is just, how can there be pain and suffering in the world?"

And so it went. A right eloquent Nietzsche in a flannel shirt, a skeptic with a knapsack on his back. Thus spake Zarathustra. We argued back, testing out the tired polemics of our Bible courses, the timid apologetics of our Sunday School lessons. We were nonetheless fascinated by his confident atheism and his lack of fear of the unknown.

We did at least have one answer, on the question of the flood. For us, the evidence seemed irrefutable; it was based on personal experience and observation. We often found fossils in our walks on the Murree hillside, evidence of ancient shellfish and other sea creatures, suggestions that Murree itself, at an altitude of seven thousand feet, had once been covered by the sea. The Genesis account had to be right, a deluge of some kind must have occurred. Even the Himalayas had not escaped the all-consuming wrath of God. We were confident that the wreckage of Noah's ark would one day be discovered in Turkey, on Mount Ararat. There were vague rumors in church magazines that expeditions were already being organized to discover the evidence that would one day convince a doubting world.

In true Christian spirit, we ended the debate by asking Hans to break bread with us, to share supper around a formica-top table in the hostel dining room. He ate like he had been fasting for a month. He spent the night in a spare room next to the nurse's office, had breakfast with us the next morning, and then continued on his weary, lonesome way. "One day you'll understand," he shouted in good humor as he turned to walk away toward Jhika Gali, the flames of hell licking at his worn leather boots. I cannot recall that even a single staff member raised objections to our brief encounter, to the odd presence of a village atheist in our hallowed midst. Sometimes, challenges were good for the soul.

On occasion, there were stories about horrible accidents involving other foreign travellers on lonely stretches of road farther west, in eastern Iran and Afghanistan. One family, heading east to Pakistan in a Volkswagen, accidently ran down a young Afghan shepherd on a lonely stretch of highway between Herat and Kandahar. The shepherd's father arrived to see his son lying dead on the road. The upset European husband was trembling and immediately offered deep apologies. He tried to offer compensation—money, cameras, anything. The Afghan father simply pointed to the young fair-haired boy riding in the back of the Volkswagen, dragged him out of the car, and shot him on the spot. Blood for blood, it was the way of the tribals. Later, everyone said that it would have been better if the family had simply driven on.

No one ever became deathly ill on our doorstep, but we did hear of tragedies involving European and American travellers from other missionaries working elsewhere in Pakistan—a young woman dying alone of hepatitis in a mission hospital outside Abbottabad, a young man disappearing without a trace on a trek in the mountains to the north. Some parents came all the way from Europe or the United States to seek their lost children or bring back their dead. The embassies offered lists of lawyers to consult, the missionaries tried to give spiritual comfort of a different kind. "He walked into Chitral and simply disappeared." "He was trying to get to Gilgit over the Babusar Pass and we never heard from him again." "She was always searching for something." "It seemed like a good thing to do, to see the world before setting off for college."

When I was older, I came across a simple marker for one such traveller in a cemetery in Abbottabad, near Murree, beside several ornate Victorian monuments to British soldiers and a set of more recent unmarked graves from the Christian sweeper community:

Shaun Paul Connolly
of
Jersey, Channel Islands
A Seeker After Truth
Died 6 May 1975
Aged 22 Years

He was buried in the Christian cemetery, probably lowered into the ground by a group of Christian sweepers, consecrated into the afterlife by a visiting Pakistani padre whom he had never met. Shaun Paul Connolly from the Channel Islands, searching for answers in Hazara, seeking after truth in the Northwest Frontier, crossing into eternity almost within the shadow of Nanga Parbat. Now, years later, old candle wax dripped across a concrete memorial stone. The site was already well on its way to becoming another shrine for local villagers to visit, a place where the poorest of the poor could lift up their hands to God.

· · ·

Not all our visitors were strangers. People from the home office, the Conservative Baptist Foreign Mission Society headquarters back in Wheaton, Illinois, also came out from time to time, to offer encouragement and to survey the slow progress of work underway. Missionaries in Africa were reporting thousands of conversions. In Pakistan, our parents counted progress on the fingers of one hand. We were up against the brick wall of Islam. Conversions almost never happened. Gradually, our calling became one of simply bearing faithful witness with the example of our lives.

One year, the Mission Board arranged for a movie producer from California to film our activities in the field. The producer had a Polish-sounding last name and seemed very worldly. He smoked a pipe and spoke slowly, as if permanently inclined toward deep thought and contemplation. His real job was to produce thirty-second commercials for national television. Rumor had it that he was from Hollywood, that Pat Boone was numbered among his friends. Every seven years, he took a sabbatical, offering an entire year of free filmmaking services to Christian ministries throughout the world. My father was asked to write a script for a movie on our work in Sind, which the film director with the Polish-sounding name planned to make.

The scenes my father developed for the thirty-minute film, which bore the title *Caught in Cross Fire*, were based on a compilation of events that he himself had witnessed. A young Christian boy, the son of a sweeper, after great hardship completes his high school education. He then looks for employment outside the sweeping profession, finding obstacles at every turn. Why would the Muslim Commercial Bank of Shikarpur want to hire a Christian clerk? Why would the local Seven Up bottling plant want the son of a sweeper in the office? Faced with rejection at every side, he rejects his own family and religion, changes his name from Paul to Mohammed, and seeks a different path. In the end, his saintly mother cuts herself while cleaning sewers. Infection sets in, followed by gangrene and an amputation. On her deathbed, she looks up in time to see Paul return to the church, re-stored to a living faith in the God who revealed Himself in Our Lord Jesus Christ, the Author and Finisher of Our Faith.

The incident about the amputation was true enough; it happened to sweepers all the time. A small cut, contracted while sweeping streets or cleaning drains. A small infection, swelling the toe and then inflaming the ankle. A surgical procedure by the local barber, who used a sharp axe to hack off half a foot. More infection, more inflammation, more surgery, this time in the local civil hospital, as effective as a slaughterhouse. Off with the leg. By now, it would be too late. Infection often did spread, carrying death and destruction in its wake, leaving half a dozen orphans at a time.

The closing lines of the movie, set against a brilliant Sindhi sun-set and taken from the Apostle Paul's first Letter to the Corinthians, moved me deeply, even at the age of thirteen. "My brothers, think what sort of people you are, whom God has chosen. Few of you are men of wisdom by any human standard; few are powerful or highly born. Yet, to shame the wise, God has chosen what the world considers foolishness, and to shame what is strong, God has chosen what the world counts weakness. He has chosen things low and contemptible, mere nothings, to overthrow the existing order."

It was a moving experience to finally see the completed film a couple of years later back in America, in a crowded Sunday evening service in a mining town in West Virginia, among a working-class Baptist congregation that faithfully sent fifty dollars each month that we might save souls in Pakistan. That was us all right, despised by the world and rejected by man, strangers in a strange and uncomforting country, sent to transform the world, marked eternally by the hand of God, saved only by His Amazing Grace. It was only fitting that we ourselves should devote our lives to the even more despised, to the *busti* Christians who kept the drains and toilets of Pakistan clean.

Another year, the Mission Board arranged a tour for American sup-porters who wanted to observe missionaries in action on foreign fields. Eight signed up, all widows over sixty sharing a spirit of adventure and a desire instilled since their rural Midwest childhoods to see the heathen saved. A young woman from the home office who worked in the public relations section and helped edit our mission magazine was also sent along, to accompany them and find out for herself what the mission field was all about.

My father was in charge of all the Pakistan arrangements for the tour. He mapped out a ten-day trip through the heart of Sind, across the desert from Karachi to Hyderabad and then up the river to Moenjodaro for a brief look at the ruins of that four-thousand-year-old city, the "city of the dead" that we had visited often since the early days of childhood. We were especially proud that among the ancient relics found there were items from Ur of the Chaldees, the pagan city from which Abraham had set out in response to the promises of God, promises that had foretold that his posterity would be as numerous as the grains of sand beside the ocean, as uncountable as the stars that lit up the Milky Way. Every time we visited Moenjodaro now, we speculated about which items on display in the museum might have been touched by Abraham, in the years before he followed God's direction and left Ur of the Chaldees for Palestine.

In planning the trip, my father momentarily engaged in one of his own grand speculations, his intriguing game of historic what-ifs. Imagine for a moment what the future of our planet would have been like if Abraham had headed east toward India instead of west toward the Mediterranean. Who knows, maybe Moses would have led his people to the promised land of Afghanistan or Burma. Maybe he already had. According to one story circulating at the time, one of the Pathan tribes to the north was actually one of the lost tribes of Israel, a chosen people destined to spend out their lives in the harsh desolation of the Hindu Kush. There was a town in the Northwest Frontier Province called Esa Khel, "Fort of Jesus." It was rumored that vestiges of Christianity, dating from the time of the Nestorian missionaries centuries ago, might yet survive.

We always revelled in the biblical touch. It was also rumored that one of the Magi who visited Bethlehem and paid homage at the birth of the Christ Child was in fact a wise Brahman from India, a Sanskrit scholar from Benares or a learned astrologer from Rajasthan. And it was a well-known tradition that Saint Thomas, one of the original twelve disciples, had himself stopped for a time in Pakistan, probably in nearby Thatta on the Indus River, on his way to convert the heathen Dravidians of southern India, a place where he would later be martyred and where his tomb can still be visited today. Several million Indian Christians traced the origins of their own community back to this early missionary, the doubting apostle who had to see the nail marks in Christ's palms before he could believe.

There were other indications, too, of the deep and lasting connection between biblical events and ancient Sind. For example, it was suggested by some that the infant Jesus had been swaddled in cotton from Sind. Cotton had first been grown in the Indus River Valley and there was a thriving trade between India and the Roman Empire. Sindhi cotton was reputed to be of the highest quality. If Jesus was wrapped in cotton, it would have been the best of cotton, and it was reasonable to suppose that it might have come from Sind.

I heard at least one sermon preached on the subject. The English, after all, had always wondered if perhaps in those ancient times His feet had set foot on England's pleasant green pastures, pointing the direction toward a New Jerusalem. One British missionary claimed that Jesus as a child had accompanied Joseph of Arimathea to the tin mines of Cornwall and speculated whether perhaps the Holy Grail might one day be found there. Strange happenings were always being reported around Glastonbury Cathedral. In a similar vein, we imagined that there might be a hidden connection between Jesus and Upper Sind. It was a comforting thought, especially at Christmastime in the stillness of another dark and cloudless Sindhi night, when the stars seemed as numerous as Abraham's progeny, when we half expected the angels to appear, shouting down from on high their ancient anthem, Glory to God in the Highest, Peace on Earth, Good Will to Men.

The tour of eight Midwest retirees continued on up to Shikarpur, where our Baptist hospital had recently been built, and then across the Indus to the historic fort at Kot Diji where, several years earlier, Fess Parker of Daniel Boone television fame starred in a film about the Crusades. "Daniel Boone was a man, yes a big man," the theme music to the television show went. "And he fought for America to keep all Americans free." I was in third grade in Georgia when I first saw the show, and it quickly became a favorite. The fact that Fess Parker had links with Sind made it seem even more remarkable. He had gotten sick in Sind, dehydrated with diarrhea. Dr. Maybel Bruce, the same Dr. Bruce who had brought me whimpering into the world, yellow as a mango pickle, saved Fess Parker's life, filling him up with antibiotics so the filming could continue on schedule. Another brush with fleeting fame. Imagine, Fess Parker-Daniel Boone, alive and well in our small corner of Upper Sind, treated by none other than our own Auntie Maybel!

(Dr. Maybel Bruce died of cancer in Massachusetts in November 1994. I was asked to sort through her papers. One letter to her parents, dated May 1963, reads as follows: "I had a call to see one of the actors from the film company making a film fifteen miles from Sukkur. They lived in Sukkur and went to an old fort to shoot the film. One of the French actors had developed a severe renal cholic. I ended up going about six times to give him morphine. After my second visit, I met the leading American actor, Lex Barker, a former Tarzan and a former husband of Lana Turner and Susan Hayward. He invited us to their farewell dinner, a very informal affair. This Lex Barker was very nice, as were all the ones we met and they were interested in our work. Not much chance of a good verbal witness, but we were able to present a little of our call and purpose in coming. It was a good break from hospital routine." I was at once both astonished and disappointed at the resiliency—and limitations—of childhood memory. It must have been Lex Barker rather than Fess Parker, Tarzan rather than Daniel Boone. It nonetheless represented, for us, a fleeting touch with wider fame.)

The tour for the Midwest retirees was a big success and I later imagined that I must have played my own part perfectly. The pale-faced, blue-eyed missionary kid, shy but helpful, meeting half a dozen American widows at the pottery workshops in Hala, giving each a blue plaque with their names inscribed in Sindhi. The missionary kid, speaking a foreign tongue, helping a group of grandmothers around the crowded bazaars of Hyderabad. The missionary kid, arranging tea in a cockroach-infested cafe by the side of National Highway Number One near Bhit Shah, chasing hungry dogs away, telling curious bystanders to stop staring, show some respect for the elderly, mind your own business, move along quickly now.

One grandmother came prepared, packing a box of religious tracts in half a dozen languages to give to the many Muslim friends she expected to meet along the way. She latched onto the cleaner in the minivan immediately. He in turn proved to be friendly enough, willing to please. Yes, Memsahib. Thank you, Memsahib. Mind the step, Memsahib. "I think he's interested in spiritual things," she told my father as the tour group left Karachi Airport for New Delhi. "Please follow up with him. He just needs to have the way of salvation better explained, by someone who knows his own language."

We heard about their adventures in India later. The seventy-year-old lady who witnessed to strangers at every turn in her minivan journey into Upper Sind was boarding an elephant at Delhi zoo. Halfway up, the elephant suddenly stood up and left her hanging on for dear life from its rough and hairy tail. Another elderly lady captured the entire episode on film, wonderful material for a missionary slide show back home.

Later, we heard the ending of another story. The woman from the home office who helped edit our mission magazine and who accompanied the tour was so moved by her Indian experience that she later returned, to head a literature crusade aimed at putting a passage from the Bible in every one of the several million English-speaking homes in that country. She met a Hindu man from Delhi along the way and later married him. I was never sure what happened after that.

Another program was developed to involve American constituencies more directly in the missionary work in Pakistan. Known as the Missionary Assistance Corps, or MAC for short, it recruited fieldworkers to assist in needed areas—teaching, bookkeeping, nursing, construction, and so forth—for shorter periods of time. Although many such workers were young people, often just out of college, retired people were also involved. On a number of occasions, the more elderly volunteers became surrogate grandparents to us, wise in the ways of the world and yet fragile and foolish, all at the same time.

One elderly man, a plumber by trade, was with us during the December 1971 war between India and Pakistan. All he could think about were the pogroms back in Russia that his family had experienced under the czar, when the family had been imprisoned because, as Mennonites, they were unwilling to serve in the Russian army or fight in the First World War. He lived in constant fear throughout our own small war. When would the Pakistani army come for us, to place us in concentration camps? How long would it be before we were marched off amid the taunts and jeers of townspeople, hostages to fate and fortune, sacrificial lambs in a slaughter that was not of our own making? There were times when my father wondered out loud if perhaps he should be sent home on the next available plane.

Other occasional visitors included the United States consul general or one of his staff, travelling the three hundred miles up from Karachi to see us in our humble surroundings. A chance to observe American missionaries in their natural habitat, a chance, perhaps, to gauge the political situation, to see what Sindhi nationalists were up to, to gather anecdotes for the next reporting cable back to the State Department in Washington. "Our recent tour to the remoter regions of Upper Sind suggests that President Ayub Khan's hold is beginning to slip." "Informed sources in the area tell us that the Basic Democracies Scheme isn't working." "An unnamed contact with knowledge of the local scene indicates that Sindhi college students are growing restive." To ten-year-old ears, it sounded impressive. We never stopped to think that the yellow diplomatic plates on the large white air-conditioned vehicles parked outside our door probably marked us as CIA for life.

The American diplomats in their huge air-conditioned Suburban land cruisers, windows darkened black to ward off the sun, were always welcome, especially when a diplomatic wife came along for the ride. She would be more attuned to our needs, more helpful in terms of our physical nourishment. More precisely, she would ensure that the diplomatic entourage brought along at least a turkey and a ham, some bacon, some cranberry sauce, some M&Ms, Cheerios, and Mars Bars for the hapless missionary children denied the usual commissary privileges. Manna from heaven! We enjoyed every minute of it, rejoicing in the unexpected bounty from a land we hardly knew and yet could claim as our own.

One visit included Mr. Tiger, the consul general, and Mr. Pinch, head of the United States Information Service and America's chief propaganda man in Karachi, whose work assignment in Pakistan must have been even more difficult than that of my father. I still remember the time when these two high officials, uncomfortably dressed in dark suits and ties despite the hot temperatures, were first introduced to our retired MAC worker, the man who worked with his hands in the plumbing trade and was devoting the last years of his life helping to build a mission hospital in Upper Sind, the Baptist in overalls whose parents had been Mennonites and who had come to the United States from Russia just after the revolution.

"Oh, Mr. Tiger, glad to meet you, I hope you don't bite," he blithely announced.

Then, "Oh Mr. Pinch, so pleased to meet you, I hope you don't. . . ." And then he stopped, embarrassed in his tracks, unable to complete the sentence. Like true diplomats, our two guests from the American consulate in Karachi did not even crack a smile.

Years later, after I myself joined the diplomatic circuit and became aware of the two separate worlds that missionaries and diplomats inhabit, different solar systems almost, I wondered if perhaps Mr. Tiger or Mr. Pinch had ever told the same story, embellishing it in their different ways, at a diplomatic function in some other foreign capital. Amazing folks, those missionaries, I imagined them saying. Did I ever tell you about the hilarious afternoon I once spent with a group of Baptist missionaries living in Sind?

# EIGHT

# Numbered Days

A strong awareness of the fragility of our lives

was instilled in us from an early age. This sense had

little to do with religious instruction or the formal

aspects of our upbringing. It was based more on

what we saw around us every day. People were

always dying; it was as if the smell of mortality

hung permanently in the air. Pakistani Christians

followed the lead of Muslims when it came to burial

customs. If someone died in the morning, they

would be buried in a seamless white shroud

before dusk.

Early in his ministry, my father buried a number of babies and young children, dead from smallpox usually, sometimes two or three in a week. The children who survived escaped with disfigured faces and haunted expressions, stares that looked emptily into a future known only too well. The facial indentations marked young girls as unmarriageable, a harsh fate in a society where to be single and female was perhaps the worst of all possible worlds. Boys who survived smallpox also tended to fall much lower in the marriage stakes. The inoculation campaigns organized by missionaries in the Christian and Hindu *bustis* were only partly successful. At least a few children always escaped the long, sharp needles, some out of fear, others because they were helping their parents keep the streets and sewers of Shikarpur clean. In my father's eyes, the fact that it was all so unnecessary compounded the tragedy.

The endless acres of anonymous burial mounds surrounding Shikarpur served as a constant reminder of the widely held sense that in the midst of life we are always in death. There was Parbata, the young wife of a Hindu sweeper who worked for us, dead at thirteen, the victim of an unexplained fever. There was the adolescent son of a local zamindar, too young even to grow a beard, shot down outside the Shikarpur courthouse where he was about to testify on behalf of his father in a land dispute. I passed by on my bicycle after doing some shopping near Lakhi Gate. A crowd was forming and the flies had already begun to appear. As the police took photographs I watched from a distance and then peddled quickly toward home. There was the anonymous old farmer who toppled from the roof of a crowded bus on the old Khairpur road. We were driving behind in our Land Rover and came across the unwrapped turban first, then a single unfastened shoe and finally the body, face down in the dust, lying in a disheveled heap just off the shoulder of the tarmac. Sometimes it seemed like the years trod heavily across our patch of earth, like a great ox breaking us all beneath its swiftly passing feet.

It seems incredible to think that the first funeral I ever attended was for an eight-month-old baby who was shot to death by a friend of mine, the son of another missionary. The facts are too awful to contemplate, a nightmare that will haunt me all the days of my life. I did not see it happen. It was never talked about again. And yet it was always there, an unknowing cloud of enormous tragedy, heavy with sadness, casting a long shadow over life in Shikarpur, a town whose very name meant "hunting-place." I must have been twelve years old at the time.

Babies were always around, our own as well as those from the nearby Christian *busti*. One *busti* baby became a favorite among the missionary children, a little doll for young girls pretending to be mothers and looking forward to the day when they too would have children of their own. We boys, playing make-believe with our sling-shots and air rifles, lived in a fantasy world of another kind. We were warriors of the great plains, hunting for game. Commanders of Arab armies crossing the desert like a hurricane, converting the infidels. Brave cowboys, clambering down deep canyons in search of rene-gades. Renowned hunters on safari in Africa, collecting trophies of the biggest lion or rhinoceros that ever crossed the Serengeti. Killers of noisy green parrots and hungry brown sparrows, exterminators of the unwanted vermin populating the mango and guava orchards nearby. Nothing ever matched the excitement of a single shot fired, a flurry of wings, and a small lifeless bird falling dead to the ground.

There came a time when the two worlds, the world of dolls and the world of air rifles, collided. The child of a Baptist missionary doctor from England, a daughter of eight or nine, was playing mother with the beloved *busti* baby on the flat roof of a nearby house. My friend was sharing the same roof, shooting at birds in a tall tree next door. The baby was thrown up into the air: rock-a-bye baby in the tree tops, when the wind blows the cradle will rock, when the bough breaks the cradle will fall, down will come baby, cradle and all. At ex-actly the same moment when the baby was thrown into the air, the air rifle was fired.

A freak accident, one that never should have happened. And if it happened, an accident that should never have caused bodily harm. We were always firing off small pellets at close range, against the back-sides of indolent water buffaloes or haughty camels. Some creatures never responded. Others simply flicked their enormous moth-eaten tails in indifferent disgust at these strange pale-faced children who seemed intent on tormenting them. Somehow, this lead pellet was different: it went straight through thin skin and finally lodged in the interior of the tiny baby's walnut-sized heart.

"Pray like you've never prayed before," my father said grimly when he told me the news at the end of a depressing day when the sky was unusually gray, when the dust hung heavy in the air and even the wind refused to blow. I had never seen him so upset, tormented even. At first I thought he was about to tell me that another missionary child had been either seriously injured or even killed. "There is a terrible tragedy and I'm not sure how it will all end."

It was the worst of all possible nightmares, one child killing another. Too late for heart massages, for emergency surgery, for trauma room heroics. A little baby whose name I cannot even recall, killed with a single pellet wound to the heart. The police were informed. There would have to be an investigation. The *busti* family decided against pressing charges. The missionary family was torn apart, contrite, devastated, beside themselves with grief. We never talked about it and I can only now imagine the weight of desolation they must have carried with them in the months and years that followed. When he grew up, their son, the one who had killed the baby with a single shot from an air rifle fired in innocence, became a medical doctor, surprising everyone with his doggedness and determination in the face of a less than brilliant academic career. He moved steadily if sometimes uneasily from the dusty streets of Shikarpur to the corridors of a famous medical school in Chicago. I later wondered if he mentioned the incident in his application essay, if he talked about it in the admissions interview when asked why he wanted to become a doctor, if it all made sense in the antiseptic world of American medicine ten thousand miles and another universe away.

Ironically, it was the missionary father who took the funeral service, leading the small group of *busti* Christians trudging wearily and yet again into the Christian cemetery outside Shikarpur, a small plot of land a short distance from the seemingly endless acres where the Muslims buried their dead. Christians were buried separately from Muslims in Pakistan, even as whites were still buried separately from blacks back in Macon, Georgia. As was the custom, the baby's father carried the corpse, a small figure wrapped in white cloth, motionless, tiny, limp, a little wraith, dead before her time, buried in an unmarked grave, into the unsettled darkness at the edge of town. I rode my bicycle to the funeral and watched in silence from a distance, until the last prayer was said and the small group of mourners took clods of earth from the ground, holding them briefly in the smallness of their hands. Then I too gathered up my measure of Sindhi earth and threw a handful of dust into the small and shallow grave.

. . .

Babies were always dying in Sind. Another time, three years later, I travelled with my father by steam train to a distant town on a branch railway line, to Dadu on the west bank of the Indus River. My father was attending a conference for local pastors that would last an entire day. A neighbor's son came by and asked if I wanted to see the town, visit the bazaar, and then go swimming in the muddy irrigation canal outside town in the lazy heat of that late winter afternoon.

I took a few black and white photographs in the bazaar with my father's new Japanese-made Pentax, the camera he had bought to take slides to illustrate talks to supporting churches back home, educating them about the work in Pakistan. After a morning of exploring the bazaars of Dadu we returned for lunch, I to rejoin my father and he to visit with his family in the mud-brick house in which they lived. A short while later he opened the door. "My nephew has expired," he said simply, in stilted English. "I will not be able to spend the afternoon at the canal with you after all."

The boy reappeared again as we were leaving to catch the evening train. He asked if I would take a picture for him and I immediately said yes, of course. Then he told me that the family wanted a picture of his nephew in death, a memory to hang on their living-room wall. It would be the only photograph of him they would ever have. Apprehensively, I went next door, ducked under a small burlap bag serving as a temporary curtain, and entered a small but carefully swept courtyard. The mother was grieving quietly in a bedroom—"eating grief," in the odd but stunningly accurate Urdu phrasing of things. The child, freshly bathed and dressed in white cotton, was propped up against a cushion, eyes closed, mouth open in what might have been a smile. I took the photograph quickly and left at once, praying all the while that the light would be adequate and that the exposure would come out right.

In the weeks after taking that photograph I often imagined my own death. I tried to contemplate the world that would still go on, long after I had unwillingly departed from the passing scene. I always seemed to return to a series of conflicting images—life as a pilgrimage, life as a journey, life as a dream, each with its own ending. And yet it somehow seemed unfair that the show could not go on indefinitely, that the only certainty upon our arrival into the world was that we would one day have to leave it. I could not help but repeat the Pushtu proverb, which said that when we die, the world should also die. In my own self-centered universe, the thought of the world continuing in my absence seemed untenable and deeply unfair.

Mansions in the clouds up yonder, where the streets were paved with gold, made less of an impression than the prospect of eternal extinction. An afterlife would be tolerable if it was just like the life we already experienced on earth. But what a fate, to be laid out to rest in a shallow grave in Shikarpur Christian Cemetery, where the dogs scavenged and a local crazy man lived, stark naked, surviving on gifts of food delivered by the kindness of strangers. Head facing toward Jerusalem (even as the Muslim graves pointed toward Mecca), Bible in hand, waiting in vain for the final trumpet call, when the morning breaks and the shadows flee away.

My parents would remember me for a time and perhaps my brother David and my sister Nancy would carry memories of our strange and wonderful childhood for a few decades longer, into their own old age. Then my brief presence would diminish still further, into a fading image preserved behind glass, a photograph that would outlive the person who took it and then the people who placed it on a wall, until the last eyes that knew me young would also be dimmed and the last surviving photograph would be consigned to the fire. And after that, what then—they too would die and be buried and with them the memories of our family and our life in Shikarpur, the happiness of our home, the glory of our habitation, the bitterness of our youth, vanished like the morning dew. The psalmist was right, we should take nothing for granted, least of all the numbering of our days.

In bed late at night I imagined the face of eternal nonexistence, the shape of things to come. The image that stayed with me most often was of an endless stream of concentric circles, each fading into the other, continuing on into infinity, for ever and ever, thousands, even millions of light years into the future. Our lives, those of our parents, those of our grandparents, of our own children perhaps, brief glimpses of distant glory, viewed as through a dark glass, followed at the end by the eternal and endless grave, bones decaying into ashes, ashes into dust, dust into ballast for yet other graves, one of the millions and millions of graves that would one day cover the entire earth, as the waters covered the sea, as darkness enveloped the remains of the day, as dusk finally gave way to endless night.

In high school, I was fascinated to read a book urging that children should if at all possible be spared the terrors of death, that it warped their imaginations, blunted their sensibilities, scarred them with psychological torment for life. The account—if I remember rightly, it was either in one of the several volumes of Bertrand Russell's *Autobiography* or in an account of one of the educational experiments he had championed—stated that superstition and religion alike could both be traced to the terrors of "primitive man" when confronted with sickness and dying. The terrors I manufactured in my mind were real enough and stayed with me for years, even long after I finally left Pakistan.

One winter, I scratched myself with a rusty nail hanging loosely out of an old crate. I was sure it would lead to tetanus and death by lockjaw, a fate too horrible to imagine. I read the short entry on tetanus in the old edition of *World Book Encyclopedia* that my parents had gifted to me, to see how long the incubation period would last. I was deeply relieved when days turned into weeks, when weeks turned into months, and when it finally became clear that I might yet survive, that I would live long enough after all to return to boarding school in Murree in the spring.

In Murree, it was fear of death by rabies that dominated the morbid imagination. Thousands of children still died of rabies in Pakistan each year, a cruel and unnecessary disease that we would probably be spared. Our parents could at least afford the painful series of rabies injections, fourteen shots with a large steel needle on fourteen successive days, each shot in the middle of the tenderest part of the stomach. I escaped the dreaded series of rabies injections but many classmates did not. One friend, Frank Pressley, was bitten by one of the rhesus monkeys that slouched around the area outside the dining room, waiting for handouts. During the fortnight of the rabies injections that followed, he walked around school like a hero in perpetual pain, the survivor of an ordeal that the rest of us had thus far fortunately escaped but would one day likely experience for ourselves.

One fall, the hillside around Murree Christian School echoed with the sounds of a shotgun. Entire packs of wild dogs were being shot because the head of one dead dog, preserved in formaldehyde and sent to the central government medical labs in Rawalpindi, had tested positive for rabies. The principal's son, Ronnie Roub, a senior in high school, roamed the ridges around the hostel, shotgun in hand, in search of the last canine to survive. Even the friendly stray dog with the hard-done-by expression who lingered outside the boarding hostel, waiting for scraps of food, did not escape. It took three shots to bring him down. The image of his bewildered expression and his white coat turning red with each explosion gave me nightmares for weeks.

And yet, in retrospect, I came to realize that the images of death and eternity I accumulated in childhood were rational and honest ones. It was right to wrestle with the fragility of our lives, with the shortness of our days, with the vastness of infinity. The facts of life went far beyond the discreet booklets my parents handed to me awkwardly when I reached the age of twelve, the small diagrams describing the miraculous reproductive systems of male and female, the lying down together of a man and a woman, the strangeness of love, the birth of children, the propagation of the species. These too were mysteries, but at times even they were overshadowed by the one dominant fact, the immutable law of finitude, which, I later discovered, was kept well hidden from most of my contemporaries in America. The great mystery there—the blank slate that was kept hidden, not only through childhood but often well into middle age—was the grave. All societies had their dark secrets and were selective on certain issues, each in their own and different way. If there was an awkwardness in certain aspects of my upbringing, it is nonetheless true that there could be few inhibitions in perhaps the one thing that mattered most, in the numbering of our days.

It would have been impossible for our parents to shield us from these facts, even if they had wanted to. In May 1969, when I was eleven and in boarding at Murree Christian School, the classmate sleeping in the bunk below me was awakened at dawn by our housefather with unaccustomed tenderness. He left the room in silence. Shortly later, we were all asked to get out of bed and meet for a word of prayer in the next room. Again, there was a pervading quietness, as if we had a premonition of what we were about to be told. When we were all gathered, we heard the awful news—David Hover's father, expected in Murree later that week, would not be coming after all. He had been killed in a car accident in Sind, driving a hospital van between Hyderabad and Sukkur. The telegram was very cryptic: "Road Accident Stop Peter is With the Lord Stop Please Inform Children." And so the children were informed, along with the rest of us. Almost certainly, we all thought the same thing—"it could have been my father, too; it could have been my father, too."

Later that same summer, we returned to Shikarpur and then travelled to the mission hospital in Sukkur where the gray van Dr. Hover had driven was parked. The front was destroyed; he had driven into a cloud of dust and been hit head-on by a bus. It bothered me to think that, if he had only started the journey five minutes earlier, he might have survived. There would have been no cloud of dust, no other bus on the road at precisely that time, no fatal collision. Life could have continued as usual; David and his three younger sisters would not have been left fatherless. How did it happen, that someone whose whole life had been dedicated to the service of God should come to such an end? What about his family? God Almighty, if he had left even five seconds later it might never have happened. It seemed inexplicable, as if it should only have been a dream.

At times, the image of life as a dream had a strong resiliency, one my sister Nancy seemed to share. Once, when we were returning from school in Murree and Nancy was less than ten years old, she turned to me and suddenly voiced for no apparent reason a thought we both must have been turning over in our minds for some time. "What if this isn't real, what if we are only dreaming, what if we are about to wake up?" My father overheard the comment. He was silent for a moment and then replied simply, "Some people think of life as nothing more than a dream." There it was, the mystery and sadness of it all, plainly stated. Perhaps we were, after all, nothing more than insignificant termites, lost in someone else's universe.

•     •     •

Possibly no tragedy affected us more deeply than the early death of Basil Barnabas, my father's longtime language teacher. He lived with his brother Leonard and a surviving aunt in Sultankot, twenty miles away. We travelled there early each Sunday morning for services. From the conversations that went back and forth between my father and my mother as we travelled to Sultankot each week it was possible to sense something of Basil's melancholy spirit, of the spiritual struggles and private fears that seemed to dominate his life. After his marriage he moved to Shikarpur, possibly to be closer to my parents.

As the years turn into decades, the images of Basil Barnabas live with me still. He supposedly had some Anglo-Indian blood somewhere in his distant ancestry, one of a small community that lingered on after partition and whose members mostly worked as schoolteachers, nurses, or railway conductors. He was very dark, had thick, sensual lips and was somewhat heavyset, the result of a diet heavy in ghee. Each week he met separately with my father, faithfully reviewing my father's Urdu sermons, marking mistakes in the margins, proposing alternative phrases, trying to help my father better capture for an audience of illiterate *busti* Christians the essentials of the Gospel message. He often asked my father for clarifications and explanations of his own, for an elaboration of an especially vague passage, for insight into what the Gospel writers had been trying to report or an explanation of a particularly difficult image rooted in the life and customs of first-century Palestine. It was one of the closest friendships my father had in Pakistan.

An owl foretold Basil's impending death. We were picnicking together in the public park at the edge of Shikarpur, near the dried-up pond where in Hindu times a small zoo had been maintained, where man-eating crocodiles once slapped the water with their huge, prehistoric tails. It was late afternoon and we were about to leave when we heard the sound of heavy wings beating against the air and saw the ungainly flash of a solitary large bird across the cloudless Sindhi sky.

Catherine, Basil's wife, was horrified. My parents had helped arrange the marriage two years before, when Basil was well into his thirties and feared more than ever that he might never wed, might vanish without posterity, might never have children of his own. It was my parents who had first met Catherine, then in her early twenties. She was teaching at a Christian orphanage run by Miss Duli Chand in Hyderabad, the orphanage in which Catherine herself had been raised. Basil too was a teacher and the match seemed like a happy one. For a time, Catherine seemed to staunch the depression that flowed just below the surface of Basil's deep and melancholy soul.

The sight of a single flapping owl while daylight still lingered was terrifying, an image of impending doom well-known throughout the length and breadth of Pakistan. "It means someone is going to die," Catherine said without a moment of hesitation, covering her eyes in horror, as if to block out the tragedies of her two decades of aloneness in the orphanage in Hyderabad, looking out over the deserts of Sind and the bleakness of her life to come.

My parents tried to calm her down. Basil also tried, offering comfort, noting that the fate of everyone was in the end determined by God alone. Perhaps he knew, even then he knew, watching with unexpected calmness as the huge owl stretched out its wings, beating them mercilessly against the daylight, setting out in search of an unlucky field mouse. Basil had been complaining of heart pains for years, only to be told by doctors, again and again, that it was psychological stress, the result perhaps of his melancholy disposition; that there was nothing physically wrong with him, and it was all in his head.

Basil died the next week, cut down by a coronary at the age of thirty-six. Dr. Shaikh tried to revive him with injections and a heart massage, all to no avail. He was the only educated Pakistani Christian in all of Shikarpur. My parents and their fellow missionaries would have to arrange the funeral. "How we wished for a funeral home," my father wrote to friends in America, trying to make some sense out of the tragedy. "The aunt asked us to wash the body. No Pakistani would turn the body of a loved one over to strangers. As in Jesus' day, preparing the body for burial is a last act of love and devotion for their departed loved one. The aunt was giving us this honor and we must accept it."

Basil's aunt came from Sultankot, where she was the only midwife in town. Locals knew her only as "Auntie," the devoted nursing sister who had delivered babies by the dozen since first being posted to the Sultankot Maternity Clinic in 1929, the year in which my father was born. Most of her own children moved to Karachi when they had grown. One son later had a son called Jonathan Marcus Welby, named after the television show, my parents told me—and also, astonishingly enough, after me. Basil had stayed on in Sultankot, managing the business side of the clinic for his aunt. He offered tutorials in three languages—Sindhi, Urdu, and English—to the sons of local landowners who aspired to an education, who wanted to take the local civil service test and looked forward to government jobs.

My father and another missionary, aided by a Muslim family friend, bathed Basil's body, then dressed it in white cotton. My father was used to measure out the funeral clothes. Frank Dobra built a simple pine coffin during the night. Dr. Maybel and Auntie Phyllis padded it with black cloth, using thumbtacks to set the fabric in place. Rose petals and perfume were laid out atop the body. New brass handles were screwed tightly onto the coffin, one at each end. "Catherine lay in Auntie's lap until the dawn," my father wrote in the diary to which he kept returning throughout the day. "She cries out bitterly, recalling past joys and sorrows. She speaks everything that comes into her mind. She tells Auntie she has no more need for servants, because now she is her slave. Catherine had been at Basil's side, loving and caring for him for two years. It must be like cutting her heart out." We could hardly imagine her own sadness and grief, her future as a twenty-five-year-old widow without children. Her life in the coming years, when she would finally renounce her Christian faith, embrace Islam, and become the wife of a Muslim doctor in private practice in Hyderabad, was impossible to foresee.

In the morning the rest of the relatives from Karachi arrived by train: Innocent, Millicent, Jonathan Marcus Welby, and the others. My father drove the Land Rover at the head of a three-car funeral procession that set out for Sukkur, the large neighboring town on the Indus River where there was an Anglican church and a Pakistani pastor named Padre Jalal. A funeral service was held at the church, followed by a second one beside the grave. There was a delay of more than an hour. The laborer at the cemetery, unaware of Basil's bulk and unaccustomed to burials involving coffins, had dug the grave too small. Hymns were sung, in Urdu and English. Padre Jalal offered prayers as the grave digger set out to work for a second time, sweating in the hot sun, shovelling out a larger space to accommodate Basil's head and feet, a place to offer up his body into the earth, as the Urdu formulation so graphically put it.

My father did the reading, from the fifteenth chapter of Corinthians, as if to silence forever Basil's fears, to reach out to him and offer assurance to him even beyond the grave. "If there was no resurrection, then Christ was not raised; and if Christ was not raised, then our Gospel and our faith is in vain. If it is for this life only that Christ has given us hope, then we of all men are to be most pitied."

The funeral party returned to Shikarpur that same afternoon, for tea and an evening meal. The men went to Basil's house beside the Shikarpur power station immediately afterward, packing furniture, bagging clothes, and boxing up household effects. Only after everyone had gone did my father finally break down and cry, lamenting a death that seemed incomprehensible. "The sound of earth striking the coffin signalled the end of a close companionship," he wrote shortly thereafter, in his periodic letter to financial supporters in the United States. "Basil's death was an irreparable loss for us. He was a dear brother in Christ who taught me Sindhi and Urdu, who corrected my messages, who confided in me his deepest problems and fears.

Now he is gone. Our tears are not merely tears of grief, but of grate-fulness for Basil's life and work. Lying here on my desk is a sermon I will preach this Sunday. Basil's corrections are carefully marked in pencil at the margins, just as he has always done, week after week, for the past many years. We had depended on him in so many ways."

## NINE

# Journeying Mercies

As missionary children, we grew up with many of the advantages of wealth without actually having it. Family income never exceeded nine thousand dollars a year, even as late as 1975, the year I graduated from high school. But that figure did not include at least one important side benefit—foreign travel. Every fifth year, on our return visit to America, we enjoyed a missionary version of the Grand Tour, usually in Europe and usually for less than a week at a time. By the time I was ten years old, I had waved at Pope Paul from St. Peter's Square, peed on one of the pillars of the Parthenon (fifth column from the left, facing west), and gotten sick on shrimp salad in a Pan Am Clipper flight from Frankfurt to New York. I thought of myself as a seasoned world traveller, even if most of our trips were brief and rarely took us beyond capital cities.

The travelling life came to appeal to me enormously. Perhaps it was a form of evasion, of living in an artificial world that demanded little other than casual observation. Perhaps it was the novelty of it all, pretending that I was doing something unusual or special or out of the ordinary. Perhaps, too, it was the appeal of the new, the illusion that entertaining the senses through a constant barrage of unfamiliar sights, smells, and sounds somehow gave a heightened sense of life itself. Regardless of the motivation, I came to think that I was lucky enough to simultaneously inhabit three very different worlds created almost entirely for my own pleasure and benefit—Pakistan, first; then the United States; and, finally, all the enormous spaces in between. In almost every case, we began our travels with a prayer. "For journeying mercies," as my father used to say.

·    ·    ·

My parents usually planned one trip into the northern areas of Pakistan every couple of years. We visited Swat when it was still a princely state, Gilgit when it was still closed off by road for most of the year, and Kaghan before the Pakistan Tourism Development Corporation constructed a string of hotels and guest houses aimed at both foreign and domestic markets. Pakistan's own middle and upper classes had not yet started to vacation extensively in their own country, and the only other travellers we met were the odd diplomat, foreign businessman, or fellow missionary. It was hard then to imagine that we were observing the twilight of a time that was about to pass away. Within a few years, the brief silence that followed the British Raj ended and Pakistan was integrated into a wider and more noisy commercial world, one that promoted tourism and even "adventure travel" as part of a concerted effort to earn scarce foreign exchange.

Our trip to Gilgit, in September 1967, was among the most memorable we ever made. The Karakoram Highway, following the Indus

River north and then continuing on to the 16,000-foot Kunjerab Pass ("River of Blood") and the border with China, was still only in the planning stages; the treacherous alternate road to Gilgit via the Babusar Pass north of Kaghan was at best open for only three months out of every year. We had to go by plane, taking the daily PIA flight, a small Dutch-built Fokker Friendship. A weather station halfway to Gilgit sent a radio message every day, indicating whether or not the cloud cover had cleared. If clouds seemed to be gathering momentum and drifting up the valley, the flight was cancelled. The pilots flew visually, following first the Indus River to Chilas and then the Gilgit River to Gilgit town.

The snow-covered mountains on each side were higher than the Fokker itself could fly and at times it seemed as if an unexpected gust of wind would blow the fragile airplane into a nearby ridge. The most dramatic moment was when Nanga Parbat came into view, on the right side of the plane. The co-pilot asked David and me if we wanted to join him in the cockpit. The mountain seemed so massive, so immovable. The plane shuddered briefly as we passed by, as if it too was impressed. Later, when Nanga Parbat had receded from view, it was possible to see K-2, the world's second highest mountain, marking the border between Pakistan and China. Remarkably, in the decades that PIA has been flying passengers on the route, there has been only one crash, in the late 1980s. The Fokker Friendship lost radio contact a few minutes after leaving Gilgit. There was a wedding party on board and also a freelance journalist from America. Several years later, as of this writing, even the wreckage of the plane has yet to be discovered.

A second trip, made in the early 1970s, this time inspired by a schoolmate, Stan Brown, involved an attempt at climbing Kutte-Jo-Kabr, "Dog's Tomb," the highest mountain in Sind, marking the border between Sind and Baluchistan. The area was controlled by the Chandios, a Sindhi-Baluch tribe famous mostly for banditry and opium processing. "The police don't go beyond this point," the son of the local chief who had agreed to accompany us announced. "I'm the law from here on." According to the old Survey of India maps, the area was marked only by "numerous sand dunes" and "stoney wastes." The last foreigners to visit were a couple of British geologists back in the 1950s, prospecting for oil.

We camped at the edge of the Kirthar mountains, the Chandios slaughtering the proverbial fatted goats and entertaining us late into the night with stories about past battles with the British, of tribal skirmishes in Las Bela, of holy men who performed mighty miracles, of brave women who would commit suicide rather than fall into the hands of an enemy. The night sky, always brilliant, was never so clear. We watched for shooting stars as the haunches and intestines of two butchered goats, placed on sharpened sticks, grew brown against the embers of the fire. The goat heads, split open with a single axe stroke, were also placed on sticks nearby, the glazed eyes staring balefully in our direction. I was not much of a meat-eater but the notion of eating a dinner cooked outside on a cloudless night, dozens of miles from the nearest habitation, was deeply appealing. Next day, we followed a crack in the mountain until we reached a spring set against an enormous rock face. It was as far as we could go. In later years, I thought of the trip as one of the finest I had ever taken, an experience of timelessness in a world increasingly driven by clocks and calendars.

· · ·

The first foreign country I ever visited was Afghanistan. I remember nothing about the trip and can only recreate what must have happened from old photographs, from my father's diary, and from the several trips we made to Kabul in later years, when I was finally old enough to understand. It was in May 1958 and my father had been asked by expatriate Americans living there to lead informal worship services over a three-week period. The road to Kabul was still largely unpaved, but signs of the great changes to come were already apparent. The West Germans had recently completed a large dam at Surabi and the Russians were beginning to lay down asphalt on what had previously been only mountain tracks. "At one point, a Russian truck came so close to us it scratched some of the paint off our jeep," my father recorded in his diary, at a time when the cold war was at its height and seeing a Russian in the living flesh was still a novel experience.

We stayed with some of my father's college classmates, who had come to Kabul with two objectives in mind. One, the public one, was to teach English at a local college. The second and more hidden aim was to try and establish the first Christian church in Afghanistan. Although the American ambassador frowned on these efforts, he himself was heading a foreign aid program that was no less subversive, aimed as it was at countering the Soviet presence and, if possible, bringing Afghanistan into the American fold. There were already rumors that the Russian-built roads were designed to specification, so as to withstand the weight of Russian tanks. The Afghan king was carrying out a difficult balancing act, thus far successfully, which tried to maintain neutrality and, at the same time, introduce new forms of education and technology into his country. We visited the King's Gardens at Paghman, the scene of bloody battles between the Soviets and the Afghan Resistance during the 1980s. At that time, all was peaceful. "It is said to be one of the loveliest gardens in Asia," my father wrote. The surviving photographs show our family standing at one edge of the garden, against a backdrop of the snowcapped Hindu Kush.

Two years later, we left Karachi by ship for my first visit to America. We sailed on the *Asia* and then, at Naples, briefly boarded the *Monte Biancamano*, a grand old liner built in 1925 and shortly destined for the breaking yards of Spain. The Italian sailors were on strike. After only one night we transferred to another ship, the *Augustus*, heading for New York. The first plane ride, from New York to Macon, was equally unpleasant. "The trip was terrible," my mother wrote to missionary colleagues in Pakistan soon after we had arrived, voicing the fears of all who have ever flown. "We did not know until later that there were tornado warnings out for the area. Every time we hit a bump, I thought it was the last time and surely we would hit the ground. Once we hit a really bad bump and Hu reached over and kissed me. 'Well it's been good,' he said. 'Good-bye.'"

A year later, returning to Pakistan by ship, we travelled across the Atlantic in grander style, aboard the *Queen Elizabeth*. We were accompanied once again by Sam and Grace Pittman, the same Conservative Baptist missionaries from Minnesota who had travelled with my parents on the *Steel King* on their first journey to Pakistan five years before. We stopped for a few days in London, then boarded the *Celicia*, an Anchor Line ship bound for Karachi. The other passengers were from India, Pakistan, or England. I have a few vague memories of the trip, most of them connected with the *gulli* man at Port Said, the Egyptian magician who entertained generations of colonial children travelling to and from British India by sea. He was an old man by this time and we must have been among his final customers. He pulled a chicken out of my stomach, a feat that did not impress me because I knew all the while that he had hidden the trembling bird in a fold of his sleeve.

Later trips to and from America, this time by plane, were much shorter, lacking the strange combination of drama and boredom that marked extended journeys by sea. For obvious reasons, our brief visit to the Holy Land was especially meaningful. We stayed in the Jerusalem YMCA, overlooking the cease-fire line. The old city was still in Jordanian hands and, looking out our window, we could see strands of barbed wire and Israeli soldiers patrolling in the distance. In three days, we saw all the major sites—the Church of the Nativity in Bethlehem, where we imagined the birth of Christ; the Garden of Gethsemane, where He prayed on the night He was betrayed; the Church of the Holy Sepulchre, where He was crucified; the Mount of Olives, where He ascended into heaven; and the walled-up Eastern Gate, where one day, on His second coming, He would finally reappear to raise the dead and call His children home. The graveyards outside the Eastern Gate seemed to stretch for acres, as if people deliberately wanted to be buried there so they could be the first to greet Christ on His final, triumphant return. My father mentioned something about Ezekiel chapter 43 and recited lines from the well-known Gospel song: "I will meet you in the morning, just inside the Eastern Gate; then be ready faithful pilgrim, lest for you it be too late."

My father had decidedly mixed views about the garish decorations and incense surrounding most of the holy places in and around Jerusalem, views that I shared at the time. The Orthodox and Catholic churches and shrines seemed much too contrived for Protestant aesthetics. "It does not seem to be the authentic place at all," my father wrote, referring to the Church of the Holy Sepulchre. We preferred instead the Garden Tomb and Gordon's Calvary, outside Jerusalem, identified by a British archeologist as the likely Golgotha because it indeed looked like a skull. The Garden Tomb Association, more in keeping with Protestant sensibilities, had planted a garden there. My parents were especially impressed with the young Jordanian Christian who answered questions and gave an evangelical witness for Christ at the end of every tour. Two years later, he was killed by advancing Israeli troops in the waning hours of the Six Day War.

The Middle East also brought the apparent conflict between Christianity and Islam into sharper relief. The Christian presence was stronger in Jordan than in Pakistan, but it nonetheless seemed to be surviving against incredible odds. In Istanbul, once the citadel of Eastern Christianity, the faith had seemingly disappeared forever. In Pakistan, Muslim acquaintances occasionally waxed eloquently about the tragedy of Andalusian Islam, of the mosques that had been captured from departing Moors and turned into churches. Islamic Spain was a sober warning for Muslims everywhere, captured most notably, perhaps, by Sir Mohammad Iqbal, the intellectual founder of Pakistan, who wondered how it could all have disappeared, seemingly without a trace. In the eastern Mediterranean, we could share some of his dark forebodings and sense of loss. The spot marking Christ's ascension into Heaven on the Mount of Olives, once a crusader chapel, had been turned into a mosque. Many of the mosques in Istanbul were also built on former churches, most notably St. Sofia's, a magnificent structure that seemed to hang atop nothingness, as if kept afloat by faith alone. Was our spiritual community destined to suffer a similar fate? After our years of living in Islamic Pakistan, it was hard not to assume the worst.

•     •     •

My first detailed memories of the United States date back to the summer of 1965, when we travelled the length and breadth of the country by road. David was ten, I was eight, and Nancy was six. My father went to collect our new, light-blue Volkswagen Variant, ordered directly from West Germany, and drove it off the New York docks himself. At that time, small imported cars were still such a novelty that we flashed lights whenever we saw a similar automobile on the highway. Our relatives in Georgia thought us slightly crazy to travel thousands of miles as a family of five squeezed into such a tiny vehicle. My father marveled at the fuel mileage we were getting.

"How grateful we are to see Mama and Papa again and looking much better than we anticipated," my father wrote in his diary soon after we arrived in Macon. My grandparents were in their early seventies at the time and my parents must have imagined that this might be the last year they would see them alive. Or, as we more commonly said, "on this side of eternity." We lived in hope that we might yet see them in the life to come.

Our travels that year also confirmed that the dramatic economic and cultural transformation then taking place across the United States was beginning to make its mark on Georgia. The Bible Belt South, already well on its way to becoming the more suburban Sun Belt, was especially affected, given the extent to which it had previously been an agrarian society, an economic backwater that had always lagged decades behind the rest of America. It was not the society my father remembered from growing up in middle Georgia, nor the country we imagined from ten thousand miles away in Pakistan. "Listened to a tape by Jim Harwell called Soft Soap in which he exposes what is happening in our country politically, judicially, internationally, socially and religiously," my father wrote in his diary, describing a recording of evangelistic sermons available at the time. "He feels that it is wrong for Christians to seek to infiltrate these areas with the hope that they will be influenced to become as we are—says we must remain separated from the world in all these areas. He feels that the liberals are merely using Billy Graham to fill their dead churches." My father never threw himself completely into the fundamentalist camp, but there were obvious temptations pointing us in that direction. Adrift from our perceived cultural moorings, buffeted by events we could not begin to understand, it was not hard to feel perplexed and even alarmed by the general drift of change.

Our one really lengthy trip, which offered even more confirmation of the changes underway, began in early July, when we travelled with my father "out west" for a series of preaching engagements aimed at raising the support needed for our next four years in Pakistan. I prepared notes for a talk on my school, which I occasionally gave to Sunday School classes along the way. We also had a suitcase of Pakistani clothes and handicrafts in the back of our car, for our various displays and presentations.

We stayed for a week in Mississippi, at O'Zion Baptist Church in Meadville, where my father had pastored while studying at seminary in New Orleans. Living on a farm for a week was somehow reassuring, suggesting that the agricultural calendar, at least, would never change. From there, we travelled on to Monroe, Louisiana, to visit the missionary woman who had scandalized the Conservative Baptists by marrying her Pakistani language teacher seven years before. "They are happy and well adjusted," my father wrote. Then it was on to Texas, Arizona and, finally, the Pacific Ocean.

California struck even my father as an amazing place. "So much of everything and so much variety," he wrote, noting with interest the cultural mix that even then was beginning to turn Californian society upside down. Various church families arranged outings, to Marine World, to Disneyland, to Will Rogers's house and Knott's Berry Farm. One family even bought tickets to a Dodgers game so that David and I could see Sandy Koufax pitch. The oddest tourist attraction we were taken to was Forest Lawn Cemetery, featuring replicas of Michelangelo's *David* and *Moses* and an enormous painting depicting the crucifixion. There was something sterile and strange about the suburban, sanitized view of death represented there. The neatly trimmed lawns and endless rows of white tombstones seemed far removed from the anonymous dirt mounds that formed the Shikarpur graveyard. Did the wealthy really believe that Forest Lawn was some sort of first-class waiting room, that burial there placed them first in line for whatever lay beyond? At a more mundane level, it struck us vividly that when Americans did anything, they did it in a big and ostentatious way.

The mountains of the Sierra Nevada were a welcome contrast and left a more lasting impression. We stayed near Yosemite National Park, at a ranch owned by two single women. Deer came up to the verandah at twilight and the following afternoon we caught several dozen bluegills and brown perch at a small fish pond nearby. "Such beauty," my father wrote enthusiastically, even after having seen the Himalayas.

For the fall, my father had arranged with the Conservative Baptist Foreign Mission Society to spend a term studying Islamics at Hartford Theological Seminary. During the three months that we were there, he preached at Baptist churches throughout New England. We stayed in a two-bedroom duplex in Newington, a suburb of Hartford. One of the Jewish doctors who had spent a couple of winters at the Holland Eye Camp in Shikarpur had a practice in Hartford and invited my parents to a party. One of his daughters was fascinated at the prospects of meeting a missionary to Muslims in the living flesh and quizzed my mother repeatedly on the audacity of their enterprise. "Why not just make them better Muslims?" she suggested. When asked at the bar what they wanted to drink, my parents both requested Cokes. It was strange and sometimes awkward to move in such rarified circles.

For our part, we children were going through cultural adjustments of our own. The public grammar school we attended was largely working-class Catholic and my parents had to write a special note to excuse us from Wednesday afternoon catechism class. The menu for Friday lunches invariably featured fish. On another occasion, my parents wrote a note requesting that we be excused from weekly dancing lessons offered as part of gym class, a note I appreciated because I always felt so awkward on my feet as well as in the warm embrace of young girls my own age. It was strange to think that, even in America, the country we thought of as our own, we should be set so much apart, even as we were in Pakistan. Here too our religion and our family life were different, so different that it sometimes felt that others viewed us as followers of some strange and threatening cult. Knowing that our time in Connecticut was brief, I focused most of my own energies on reading, winning a school prize for most books read during a single term. I purposefully chose thin volumes with lots of pictures, in a successful effort to inflate the final total.

We returned to Macon in time for Christmas and the beginning of a new school term at Bruce School in South Macon, near Mikado Baptist Church. Memories here begin to grow more dim. We often visited Papa and Mama and most of the rest of the Addleton clan living on

Ben Hill Drive in North Macon. Granny, my mother's mother, lived on the west side off Broadway, in a rented apartment in a neighborhood that would soon be almost entirely black. We ourselves lived in a clapboard house on Guyton Street, near busy Houston Avenue. Our next-door neighbors were not churchgoers but we nonetheless tried to bring them into the fold. Their youngest son had an inoperable tumor at the base of his spine, which made him a hunchback and, we were told, seriously affected his life expectancy. Once, in connection with an upcoming revival at Mikado, I plastered the neighborhood with tracts and notices. I vaguely recall an adult taking me aside to inform me that Martin Luther King was a "communist" and should never have been awarded the Nobel Peace Prize. I briefly fell in love with my third grade teacher, Miss Carmichael. I looked forward to our planned return to Pakistan.

We were scheduled to return by ship. It was the middle 1960s, the last time when it would be as cheap to travel by sea as to fly. Our bookings on the *Queen Elizabeth II* had already been made and our barrels and crates had already reached New York when my father's mother was hospitalized in critical condition following a stroke. Her heart, never strong, was finally giving out.

"Today is Friday the thirteenth," she told my father, as he sat beside her bed, watching the glucose drip slowly into her arm.

"Oh, you are not superstitious, are you?"

"But I had a dream last night that I was very sick and couldn't get well."

Later that week, my father cancelled our travel plans, waiting for her to either die or stabilize. "Mama pulled through," he was able to write a few days later. "She was in the valley of the shadow of death. Papa feels we should remain as long as possible. He feels that Mama can't tarry much longer. I found it impossible to say farewell while she was so very close to death."

When her condition finally stabilized, my father once again set in motion plans for our return to Pakistan, this time by plane. We left early, at 7:30 in the morning on June 2, 1966. My father spent half an hour alone with his mother and then brought the grandchildren in, one by one. "Mama," he said when I entered. "Jonathan wants to take your picture. Do you mind?" I held a small plastic camera, a gift from a good-bye party held some days before. I adjusted the flash, took the photograph, and left as my father returned for a final few minutes with his mother. "I prayed and was able to get through it," he wrote later that evening, from our room in the Conservative Baptist guest house, a stone tenement on West 92nd Street in Manhattan. "It was so hard to pull myself away. She sobbed as I kissed her. There are experiences that must be borne. The pain and heartache are there and no comforting words can alleviate it."

We had travelled in separate cars to the Macon airport, where several dozen friends and relatives were waiting to see us off. As I climbed aboard the Delta jet, the camera strap broke and the camera fell to the ground, bursting open. Four days later, in Pakistan, we nonetheless took the role of film into a photo studio for processing. All but six and a half pictures on the thirty-six picture spool of black and white film had been destroyed. The half-picture was the one of Mama looking up from her bed, oxygen tank off to one side. She was smiling faintly and there was a gentleness about her eyes that must have reminded my father of something from his childhood. He immediately got enlargements made, one for each of his twelve brothers and sisters. It seemed like too much of a coincidence, that this last picture of his mother should have been one of the very few photographs to survive.

Less than a month later, the telegram came from Macon informing my father of his mother's death. The letters from his surviving brothers and sisters came later. "I am transported home each time I read them," my father wrote. "I feel the sorrow and anguish. But, being so far away, I cannot miss Mama as they do. It seems strange not to, and it seems like a dream to think that she is dead. I won't really miss her absence until four years from now."

•       •       •

Four years later, in the United States for our final furlough before I graduated from high school and left home for college, a more accurate mental map of Macon finally became firmly planted in my mind. Ben Hill Drive, in north Macon, across the Ocmulgee River and near the Jones County line, stood at the center of everything. My grandfather,

Ben Addleton, now in his eighties and known to us as Papa, was still alive and several relatives had built houses on what had once been his farm. The road was still unpaved. We gathered there often, for family reunions and on special occasions. Papa had remarried by this time, to a frail woman, several years younger, whom we called Miss Esther. They were living in a house trailer now and one of her chief complaints was that he spent too much time playing pool. Unfortunately the marriage did not last. Miss Esther moved into a high-rise for the elderly, first on Vineville and then just off the Gray Highway. Papa moved back in with one of his daughters, who lived at the house he had built with his own hands out of old railway two-by-twos on Ben Hill Drive.

My mother's family was more scattered. One brother and sister still lived in the middle Georgia area, but the others were spread throughout the country—in Colorado, Michigan, Ohio, and Massachusetts. To a certain extent, the tragedies of a hard childhood were still being played out on some of the children. We visited one sister briefly at the state mental hospital in Milledgeville, where she had committed herself for treatment that seemed to be working. We talked in the visiting area and, as we were about to leave, she asked for a "nutty buddy," an ice cream bar sprinkled with walnuts. "Oh yes, a nutty buddy," she exclaimed again, "that's just what your dear aunt needs, a nutty buddy." It was one of the more likeable qualities of the Simmons family, that even in adversity they were able to laugh about it. Even now, I cannot order a nutty buddy and keep a straight face.

We ourselves lived in South Macon once again, on Flamingo Drive, near Mikado Baptist Church. We had to find a house that rented for less than $125 a month and the place we found was surprisingly spacious. We each had our own bedroom. The senior John Birch family lived down the street, an elderly retired couple whose missionary son had been killed by the Chinese communists in the late 1940s and whose memory had been taken over by the far-right-wing organization which now bore his name. The neighborhood itself, historically white, was just beginning to turn black. It was 1970, the year when court-ordered busing finally came to Macon, Georgia. Several churches had already formed all-white private schools, in part to escape the heavy hand of a national government they perceived as increasingly hostile. One of them—Macon Christian Academy, at Gilead Baptist Church in South Macon, just off Rocky Creek Road—offered full scholarships to us, the missionary family. Class size was limited to twenty-five students; in our case, they were generous enough to bend the rules and allow a twenty-sixth.

David, at that time, impressed perhaps by Dr. Holland's example, was entertaining notions of becoming a medical doctor. He was concerned that the poor quality of math and sciences in the public schools would set him back when we returned to Murree the following year. To my surprise, he opted to spend tenth grade at Macon Christian Academy. My sister was given no choice in the matter, she had to go—my parents were no doubt concerned about the lurid tales they heard about the newly integrated public schools; transportation arrangements were also becoming increasingly complicated. Macon Christian Academy was extremely strict, even by the standards of Murree Christian School. Both my brother and sister occasionally got into trouble with the administration, doubtless embarrassing my parents.

For reasons that even now I do not completely understand, I was adamant that I should attend a public school. I did go, along with twelve hundred other eighth and ninth graders, to the old Ballard Hudson Junior High, recently amalgamated into the Southwest School District. My father laughed out loud when I returned home one day, band uniform in hand. It was the purple uniform of the old Ballard Hudson Wildcats, the historically black high school famous throughout Georgia for its marching bands and football teams. I played saxophone, with all the woodenness of someone suffering from white man's disease. Fortunately, at that time we had not yet started marching—I would have found it difficult to walk a straight line and read music at the same time.

More than two-thirds of my classmates that year were black. It was a familiar enough scenario, like living in Pakistan among the Islamic believers, like living in Connecticut among the children of working-class Catholics whose very toughness pulverized me into silence—once again, I was an oddity, a stranger, a small piece of discarded flotsam tossed about on an unfriendly cultural sea. As always, I kept my distance, watching the passing scene from afar. It was almost as if I was watching a movie or a theatrical performance. I did not know if I was observing tragedy, comedy, or farce, the themes changed so often. There were occasions when I wanted to applaud from the sidelines and other times when I wished for a long and extended intermission. In the end, I came to love it. I had a front-row seat on an intensely human drama and I would not have changed it for anything.

In the year that busing finally came to Macon, attempts were made to develop new institutions and instill new pride. It was partly successful and, in later years, Southwest did go on to become a state powerhouse in basketball, sending some players to national prominence and a few to the NBA. Nonetheless, it was a difficult first year. The formation of new school districts effectively eliminated several long-standing traditions—including, in my father's case, his old school, Sidney Lanier High. I was sorry to see the name of his old football team—the Poets—consigned into the dustbin of history. Was the name chosen to inspire fear in the hearts of opponents, or to reduce them to helpless laughter when they realized who they would be playing against? Regardless of how it was chosen, it still seemed like an inspired way to honor Georgia's poet laureate who had in fact lived in Macon for many years. In contrast, a bureaucrat without a sense of humor decided to call our new team the Southwest Patriots. Perhaps the naming of names in this case reflected a patriotic hope that integration would somehow work.

I went to school that first day with some trepidation, joining the hundreds of other thirteen- and fourteen-year-olds lining up to go into the enormous basketball gymnasium where a teacher, shouting through a megaphone, assigned us to our various homeroom classes. For most of the rest of the year, I remained as I was on that first day— a silent and anonymous observer, watching events and only responding to them if and when I was asked. I made few friends. One was a white girl whose name I have forgotten, a frail adolescent with dark hair and acne whom I admired immensely because she witnessed frequently about her faith. I discovered that she went to a Pentecostal church pastored by one of my uncles and became even more impressed. Despite her frail appearance, she was not intimidated by the skepticism of those who surrounded her. The other was a slight black student named Tyrone, unathletic in the extreme but with a sense of humor that I appreciated. We corresponded for several months after I returned to Pakistan and then, quite suddenly, stopped writing.

Our principal was a Mr. Alderman. Once, a fellow student muttered something about how he must be "a relative of mine." "He is not," I fired back fiercely, outraged that someone could even associate my last name with someone in authority. For a time, my father earned some extra money by serving as a substitute teacher in the Bibb County School System. I was petrified that he might one day sit in for one of my own teachers. I definitely would have died of embarrassment.

The teachers at the old Ballard Hudson Junior High were as memorable as those I knew at Murree Christian School. One, a black man in his late forties, was known as "Rev" Wilson. He was a tiny man with a small moustache, a shrill voice, and a sense of humor that in another setting I probably would have come to love. He pastored a local streetfront church and also taught civics and Georgia history. Even then, I thought it odd that he should be teaching an essentially white man's version of the settling of our state, of Oglethorpe's colony, of the days of slavery, of Confederate heroes. For some reason, he was incapable of controlling a class. There were no lectures. We were simply given a specified number of pages to read each day, as he did verbal battle with some of the more surly members of the class. Sometimes he shouted as if he was reaching the climax of a sermon on hell, all to no avail.

In contrast, Miss Agnew, a white science teacher, was one of a very few who ever successfully controlled her class. She was comparatively well educated, and gentle but sharp at the same time; once again, I almost fell in love. A failure in science at Murree, I did well here, almost certainly because the academic standards were so much lower. She taught science; I was more interested in the culture and history of science. When we edged into biology and briefly crossed over into discussions on evolution, I seized the moment. I had recently read in *Time* magazine an article stating that Neanderthal—or was it Cro-

Magnon man?—had more of a spiritual life than he had previously been given credit for, that evidence had been found suggesting funeral rites and possibly even a belief in an afterlife. "So there," I said.

It was one of the very few times during the entire school year that I became vocal about anything. Science was more culturally rooted than was generally realized, I suggested. The kind of "ascent of man" drawings featured regularly in this generation of *Time-Life* books or *National Geographic* magazines would doubtless be outdated by the turn of the century. The latest science popularizers were no different than the religious propagators of previous centuries, their drawings as crude and improbable as illustrations from a Sunday School manual. As for the paleontologists, they could argue until they were blue in the face, but why were they always bending entire theories to accommodate the latest fossil find? If the earth was indeed billions of years old, by what arrogance did they presume to resolve the riddles of the universe in their own brief lifetimes, mere blinks in the long stare of eternity? Were they really motivated by metaphysical truth, or was it more a matter of consolidating academic reputations and ensuring tenured professorships in the here and now? Why were new fossil finds so often billed as yet another "tremendous discovery"? Remember Piltdown Man, that classic of scientific deception? I was an imbecile when it came to understanding the scientific method but I like to think I was a convincing apologist when it came to arguing with others over something neither of us knew anything about.

I suspect Miss Agnew watched all this with some amusement. At the end of the year, she justified a field trip to Stone Mountain near Atlanta, an unusual outing for students living in the public housing projects in the poorer sections of Macon. When several students said they might not be able to pay even the modest amount requested, she dipped into her own pocket to make sure the entire class was able to participate.

I looked on with pride every time there was an article about our school in the *Macon Telegraph and News*. Expulsions figured there from time to time, and there were also a couple of knifings. My parents, my mother especially, were anxious about what I might experience. I was usually quiet and did not give much away. There were embarrassments and occasional scuffles in the showers after gym class. There were the pornographic photographs from a magazine passed around the back row in a mathematics class. There were a couple of confrontations in the hallway, requests for money mostly. For obvious reasons, I made sure to never find myself in a situation where I might be alone.

But, looking back, what I remember most vividly about that year in Macon is the enormous tension that pervaded Southwest Junior High on March 8, 1971, on the day of the Ali-Frazier fight. It was billed as the fight of the century and the anxiety in the days leading up to it was palpable. Most black students rooted for Mohammad Ali; most white students secretly hoped for a Frazier win. Both boxers were black, but Ali seemed to exude arrogance; Frazier, less flamboyant, had the smaller mouth. Frazier won this time around and the relief among the minority of white students in school the next day was palpable. "So there," we wanted to say. It seemed to be the familiar retort of minorities, always and everywhere; after all, in this particular milieu, we did in fact represent a definite minority. Don't presume too much, we would have wanted to say; you won't always have it this good; we may be humiliated now but the wheel always turns; our day is coming soon. "So there," we wanted to shout, if only we had the courage to verbalize what we really felt within the deeper recesses of our subconscious, and presumably racist, minds, little realizing the extent to which attitudes toward this fight would become a metaphor for the changing face of race relations in the United States in the years to come. "So there, so there, so there."

TEN

# Remember Where You Stand

A lingering concern throughout our final

furlough in Georgia was the fear that we

might not return to Pakistan. Visas were one

possible stumbling block, the political

situation on the Indian Subcontinent another.

For a brief time, my father also considered an

alternate career, one that would have kept us in

the United States forever. I desperately wanted

to graduate from Murree Christian School and

would have been bitterly disappointed had we

not gone back.

The visa situation was always problematic, even in the 1950s when my parents first arrived in Pakistan. From time to time, articles appeared in local newspapers demanding that all missionary schools be nationalized and that all foreign missionaries be immediately expelled. On those few occasions when the military did allow a national parliament to meet, debates were held and motions tabled to the same effect. One, introduced by a Mr. Abdul Aziz from Karachi in the early 1960s, noted that "the foreign missionaries work as political agents hand in hand with their respective Governments, all the while using religion and philanthropy as a cloak for their real intentions, subversive activities and espionage." Editorials and letters to the editor appearing in national newspapers took on the same tone. Friday sermons at local mosques were even more caustic.

Such views were understandable in what was after all an Islamic republic. Over time, the numbers of missionaries were gradually reduced. Those working in remote regions or conducting evangelistic work along the Indian border or in the strategically important northern areas were obvious targets and among the first to go. Each missionary family had its own file with the Pakistan Civil Intelligence Department, some of them quite large. Eventually, an accumulation of damaging local reports could lead to either an immediate expulsion or the refusal of an essential entry visa. By early 1971, when my parents were preparing to return to Pakistan, the number of Baptist missionaries in Sind had been cut almost in half, seemingly as part of a larger nationwide effort aimed at reducing the missionary presence in Pakistan from a few hundred missionary families to a few dozen.

Returning to Pakistan as part of such a lonely and diminishing band must have been hard for my parents and I sensed at times that, for them, a visa refusal might almost have come as a relief. It would be a credible, even graceful, way of bowing out of a difficult and largely unresponsive mission field—evidence that a door was being shut, that God had spoken, that my father would have to seek an alternative ministry. In the end, some weeks before we were due to return to Pakistan, we received a letter from Pakistan's consulate in New York. My parents opened the brown registered envelope containing our passports and noted with a combination of relief and regret that the necessary entry visas had been stamped in. "And a door was opened unto me of the Lord," my father wrote in his next prayer letter, citing a familiar passage from Second Corinthians. "While other missionaries have been unable to get a visa to enter and when there has been much trouble inside the country, we feel it is clearly the Lord's will that we return to the work of the Gospel there."

The political situation was equally problematic. Pakistan was on the verge of self-destruction. National elections were held in March 1971, not long after the cyclone in East Pakistan left almost half a million dead. The party advocating independence for East Pakistan won in a landslide and the army immediately declared martial law, provoking a civil war that led to tens of thousands of deaths and the departure of as many as ten million Bengalis as refugees into India. Colleagues still serving in Pakistan wrote to my parents in Georgia about the growing unrest. Television reporting from refugee camps in India brought the prospects of war even closer to home. In the end, and once again to my enormous relief, my parents determined that we should return. "With your prayers and encouragement we'll make it," my father wrote in his prayer letter to our financial supporters, once again citing Paul's Letter to the Corinthians: "Now thanks be unto God who always causeth us to triumph in Christ."

The final concern was more personal, one I sensed in the hushed conversations my parents occasionally had about our future. They seemed to be discussing an unexpected proposition coming out of the home office in Wheaton, Illinois—that my father should stay in America as the Conservative Baptist Mission representative covering the entire southeastern United States. Perhaps it was in the context of the deteriorating political situation in Pakistan and the prospects that a visa might not be granted. At least some other Pakistan missionaries had, after all, made such decisions—one colleague became head of the Mission Board and another was personnel director. My father would have been a natural for the job. Conservative Baptists were spread almost everywhere in the United States except in the American South, dominated as it was by the Southern Baptist Convention and a multitude of independent Baptist churches.

It would almost be a mission field in and of itself, to represent a relatively new Baptist denomination and help draw support for missionaries in a part of the country that seemed like an essential future constituency, a recruiting ground for potential new missionaries as well as a potent source of financial support. My father's sermons were well received; he had a low-key, nonthreatening style, he mixed well across lines of class and culture, and he knew the complex theological terrain in a part of the country in which Baptists predominated but often disagreed among themselves. He would serve as a natural bridge between theologically conservative churches in the Midwest and likeminded believers in the South. Most importantly, he was from the South, spoke with a southern accent, and had shared in the experience of so many of his contemporaries—a large family, a rural upbringing, an adolescent experience with the Almighty, and an adulthood that had brought enormous change and even a degree of material wellbeing that would have seemed improbable at the height of the Great Depression only thirty-five years before.

Secretly, I suspect my father was flattered and even briefly tempted by the offer, as he might have been several years later when he was offered a position as "Professor of Missiology" at Jerry Falwell's new institution, Liberty College in Lynchburg, Virginia. In career terms, it must have seemed attractive—to be asked to serve as area director for the Mission Board or, in the case of the offer from Lynchburg, to have the prospects of eventually becoming a tenured professor at an institution that was already patterning itself as a Notre Dame for Baptists. But, in the end, my father determined that his real calling was living out his life as a foot soldier in the great missionary endeavor overseas, not in speaking on it or canvassing for it or teaching about it. I was relieved, proud, and enormously grateful, all at the same time. We would not succumb to the attractions of a settled life in America and I would not become one of the anonymous thousands, shuffling my way through a large city high school somewhere in Georgia. I was elated. We were returning to Pakistan and I would have my final fours years in Murree after all.

•     •     •

There were times, especially during my last year in Murree, when I consciously and overtly gave grateful thanks for everything I had. It happened most often in the late afternoon, as I looked toward the highest range of mountains, toward the mountains of Kashmir. The view was framed by *chir* and *deodar* trees and the light came from two directions, from the setting sun first and then from the reflection of light off ice and snow on distant peaks. When the sun finally disappeared, the light still lingered for a time, shining off the mountains and clouds, red first, then pink, and finally deep purple, as if the night sky was being fitted out to become the canopy of God. Darkness followed quickly, though sometimes a full moon was enough to illuminate the mountains. Early evening was the best time to see falling stars and, occasionally, a satellite in orbit, coursing its way slowly across the sky. It was hard not to think, with the setting of the sun, that this was one day like no other; that it would not happen twice, that never, in all of history, would we see the same combination of mountain, cloud, and sky. The sun would set, the moon would rise, the stars would tumble forth again—but this day, this hour, this moment in time was a gift, the likes of which would never be repeated.

The size of Murree Christian School accentuated our smallness, lost as it was in the vastness of the mighty Himalaya. There were forty-four students in high school in 1973, when my brother graduated; there were thirty-four two years later, when it was my turn to leave. We could all fit easily into a single school bus and even the simplest of school outings inevitably involved virtually the entire high school. Events were scheduled by student committee and usually included at least two camping trips each school term. Rawal Lake was one popular destination, the nearby hill stations of Patriata and Nathia Gali another. Sometimes we went even further afield, to the Indus River at Attock, to the Story Teller's Bazaar in Peshawar and, on a couple of occasions, as far as the Khyber Pass, where bricks of hashish were freely sold on the open market. Pakistan was only then starting to promote a mass domestic tourist industry and it was still just possible to imagine that we were doing something out of the ordinary, that we could still aspire to be something more than just tourists passing through.

But, more than anything, it was a time when our universe was bounded by the single mile separating Jhika Gali, where we boarded, from Gharial, where we went to school. Given so few students, it was possible to be involved in some way in almost everything. There were too few boys to field even the necessary two sides of a soccer team. Almost anyone who cared to could participate in a drama production, either as part of the cast or as part of the stage crew. I was too inhibited to try out for a part that required anything more than a few lines but, for a while, I imagined that I might make a mark on the sports field. In retrospect, I realize I never rose above mediocrity. At the time, I still thought I had a chance for some semblance of success.

Soccer, requiring eleven starters and two substitutes, seemed the right place to start. Our team was called the Jesters, largely on account of a collection of hand-me-down sweatshirts featuring four large squares in varying shades of green. We resembled—and played like—a troupe of medieval comedians. Ian Murray, science teacher and soccer coach, posted the team on the school bulletin board at noon on the day of every game. If a regular happened to be sick or away, I imagined that I might at least be able to suit up as a substitute. Almost inevitably, if I was listed at all, it was as a linesman, assigned the thankless task of trotting up and down the sidelines with a flag, waving whenever a ball went out of bounds. I was in eleventh grade before I finally started as a regular player, and even then only because a key player had to leave for the United States on short notice because his mother had recently been diagnosed with cancer.

I started my first game as goalkeeper against Lahore American School and I was terrified from the moment the ball was first kicked in my direction. After it was all over and we had lost by a score of six to one I slowly trudged off the field, numb and in shock. Off in the distance, above the shouts of players from the opposing side, I heard the Lahore coach give his team a final admonition: "Remember to shake hands with the Murree goalkeeper!" Long afterward, after I had returned to Pakistan as an adult, I met Sergie Panu, one of the Lahore players, in the transit lounge at Lahore International Airport; his father was an Italian businessman and, seemingly, he was following in the same direction. I approached him and asked if he had ever played soccer for Lahore American School. "Oh, yes," he laughed, "I was the one who scored all the goals." I hesitated for a moment, then replied. "And I was the one who let them in."

Despite this first debacle, I continued to experience firsthand the loneliness of the goalkeeper. I sometimes confused rolling around in the dirt with on-field heroism; as the last line of defense, I felt that the few times I touched the ball somehow had greater import than if I had been a midfielder. I also secretly hoped to leave each game with a few scratches and, if possible, some blood about the shins, as a visible battle wound. When I finally made the team, I enjoyed the away games most of all, especially those against Lawrence College, on the other side of the hill, facing toward Rawalpindi. When the game was over, we all marched up to their dining hall, the walls lined with flags and coats of arms and honor boards listing the names of prefects and house masters from half a century ago, English names all until 1947, when they were replaced by new generations of Pakistanis. Tea was served around a long wooden table as we stood about in our cleats and knee pads, trying to make small talk amid the echoes of a receding imperial past. We might as well have been knights in rusted armor, socializing after a jousting tournament. After it was all over, we headed back to school in an open '56 Chevrolet pickup truck, bought from a departing missionary who had been refused a visa some years before. Ian Murray drove, shouting occasionally out the window for us to get a grip on ourselves, to calm down and keep quiet for the duration of the journey. Meanwhile, we hung crazily out the back, shouting all the verses of "A Hundred Bottles of Beer on the Wall" as we returned to school.

In 1973, Murree Christian School was invited to join the association of State Department schools spread across the region—Karachi American School, Lahore American School, the International School of Islamabad, and the American-International School of Kabul. The Murree school board approved, on the understanding that we would not participate in the final dance party held at the conclusion of every sports tournament. It was our first real exposure to how our counterparts in America might be experiencing their adolescence, our first clue to what we might eventually have to go back to. We were doubtless regarded as well-meaning imbeciles, polite, well mannered, the frequent recipients of good sportsmanship awards, and the losers of almost every game we played. We felt like poor cousins at the outset, like a class-B country school set against the triple-A giants of the city leagues.

Confusion and misperceptions abounded on both sides. At the start of one basketball tournament, when the school administrator from the International School of Islamabad opened the proceedings, he glanced up at the threatening monsoon clouds gathering in the sky and made a passing reference to his hopes that "the old man up there would delay the rain." It struck me then as sacrilege. After all, the deity was not simply some "old man"; He was our Father in Heaven, He knew us by name. We started our own games with a team prayer and sometimes concluded them with a prayer as well. At the same time, our entirely secular tradition of "testing the wind" by licking a finger and raising it skyward whenever we shot free throws led to rumors that we were in fact trying to enlist God's aid (actually, it was our own sarcastic protest against field conditions in Islamabad, where the swirling wind made outdoor play difficult). During one early game, against Islamabad, the scoreboard showed Lions 40, Christians 30, as if we were destined to always lose. "Are boys allowed to talk to girls?" ran one question from the other players. "Do you have prayer meetings and church services every day?" went another.

We had one moment of glory, during the sports tournament in Kabul, Afghanistan, in the spring of 1974. The entire high school from Murree went by road; the other schools typically flew in by plane. We were farmed out to houses in the diplomatic and business community, marveling all the while at the imported Ethan Allen furniture, elaborate wall hangings, expensive oriental carpets—and vast kitchens, manned by uniformed servants and filled with imported groceries bought from the local commissary. When Murree students met up again, after housing assignments had been made, the first topic of conversation was almost always about food.

I represented Murree Christian School in chess at the Kabul tournament, promptly losing all four games. But basketball was the main feature, the event most of us had come to see. In view of our last-place finish the previous year, we were scheduled to play the two top-ranked teams—Karachi and Kabul—first. Somehow, we managed an upset win over Karachi American School. I played three minutes and scored three points, the most playing time I ever got. Game two, against Kabul, thus became critical. We were awed by the discipline displayed in their pregame warm-ups, by their new black and gold uniforms, by their height; it was as if giants walked the land. The best Kabul player was rumored to be destined for a college basketball scholarship. Even the Kabul coach, Bill Heim, a tall and weathered former Peace Corps volunteer who reportedly had once played professional football for the Philadelphia Eagles, looked intimidating as he strode around the court in his sweatsuit, weights attached to each of his ankles. Kabul was expected to dominate the tournament and looked larger than life.

As usual, Murree quickly found itself behind, this time by nine points. In the second half, three Murree players—the three who would eventually make the tournament all-star team—fouled out. And then the shots started falling in; it was as if we could do no wrong. Substitutes came off the bench and scored twelve quick points. As the Kabul coach stared incredulously into space, shaking his head from time to time, Murree came from behind for a 55–51 victory. I never left the bench, never played even a minute or scored a single point. And yet it was possibly the proudest day in my high school athletic career. After the game, the Murree crowd huddled together, embracing and shouting into the late afternoon. Most of us had played together since first grade; it was as if we had spent our whole lives preparing ourselves for this occasion. We went on to win the final two games, against Lahore and Islamabad. I almost cried when our captain, Dudley Chelchowski, wearing a white polo-neck shirt and double-breasted suit jacket, collected the trophy on our behalf at the awards ceremony, when it was announced that he and Mark Pegors and Paul Johnson had all been voted onto the all-star team. It seemed so improbable and yet so right, as if perhaps there was a God in Heaven after all.

(The night after I wrote these lines, my brother David called long-distance from Atlanta to tell me that Dudley Chelchowski had shot and killed himself. Dudley, the goalkeeper I replaced when his mother was dying of cancer; Dudley, the basketball captain who gave us our few moments of glory under the Kabul sun. I still cannot believe it. His biography was different than most of the rest of us, his road almost certainly more difficult. His father was Polish, a United Nations official assigned to the peacekeeping force monitoring the ceasefire line separating India and Pakistan-held Kashmir. I return to the pile of old high school annuals—the *Kahani*, as we called it, Urdu for story—now lying about the floor. Under Dudley's eleventh-grade photograph the caption reads, "A great nose indicates a great man." Come to think of it, he did have a rather large protuberance. Under Dudley's twelfth-grade photograph the caption reads, "If thou dost play with him at any game, thou art sure to lose." He was competitive, as competitive as anyone I have ever met.

In retrospect, it is hard to understand how victory on the basketball court could have meant so much to me, even become one of the defining moments in the first eighteen years of my life. It seems ridiculous that I should even remember the final score after all these years. I contributed nothing, and yet I regarded it almost as a personal triumph—not in an individual sense, but because I was part of a larger collective. It was as if we were trying to overcome a long-held sense of inferiority, overturning a stereotype that seemed to dictate that we were good sports incapable of ever winning. After a while, it seemed natural to play the part of the underdog. We revelled in secondhand compliments, in the news that someone had heard that "Murree kids were considered well behaved" or that "Murree kids were so polite." More likely, we were thought of as sanctimonious bores who took themselves much too seriously. And yet the feeling when it was all over, when we had demonstrated that "missionary kids" could somehow play in the same league as the progeny of diplomats and businessmen, brought with it an enormous sense of satisfaction and relief, as if the Himalayan-size chip we carried on each of our shoulders had somehow been shattered. We savored the string of four straight victories all the way back home, through the Kabul Gorge and on to the Pakistan frontier, following a route that would become a killing ground for hundreds of Soviet soldiers within the decade. Even now, the memory of our inane shout—"We're number one, we're number one"— echoing off the Hindu Kush brings some latent satisfaction, reminding me of a time when a basket, a ball, and a slab of concrete was, for one brief moment, all that it took to define true joy.

On his return to the United States in 1974, Dudley became a policeman, eventually joining the police force in Alexandria, Virginia, across the river from Washington, D.C. In the late 1980s, he and a fellow officer were part of the SWAT team sent in to free a hostage being held at gunpoint. Drugs were involved. The siege was almost over when the drug dealer came out shooting. Dudley ducked and was badly injured, taking the full force of a shotgun blast in both legs. His partner was killed. The entire scene was captured by local television crews and, later, written up in *Reader's Digest* under the title "In a Frenzy of Evil." After recovering, Dudley was invited to meet President George Bush and celebrated as a momentary hero in the national "war on drugs" then briefly dominating the media. He was too injured to return to the streets, but the Alexandria Police Department found a desk job for him. Later, he married a police officer on the department who already had a family of her own. I last saw him two and a half years before he shot himself, still struggling with the fact that he had survived while his fellow officer, standing behind him, had been killed. The physical pain associated with the shooting seemed permanent. I did not sense then that he was also suffering from deep depression, that he would one day become the first of my own school contemporaries to die.

·     ·     ·

I am almost finished and I still have not mentioned one other fact that dominated so much of my later adolescence—the inadequacy of my physical body, the feeling that I was trapped inside a misshapen collection of flesh and bones that would one day betray me. I was not an especially sickly child, but there were occasional brushes with the medical world that impressed me early with the precariousness of our existence on earth. I had what, in retrospect, seems to have been at least one childhood bout with rheumatic fever, leaving me with a permanently damaged heart valve. Another time, in boarding school in Murree, I spent several days in the school dispensary, falling asleep with a high fever on Monday evening and waking again, bewildered,

Thursday morning. The nurse came in with a cup of tea and a thin slice of toast covered with honey. I remember to this day her gentle hands, the softness of her voice—and the taste of honey, so thick and sweet and delicious.

My first encounter with the surgeon's scalpel came in July 1966, shortly after I turned eight. The diagnosis, made at the Murree Summer Missionary Clinic by Dr. Peter Hover, was acute appendicitis. My father left in our Land Rover immediately, driving across the mountains to the mission hospital in Abbottabad. There was only a single missionary doctor there and it had been years since she had performed an operation. The regular anesthetist was absent. The decision was nonetheless made quickly to operate, using a spinal anesthetic rather than the more usual ether, which would have rendered me unconscious. As I later found out, a spinal was rarely used on children—but even greater concerns surrounded the use of ether in the absence of a proper specialist.

I vaguely recollect the long needle, the tussle to fix it against my lower spine, and then the gradual loss of all feeling below the waist. What if the growing numbness, beginning with my toes and going up my legs to my middle, did not stop there but continued further on, up to my neck and then beyond? The thought briefly crossed my mind. A cloth of light cotton, held up by two thin metal wires, shielded me from what was going on down below. My father watched from a clear window outside, occasionally smiling in my direction. Near the end, the feeling in my lower body began to return, first as a scratching, then the more sharp sensation of skin being stretched and sutures being tied together. "What do you feel?" the doctor said, a brief look of anxious concern crossing her eyes. She motioned for two nurses, who held my arms against the cold metal operating table as the final stitches were sewn into place. "Only a little longer," she said at one point. "We're almost through. Try to hold on a little longer if you can."

I was unsure about the accuracy of my own recollections of the operation, until my father showed me the entry for his diary on that day—the same day, as it happened, that his own mother died of heart failure back in Middle Georgia Hospital in Macon. "Dr. Phyllis Irwin did surgery which I watched through the window," my father wrote.

"He was given a spinal and so was conscious. Toward the end, while putting in stitches, he began to feel pain. But Dr. Irwin encouraged him to endure it for those last few stitches so she wouldn't have to give him ether. She told us later that she did not like to give spinals to children."

All this became the backdrop for a much larger concern that became apparent as I crossed the threshold from childhood to adolescence. It started with a bump in the middle of my chest, to the right of my lower sternum. I mentioned it to the doctor who did our physicals in Chicago during the summer of 1970; he touched it briefly, then announced that it would likely disappear soon, it was all a part of growing older. A couple of years later, back in Pakistan and halfway through high school, the bump became noticeably larger and my parents also became concerned.

For me, the issue was mostly cosmetic. I hated PE classes, especially when groups were divided into "skins" and "shirts" to play basketball or soccer. It seemed as if I was always taking off my shirt, trying to shield my misshapen chest with my elbows. Seeing a group of senior girls pass by was even more humiliating; it was as if they were staring in my direction and all thinking the same thing—"I wouldn't be seen dead with that miserable plucked chicken, with the scrawny chest and the strange doorknob growing at an odd angle outside his sternum." I never became as desperate as Somerset Maugham's Philip in that classic of adolescent angst, *Of Human Bondage,* praying at night in the fullness of faith that his clubfoot might be removed by morning. I nonetheless wished on many occasions that it might disappear. A disease, a fever could come and go and conceivably might be prayed away; this protrusion seemed lasting and permanent, part of my body, as physically stolid as my arms and legs. I convinced myself that it would take an operation to remove it.

Sometime later my parents consulted with Dr. Bowes at the United Christian Hospital in Lahore, a leading missionary surgeon who had reportedly performed Pakistan's first open heart surgery. My father flew up from Sind; I took the rail car down from Rawalpindi. The doctor ordered a series of x-rays, then pummeled my chest in an effort to get to the bottom of it all. "My only concern is that it might get bigger," he said, recommending immediate "exploratory surgery." He wanted to make sure that it was not a tumor after all. He also promised, whatever happened, to "shave away as much of the bump as possible." I was secretly elated. I knew I lacked the faith necessary to move mountains, to simply pray it away; but I wanted to wake up after the operation and experience the kind of normalcy that I longed for.

After the consultation, my father and I went out to a Chinese dinner in Gulberg and once again I wondered, as I had so often in the past, "What if I don't wake up at all, what if I don't wake up at all?" The thought also crossed my mind that afternoon, swimming by myself in the pool at the Lahore American School, feeling the hard knot of gristle, cartilage, and bone as it brushed against the water. I thought about it a third time that night, trying to go to sleep in a rope-slung bed in the Bowes's guest bedroom. But even as I thought of eternal extinction, I also thought about the here and now—in this case about Dr. Bowes's two daughters who attended Lahore American School, who were dark and had long dark hair like figures in the Song of Solomon. At dinner, I had been too self-conscious to say hello; now I was trying to write a poem. Under the covers, I hoped that the surgery might make a martyr of me, that they might yet be willing to visit me in my hospital bed.

It was the first operation on Dr. Bowes's schedule. I vaguely recall being wheeled into the operating theater, falling into a deep sleep, and then waking up under what seemed like the weight of a large concrete block. My father stayed with me while I recuperated, from time to time supplementing the hospital fare with tubs of ice cream and tinned peaches and pears. There were no visitors my own age. Some days later, when the bandages were taken off, I looked anxiously for what I hoped would be a miracle. Nothing had changed. If anything, the bump was bigger, made larger by the swelling. My father, at least, was relieved—it was not a tumor after all, simply a fusion of the sternum with the structure of my rib cage; it might grow somewhat larger, until I reached my full height. It was useless to contemplate even cosmetic surgery until I stopped growing.

I flew back to Rawalpindi devastated, as my father took a flight south to Sukkur. Some weeks later, dressing out for another basketball game, a classmate—Dudley Chelchowski, as it happened—looked in my direction. "What's that," he said, "I thought you had an operation to make it better." "Oh, it's just the normal swelling after surgery," I said lamely, "it should get smaller." I cringed, knowing all the time that the bump was as big as ever, that I had better get used to it. I wore bandages for as long as possible, believing that they at least offered a partial explanation. Awkward with girls my own age, I attributed it all to the growth in my chest, to the large doorknob not far from where my heart was supposed to be.

· · ·

The dominant issue during my last year of high school was the decision on what to do next. There were fifteen students in my senior class, and almost all of us would go on to college, mostly the kind of Bible schools or Christian liberal arts colleges that actively recruited missionary children. Financial aid packages were based on financial need, and most of us were eligible for the maximum extent possible. My brother, intent on becoming a doctor, had deliberated between Boston University and Wheaton College in Wheaton, Illinois. In the end, he had chosen Wheaton—some of my parents' colleagues lived nearby, the Mission Board was headquartered in Wheaton, and some of his own friends would also be attending. There was a strong expectation that I might go there too.

I was not so sure. Other than an affinity for camping and travelling—and an ineffectual sports career—my major "outside" interest during high school had been journalism. I helped reactivate the monthly school publication known as the *Akhbar,* Urdu for newspaper. It was the publishing aspect of my father's own work that most excited me, even as seeing the latest mimeographed issue of the *Akhbar* roll off the Gestetner machine in Murree gave me a special thrill. I would spend hours in the typing room, measuring out the columns, scratching out the headlines with a special pen, repairing the damaged mimeo forms, trying to ensure a quality final product. I even persuaded our staff advisor to enroll Murree in one of the U.S.-based Scholastic Press Associations operated out of Columbia University. For thirty dollars annually, we got a magazine subscription and discounts on books related to journalism. We could also send sample copies of the *Akhbar* to their annual competition. I was thrilled, later in the year, when we received a "first rating" from the Columbia Scholastic Press Association, scoring 875 out of a possible 1,000 points in the category for "mimeographed newspapers from schools with an enrollment of less than 150." I did not realize at the time that the competition must have been slight, that we must have been among the only schools anywhere in the world to have made a submission in that category.

In the end, I narrowed my choice of colleges down to three. First, there was Wheaton College. David was finishing his second year there and it would be easy for me simply to follow in his footsteps. I would likely major in history or literature, postponing until later any decisions about what to do with the rest of my life. I felt my mother in particular pointing me in that direction. For obvious reasons, there were fears that my parents might "lose" me if I ended up going to a "secular" institution of higher learning; a college that was overtly Christian might, at the very least, help cushion the shock of my return to America.

Second, there was the University of Georgia, in particular their School of Forestry. I lit upon this option while scanning a guide to colleges and universities, thinking all the while that it would put me close to relatives. I briefly thought of myself as a forest ranger, even as some years before I had thought of joining the Coast Guard or attending West Point; the notion of spending the rest of my life looking after trees in national parks had a strong, if unrealistic, appeal.

Finally, there was Northwestern University or, as I more usually said it, with an air of self-importance, "the Medill School of Journalism at Northwestern University in Evanston, Illinois, just outside Chicago." I would combine my interest in writing with my love of foreign places and become a foreign correspondent. Watergate was still recent history, there were tens of thousands of aspiring journalists, and I was certain that I could compete successfully with the best of them.

The decision weighed most heavily on me during winter vacation; I had to decide, one way or another, by the end of March. "Seeking God's guidance" was a familiar phrase, one I had heard since early childhood. Nothing could be more important than the choice of college or university and the decision about a possible future vocation. And yet it was almost impossible to fully understand what that phrase meant. Was it a feeling of "rightness" about a decision? A shout in the dark, accompanied by trumpets and tambourines? A still, small voice? Did it involve a "testing" of God, the laying out of a fleece? Or was it simply a matter of waiting patiently to see which doors opened and which doors closed? I was not sure, but I felt there needed to be some drama, some soul-searching to whatever came next.

I purposefully decided that I would make the final decision in February 1975, during our forthcoming vacation at Karachi beach. The Baptist Mission owned a small two-room shack on Hawkes Bay, between Sandspit and the Canadian-built nuclear power plant beyond French Beach, Pakistan's first such nuclear facility. We had spent a week there each year for as long as I could remember; it was one of the few constants in our life. After elaborate efforts to rat-proof the structure, we settled in for our five days of swimming, sunsets, beach-walking, table games under a hurricane lamp, and long evening walks looking for great sea turtles. The port facilities at Karachi Harbor were insufficient and, at night, it was possible to see lines of ocean freighters, lights on, waiting their turn to dock. I had not yet had the opportunity to hear Otis Redding's song, "Sitting on the Dock of the Bay," or even to realize that he came from Macon, Georgia; if I had, I probably would have spent the whole week listening to it, his mood of melancholy so often matched my own.

I always appreciated high drama and, each day, I walked up and down the beach alone, trying to force a decision. In the end, I chose Northwestern, for reasons that seem so trivial now: they had the best brochure; they talked about their institution as "combining the qualities of a small liberal arts college and a large university." And nearly all their published material included a reference to possibly the only surviving remnant of their distant Methodist past, a passage from Philippians: "Whatsoever things are true, whatsoever things are honest, whatsoever things are just, whatsoever things are pure, whatsoever things are lovely, whatsoever things are of good report; if there be any virtue, and if there be any praise, think on these things." It was perhaps the first illusion that I was disabused of when I arrived, that journalism school would have anything at all to do with truth, honesty, justice, purity, loveliness, or things of good report. Given my frame of mind at the time, it was nonetheless appealing to think that I was about to embark on a endeavor that had at least some spiritual overtones, that there might be, in at least some vague sense, an aspect of a "calling" to my own prospective newspaper career.

A couple of years later, attending the only creative writing class I ever registered for at Northwestern University, I remembered that decisive moment on Hawkes Bay with a feeble attempt at the mandatory first poem:

I am come as in another life,
To a place of quiet sadness.

The dreams of another time
Are diced away and gone forever;
The evening has become broken,
Like the loosening of shattered stone.

My brother said to watch the sky:
I saw the clouds;
My sister said to watch the sea:
I saw the waves.

Beyond the grass the jackals howl,
Across the water the fires burn.

It was a weak first effort that nonetheless elicited a few favorable comments from the instructor. "Interesting syntax," he wrote on the first three words, perhaps unaware that I had plagiarized the phrase from the New Testament. "Clever verb," he commented on *diced*, perhaps not realizing that it came from the same source.

His final comments, written in pen at the bottom of the page, were most telling: "A bit too much deep structure has not been transformed into surface structure. The title and the poet hold clues a reader can only hint at. I like the rhythm to the lines, their calm pace, and the opening and closing set-ups. I want just a bit more from the body of the poem. Sorrow for what? Why watch sky and sea? It can go at least two ways, and the ambiguity might not be in your best interests."

The critique captured more than even John Jacob, my English instructor, might have realized. He was right: it was almost impossible to bring to the surface most of the "deep structure" of my early childhood; I could only hint at it obliquely. The common experience essential for a more direct approach—the cultural touchstones, the shared events, the lived-together past—was largely absent. How could I begin to describe—much less "share" with the rest of the class—life in Ratodero and Shikarpur, school in Murree, drives across the desert, trips into the Karakoram? And how could they in turn convey to me solely through words their own, equally unique way of life, one that I could only dimly comprehend?

In the end, even a shared biography and a common language might not suffice. After all, it was not unusual for words to be inadequate to describe our feelings even among those closest to us, with those whom we ought to have loved most of all. We could look at the same sea and see something different, watch the same clouds and imagine varying shapes, observe the same event and still come away with conflicting interpretations. Words alone were inadequate to fully capture all we were or wanted to be. More often, gesture, rhythm, and tone were what mattered most, providing intimations of glory, hints of sorrow, forebodings of tragedy, expressing in some sense that which is known but which can never be fully told.

If it all sounds ambiguous, it is because it was—wholly and purposefully so. In time, I came to accept that ambiguity was a necessary condition for my own emotional survival, that it would be foolish to ever try and eliminate it entirely, either within myself or in my relations with others. At first, I imagined that the strong sense of "apartness" that I carried with me had its roots in my upbringing in Pakistan, in the fact that I was forever having to negotiate across so many different frontiers of race, class, culture, and religion. Only later did I come to understand that cultural displacement was one of the defining features of the twentieth century, that one of the greatest gifts my parents ever gave me was an ability to cross an ever-increasing number of boundaries and still not be bound by them, to travel the world and still maintain a sense of who I was and where I came from. To borrow a phrase, the origins of which escape me now, I was somehow fated to acquire early in life the ability to be partly at home everywhere—but not fully at home anywhere. More than anything, it was this gift that allowed me to survive my first months alone in America.

•     •     •

Graduation from high school was a fitting afterword to the only life I knew. I was part of the eleventh class to ever graduate from Murree Christian School, and yet the traditions associated with graduation already seemed as if they had been around for centuries. A baccalaureate service was scheduled at Holy Trinity Church in Murree, even as it had been held for the three graduates representing the class of '64 eleven years before. The processional music, number 414 in the hymnal, "God of Our Fathers," was the same. In our case, we also had special music—"The Prayer of Saint Francis of Assisi" as rendered by Pat Nye—followed by a sermon, a congregational hymn ("Be Still My Soul"), and a recessional ("A Mighty Fortress"). After it was all over, we gathered outside for photographs with Ian and Isabel Murray, our class advisors. We also posed for family photographs, an event that two years earlier had gotten my father into so much trouble with one of our supporting churches back in Macon, Georgia: my brother David's hair was too long; my sister Nancy's skirt was too short; and my mother wore a pants suit. The church, disturbed at this particular set of missionaries who did not live up to expectations, dropped their financial support on account of the photograph.

We felt very self-important that day, overtly religious and spiritual-minded, as if this really was a special launching out into the wider world from which we had been so insulated these past many years. There was a certain pensiveness as well, a feeling that we were watching an event in slow motion rather than actually participating in it ourselves. Our parents had taken us this far. Now we were on our own, to spread across the globe within the week, strengthened in parting only by the lingering words of a last sermon, a farewell hymn, and a final prayer.

The gifts we received from other parents and teachers emphasized the spiritual aspect of our departing, often including as they did a Bible verse to "take with us," along with the obligatory five- or ten-dollar checks. The Roberts, Australian missionaries working in Quetta, gave me Deuteronomy 31:8 ("The Lord himself goes at your head"). The Wilders, Presbyterian missionaries working in Lyallpur, gave me Psalms 84:11 ("The Lord will hold back no good thing"). Liz Legget, the English teacher from Scotland, passed on an odd verse from the Psalms, Psalm 34:11 ("Come my children, listen to me: I will teach you the fear of the Lord"). Eva Hewitt, the school librarian, now in her seventies, gave perhaps the most familiar verse of all, Philippians 4:13 ("I can do everything through Christ which strengtheneth me"). Hoyt and Edna Smith, Methodist missionaries working in Punjab who arrived in Pakistan even before independence in 1947, now nearing retirement, offered a verse from Hebrews that resonates still, nearly twenty years after the event: "Remember where you stand: not before the palpable, blazing fire of Sinai with the darkness, gloom and whirl-wind, the trumpet-blast and the oracular voice. . . . No, you stand before Mount Zion and the city of the living God." I stood before a mountain, that was for sure; I also imagined I stood before the living God, who knew what lay ahead even if I did not. In fact, we had been taught as much. "We can't know the future," one of my teachers said, so often that I grew tired of it. "But we can know the one who holds the future."

Spiritual themes also dominated the commencement exercises held in the cavernous MCS school auditorium the following week. We marched solemnly, in time to a recorded rendition of "Pomp and Cir-cumstance," and then Don Calderwood gave the invocation. Ellen Christy gave the valedictory address, striving mightily to offer a new twist to themes of parting that already, in the short history of Murree Christian School, were becoming stereotypical—appreciation for all that had been given us; a few backhanded compliments and cynical musings to maintain credibility, to suggest that there had been times when those around us had failed to maintain the high ideals that had been set before us; and a final recognition that, whatever may have happened in the past, we were now on our own and nothing much else could be done for us.

Ellen, slight and with short hair, spoke softly and my parents later told me that they could only barely hear what she said. She stood on an upside-down crate so she could see over the podium and into the audience below. As always, I admired her from afar; she seemed good at everything she did, even as I continued to struggle with my own inarticulateness, my own feelings of emotional inadequacy, my continuing habit of lighting upon the awkward turn of phrase that so often degenerated into a stutter. Chuck Roub responded to the speech with grace and understanding and a few jokes, as he had in so many other commencement exercises over the past decade. Dr. Norval Christy, Ellen's father, a medical missionary from Taxila who, like Dr. Holland, specialized in cataracts and had himself restored sight to an estimated one hundred thousand people, distributed the fifteen diplomas in turn. Then we marched out into the night to the lingering lines of our school hymn, sung so often in Friday chapel services over the past twelve years:

Nestled neath the great Himalayas, far above the plain
Stands the school we love and cherish, more than earthly gain.

Built upon a firm foundation, in God's hands a tool:
Shaping lives of dedication, Murree Christian School.

There was a reception line outside on the basketball court, then refreshments provided by all the high school mothers. Portraits of the fifteen graduates representing the class of '75 were posted on one wall. At the receiving line, one elderly missionary embraced each mother in turn, repeating the same phrase over and over again. "A fine son, a fine son," he announced gruffly before moving on. "Ma'am, you have a wonderful son." By late evening, the crowd began to thin and, after a time, only we graduates and our families remained, talking quietly among ourselves. It was over, it was really over—there would never be a night quite like this, not for us anyway, an evening so full of promise and yet so tinged with all the sadness and inadequacies of adolescence. There was so much I wanted to say, so much I longed to do; but, as happened so often, I held back, keeping emotions inside that at this, of all possible nights, should have been on open display for all the world to see. I felt empty when I said my final good-byes to people among whom I had spent almost my entire life, leaving in most cases without so much as a final handshake.

My brother and I walked back to Murree together that last night, along the three miles of winding road to our house at O'Spring, just below Kashmir Point, hardly a mile from where I had been born eighteen years before. He had returned for my graduation, after finishing his first two years at Wheaton College. Even his accent had changed, inflected as it was by the latest in student jargon at that particular campus. Almost every sentence seemed to start with a "hey jack this" or "hey jack that," as if to underscore the growing distance that I feared was developing between us.

We talked about his two years in America, about what I might expect to find when we would next meet, at the Greyhound bus station in downtown Chicago six weeks from now. We could not aspire to follow in the footsteps of the missionary children of a previous generation, the Henry Luces who founded magazines, the John Herseys or Herman Hesses who wrote books, the learned scholars and prominent diplomats who grew up overseas, the progeny of missionaries, becoming experts on China and Japan and the Middle East. We were of a different time, representing a life experience that had already moved to the fringes of American society or at least American academia, where notions of a life motivated by love of God or orders from God seemed alien, even threatening.

There was a time when the missionary endeavor might have stood at the center of the ruling American culture, when the progeny of missionaries would be welcomed, first into fashionable prep schools and then into the Harvards and Yales and Princetons of the land, schools that had themselves once been rooted in a missionary vision of sorts. But the missionary era after World War II was different; our family histories were different and our social origins had vastly changed. The so-called mainline churches that had once established a mainline Protestant culture for the entire country were either confused or

beginning to wither and die. All too often, the evangelical and fundamentalist churches that tried to replace them seemed shallow and in-
consequential, incapable of contributing much to any unifying cultural
or spiritual themes.

I would feel the cultural shift in far more personal ways, in the
academic community I would shortly join. "Oh, your father is a
missionary," was the usual comment, once it sunk in that such types
still existed. "How interesting." The thought behind the expression
seemed to be saying something quite different. "Oh, your father is a
missionary," it suggested. "That explains everything." "You're grown
up now," a professor said to me a few weeks later, not long after I arrived in Chicago, jumping to conclusions, little realizing the shaky and
impermanent ground upon which his own philosophical premises so
blithely rested. "You've got to stop believing these things."

Continuing on toward Murree, David and I talked about the trip I
was embarking on early the next morning, with classmates Stephen
McCurry and Mark Pegors. The three of us were going overland,
by bus and train, to Paris. The route—Peshawar, Kabul, Kandahar,
Tehran, Tabriz, Istanbul, Belgrade, Vienna, Munich, Amsterdam, and
finally Paris—tripped off the tongue like poetry. I could not imagine
the turbulence that would mark at least the first half of our itinerary
in the decade ahead. Again, I felt grown-up and self-important, as
if setting off on a ten-thousand-mile journey across the wilds of Asia
was a test of manhood. It would take ten days to reach Istanbul, at
a cost of forty dollars, all transportation, meals, and cheap hotels
included. There, waiting for a bus to Vienna, we would be asked to
carry a cache of hashish; only Steve's immediate refusal spared us
from what might have turned into a lengthy term in a Turkish jail. In
Switzerland, Mark and I would briefly have a falling-out over a trivial
matter, each nearly deciding to go our separate way. In Paris, we
slept our last night on benches in a park near the Eiffel Tower, almost
missing our two-hundred-dollar chartered flight to New York. We
were met the next morning at John F. Kennedy Airport by Dudley
Chelchowski, who had graduated from Murree and left for America
one year before us, and was even then contemplating becoming a
policeman.

All this seemed far away on that last night in Pakistan, as far away and incomprehensible as the stars. Ellen. William. Joel. Virginia. John. Nancy. Robert. Stephen. Deborah. Mark. Susan. Elaine. Emily. Margaret. Jonathan. Other names also, the names of our near contemporaries at Murree Christian School, those who had gone ahead and those who would shortly follow after. It was impossible then to imagine the different roads we would take, the choices we would make, the lives that were to come. It would have been a harder parting had we been gifted with a second sight, had we been able to peer into the future and know what would become of us.

David and I walked in silence for a time, words once again proving inadequate for the occasion. Suddenly, just below Rock Edge, at the halfway point between Jhika Gali and the Murree Post Office, my brother David stopped and looked across the mountains. Up the hill, at Rock Edge, was the house where I was born, the gray house with the corrugated tin roof and the thin wooden walls where my parents had lived when they first arrived in Pakistan two decades before. Kashmir was behind the mountains, beneath the Pir Panjal where snow was visible, even in summer, against the moonlight of the cloudless sky, the sky that stretched toward Nanga Parbat in one direction, toward the plains of Punjab and Sind in the other. It was the same sky that David and I had looked up at each night from our rope-slung beds, underneath sagging mosquito nets, on the mud roof of our Ratodero home, my father pointing out the constellations, my mother saying it was time to stop talking, time to be quiet and go to sleep. It seemed so astonishing, that all this should ever have happened, that all this was about to end, that I was finally leaving Murree and Shikarpur and Ratodero behind, that it was unlikely that I would ever have an opportunity to return. We stopped, we gazed up at the night sky, at Orion, Taurus, the Pleiades, at the expanse of the Milky Way, whole universes improbably shaped and formed, as improbably shaped and formed as we who watched them now. The words that finally came were short and to the point, understated and brief, acquiring meaning only in later years, when I once again recalled the mountains and the sky, a sky that seemed to go on forever, a sky that had not yet been dimmed by the glow of a hundred cities, the lights of a thousand street lamps, the electricity of a million homes. "Look carefully," my brother said, casting a final glance upward at the sky that had sustained us all these years, that gathered round about us even now for this last and final time. "Look carefully," my brother said. "It will be a long time before you see stars shining this brightly again."

JONATHAN S. ADDLETON was born in
Murree, Pakistan. He has a B.S. from
Northwestern University and a Ph.D. from
Tufts University. A foreign service officer
with the U.S. Agency for International
Development (USAID), he has worked in
Pakistan, Yemen, South Africa and, most
recently, Kazakstan.